Blake and Homosexuality ✵

Blake and Homosexuality ✳

Christopher Z. Hobson

palgrave

First published 2000 by
PALGRAVE™
175 Fifth Avenue, New York, N.Y. 10010 and
Houndmills, Basingstoke, Hampshire, England RG21 6XS
Companies and representatives throughout the world.

PALGRAVE™ is the new global publishing imprint of St. Martin's
Press LLC Scholarly and Reference Division and Palgrave Publishers
Ltd (formerly Macmillan Press Ltd).

ISBN 0-312-23451-1

Library of Congress Cataloging-in-Publication Data
Hobson, Christopher Z.
    Blake and Homosexuality / Christopher Z. Hobson.
        p.   cm.
    Includes bibliographical references and index.
    ISBN 0-312-23451-1
    1. Blake, William, 1757–1827—Criticism and interpretation.   2. Ho-
mosexuality and
literature—England—History—18th century.   3. Blake, William,
1757–1827—Knowledge—Psychology.   4. Sex in literature.   5. Homosexuality, Male, in
literature.   6. Homosexuality and literature—England—History—19th
century.   I. Title.
PR4157.H63 H64   2000
821'.7—dc21   00–040446
            CIP

Design by Letre Libre, Inc.

First edition: November 2000
10   9   8   7   6   5   4   3   2   1

Children of the future Age,
Reading this indignant page;
Know that in a former time.
Love! sweet Love! was thought a crime.

—"A Little Girl Lost" 1–4

For Man cannot unite with Man but by their Emanations
Which stand both Male & Female at the Gates of each
  Humanity

—*Jerusalem* 88:10–11

Contents

List of Illustrations

Preface ✳

B etween the two poems that supply my epigraphs, William Blake undertakes a journey of nearly thirty years that develops and changes his view of their common subject. He begins with a sense of love's sweetness that is expansive and restrictive at the same time, for it celebrates some kinds of love while ridiculing others. He ends by rejecting and criticizing his own narrowness, embracing love's forbidden forms, and finding in them tokens of humanity's unity and possible redemption. Along the way, like his protagonist Los, Blake takes "his globe of fire to search the interiors of Albions / Bosom" (J 45/31:3–4) and encounters "the crue[l]ties of Moral Law" (M 5:12, copy D) in their most barbarous form. But he also meets the defiance that opposes "Naked Beauty!" to Satan's law (M 4:28, copies CD), and the innocence of female love on the banks of Albion's river (J 19–20), experiences that add to his belief in sexual liberty and the centrality of tolerance in a cleansed society. At the end of this process Blake has attained a more complex understanding of gender relations in general and homosexuality in particular and, on this issue, stands with one or two others as a prophet to "the future Age." This, in brief, is the story *Blake and Homosexuality* relates.

This study follows a separate work on Blake's social and political ideas, *The Chained Boy: Orc and Blake's Idea of Revolution* (1999). Throughout the present work, as in that one, I assume that Blake's emblematic characters and symbolic entities refer simultaneously to social, psychosexual, religious, and other areas of experience. Here, of course, my primary focus is sexual, but I postulate Blake's overall concern with a human renovation that takes place in society, not only—as much traditional Blake interpretation has supposed—in the psyche or imagination. Where necessary, I refer briefly to points made in the earlier work. In common with that book, this one reads literary texts in relation to history, in this case both the detailed history of homosexuality in the eighteenth and early nineteenth centuries and the English political-dynastic history that deeply concerned Blake.

The opening chapter offers a double sketch: of homosexuality in eighteenth- and early nineteenth-century England, the subject of voluminous recent historical research that I summarize with incidental contributions of my own; and of the treatment of homosexuality by the republican tradition in letters, which Blake inherits, at first shares in part, and then distances himself from. The two following chapters, on Blake's early narratives and on *The Four Zoas,* trace this shift primarily through textual and pictorial analysis, though with reference to contemporary history and historiography. The fourth and fifth chapters deal with Blake's *Milton* and his assessment of Milton's legacy. Portions of these chapters relate episodes in *Milton* to seventeenth-century political and sexual history and to contemporary sexual repression in what I hope is detailed and regular enough fashion to be worth readers' serious consideration. These chapters also deal with Blake's illustrations to Milton's works, and his integration of homosexual content into pictorial images of prophetic vocation. The sixth chapter, on *Jerusalem,* finds in that poem a synthesis of Blake's handling of homosexuality, sexuality in general, and themes of social-political oppression and liberation. My conclusion sums up what I take to be the importance of homosexuality in Blake's overall thought and the implications of this issue for the more general question of Romanticism's treatment of sexuality and its now much-disputed status as social-utopian vision.

Blake's references to homosexuality are substantial in aggregate, if not dominant in any one work. They include brief visual and textual allusions in works of the 1790s; depictions of homosexual acts and gnomic text references in *The Four Zoas;* relatively explicit text episodes and other coded or symbolic references in *Milton* and *Jerusalem,* together with homoerotic artwork in the former; and suggestions of homosexuality in illustrations of Milton's works. All are of interest in themselves, but they are also significant for their connection with Blake's other deep concerns—with moral hypocrisy and cruelty, with male aggression and the battle of the sexes, and with war, the foundations of tyranny, and the possibilities of establishing a cooperative commonwealth.

Though Blake's references bespeak a substantial interest in homosexuality, his attitudes on the subject, their relation to the issues just mentioned, and their importance in his poetic development can be demonstrated only with probability, not certainty. Even if the homoerotic reference and thematic relevance of the episodes I discuss is accepted (which will not always be the case), the difficulties of pinning down meaning in Blake's texts and art are notorious. In this case, they merge with the ambiguities of expression and intention typical of other eighteenth-century homoerotic representations.[1] Inevitably, then, there will be room for disagreement with portions of my argument, my assessment of Blake's development, and my overall judgments. I ask readers' patience in examining a pattern I build up through all my chapters; their critical evaluation of my own readings of direct statements, fugitive tonal qualities, coded uses of place names, resonances with contemporary history, and the like; and finally, their overall judgment of whether Blake's homosexual references, relatively infrequent yet appearing at crucial points in his narratives, constitute, as I think they do, a clue to the direction of his thought.

❊ ❊ ❊

This book seeks to contribute to an ongoing debate about Blake and sexuality, with broader implications for our thought about Romanticism. Nearly twenty years ago, W. J. T. Mitchell proposed a future focus of Blake studies on the "Dangerous Blake." Mitchell argued that the battle for an Apollonian "Blake of sweetness and light," waged by early interpreters against the image of the "mad" poet, and crowned by Northrop Frye's magisterial[2] synthesis of Blake's mythic and poetic contexts in *Fearful Symmetry* (1947), had been won ("Dangerous Blake" 410). Mitchell hoped that future scholarship would turn back to the rough edges buffed up by this polishing job—to "the dangerous Blake, the angry, flawed Blake, the crank" (410), and specifically to three of his aspects: his "madness," "obscenity," and "incoherence" (411–16). Mitchell complained that in Frye's and later treatments, "Blake's obscenity has been domesticated and sanitized in the name of higher sublimations. . . . Perhaps now that he has passed safely by the Victorian censors and the modernist strategies of desublimation we can return to Blake's images of rape, lust, sado-masochism, and other scenes of abnormal sexuality. . . . Blake was not a nice man: he was filthy with work and visionary conviction" (414). Mitchell specifically asked, "Why are there scenes of homosexual fellatio in *Milton,* and what do they have to do with the presentation of Satan-Hayley's effeminacy in the Bard's Song?" (414); elsewhere, Mitchell suggests that Blake uses these plates and the Bard's Song to contrast positive and negative kinds of male love ("Style" 67). While different from my own, Mitchell's view opened up the topic of Blake's treatment of homosexuality, suggested its complexity, and presented one of the ideas ("abnormal" or perverse sexuality) I use to explore it.

However, by and large later scholars ignored all three of Mitchell's guideposts, instead sculpting two more recent Blakes that became influential in studies published in the 1980s and 1990s: a deconstructionist Blake and a (frequently) antifeminist Blake. The former will hardly concern me, but the latter appears in my discussions of Blake's earlier works, in references throughout, and as a topic of interrogation in my conclusion. There has been no unified feminist reading of Blake; at least three trends have emerged, ranging from those that celebrate Blake's attacks on patriarchy and repression, through mixed readings that discern both antipatriarchal and antifeminine threads in his work, to those that believe he firmly subordinated women to men.[3] My own readings would fall between the first two positions, but closer to the second; my discussion takes up the issues raised by—and looks at the weaknesses in—the third. These studies have approached Blake's early apotheoses of masculine aggression mainly in polemical fashion, noting that Blake in the 1790s was not as advanced in his thought about gender as some women writers of the time, but ignoring the sources and ramifications of Blake's "poetics of masculinity" in the republican poetic tradition and overlooking or becoming embarrassed by Blake's explorations of perversity (see chapter 2); and they have remained largely unaware of his critique of aggressive male phallicism in later work (see chapter 3). Most of all, they have been unaware of the importance of homosexuality and its persecution in Blake's culture and the impact of these factors on his work. This lack of awareness has contributed to their image of an enduringly masculinist Blake, which a knowledge of his treatment of homosexuality undermines.

While not unknown, discussion of Blake's view of homosexuality has been relatively rare. Commentaries on Blake's artworks have noted the homoeroticism of some of his images but (with a few exceptions) have not attempted a thematic reading of the images or connected them with analogous textual material.[4] Textual interpreters, on the other hand, have generally assumed that Blake was critical of any but heterosexual relations. S. Foster Damon, adopting a quasi-Freudian view of homosexuality as resulting from failure to undergo a complete heterosexual development, notes that Blake "did not condemn the practice [of sodomy] as such," but rather "the negative inhibition involved" (*Dictionary* 376). Several later accounts are considerably less generous—their Blake is marked by a strident male-centered heterosexuality that conceals latent homosexual fears, or, alternatively, by idealized homoeroticism that wards off threatening female presences (Storch, *Sons;* Webster, *Psychology*). Brenda S. Webster, for example, in brief sections of her critique of Blake's sexual ideology, argues that Blake's poems construct a masculine ego that represses homosexuality and displaces it as accusation or aggression against others. Blake, Webster believes, can sometimes envisage "egalitarian male homosexuality," but only as a way of "dispens[ing] with women altogether" (*Psychology* 22), and homosexual panic usually thwarts even this misogynist choice. Such treatments, however, overlook or misread important episodes involving homosexuality in Blake, omit or misunderstand the contemporary antihomosexual culture that Blake reacted against, and fail to perceive Blake's growing consideration of different kinds of perverse sexuality over time. The more affirmative treatments of Blake and women have generally left the topic of homosexuality alone.

As against these rather fragmentary and dismissive assessments, a few commentaries, while not focusing on homosexuality as such, have assumed or argued Blake's acceptance of it in some instances, along with his more general sexual openmindedness. These include W. J. T. Mitchell's brief but nuanced and sensitive comments on the lesbian scene in *Jerusalem* (*Composite Art* 206–207), as well as his view of "Dangerous Blake" already mentioned. Jean H. Hagstrum's "Babylon Revisited, or the Story of Luvah and Vala" (1973) and his chapter on Blake in *The Romantic Body* (1985) provide germinal explorations of several topics I take up, such as Blake's critique of male phallicism and his late reaffirmation of sexual love, though Hagstrum also assumes that Blake saw homosexuality as part of "fallen" sexuality ("Babylon" 109–111, 115–17; "Arrows" 120; see chapters 3, 6). Among newer works, Warren Stevenson's *Romanticism and the Androgynous Sublime* (1996) provides suggestive discussions of Blake's treatment of androgyny and its appearances in *Jerusalem;* Stevenson, without discussing the topic specifically, seems to assume throughout that Blake accepts homosexuality. These studies provide an ongoing countertradition to the negative commentaries just mentioned, one to which this book hopes to contribute.

❋   ❋   ❋

While this book is not meant as a theoretical study of homosexuality, the reader is owed some specification of its terminology and assumptions. My discussion refers to "homosexuality," rather than "sodomy," for the book's general topic, though it often uses the latter term and its derivatives to refer to the male homosexual world and its practices; these terms were used in Blake's time, while "homosexuality" was unknown until the late nineteenth century. "Sodomy" technically referred only to acts of anal penetration but in practice was used for all the specifically sexual acts by males that we would consider homosexual. Despite this relative flexibility, and the risk of anachronism, and in agreement with G. S. Rousseau, though for partly different reasons, I prefer the more modern term. Rousseau's concern is that "sodomy" is too narrow to cover a "number of homosexual practices . . . ranging from restrained platonic friendship . . . to diverse forms of transvestism and anatomical penetration" ("Pursuit" 132). Mine is twofold. First, "sodomy" does not include lesbianism, one of Blake's topics. Second, "homosexual" and "homosexuality" connote a proclivity or identity as well as specific acts, while "sodomy" and "sodomite" are presently understood to refer only to the acts themselves and those who perform them.

This latter point, however, requires separate discussion in light of Michel Foucault's casually argued but enormously influential thesis that sodomy was viewed only as a practice, not an identity, until the medicalization of sexual discourse in the later nineteenth century. Foucault's view has shaped a generation of historiography and literary criticism on homosexuality—which has been, moreover, virtually the *first* generation of study of its manifestations in the eighteenth century.[5] Foucault's statement of his thesis is worth recalling specifically:

> This new [nineteenth-century] persecution of the peripheral sexualities entailed an *incorporation of perversions* and a new *specification of individuals*. As defined by the ancient civil or canonical codes, sodomy was a category of forbidden acts; their perpetrator was nothing more than the juridical subject of them. The nineteenth-century homosexual became a personage, a past, a case history, and a childhood, in addition to being a type of life, a life form, and a morphology, with an indiscreet anatomy and possibly a mysterious physiology. Nothing that went into his total composition was unaffected by his sexuality. It was everywhere present in him: at the root of all his actions because it was their insidious and indefinitely active principle; written immodestly on his face and body because it was a secret that always gave itself away. It was consubstantial with him, less as a habitual sin than as a singular nature. We must not forget that the psychological, psychiatric, medical category of homosexuality was constituted from the moment it was characterized—Westphal's famous article of 1870 on "contrary sexual sensations" can stand as its date of birth—less by a type of sexual relations than by a certain quality of sexual sensibility, a certain way of inverting the masculine and the feminine in oneself. Homosexuality appeared as one of the forms of sexuality when it was transposed from the practice of sodomy onto a kind of interior androgyny, a hermaphrodism of the soul. The sodomite had been a temporary aberration; the homosexual was now a species. (42–43)

Foucault is obviously speaking of professional, quasi-official attitudes, not how homosexuals viewed themselves, and yet later discussions have not observed a rigid line between definitions by self and other. Nor does a rigid line seem possible to draw in practice: Aside from official bodies that might deal with sexual crimes, such as courts, hostile individuals and even homosexuals themselves may pick up and use definitions derived from the dominant culture, along with others (even contradictory ones) derived from their own ideas. Hence, scholarly discourse has sometimes assumed that there can have been no *self-conception* of homosexuality as an identity rather than a practice prior to Foucault's "medicalization" of the mid-nineteenth century.

Such discussions, as those who follow scholarly debates about homosexuality know, touch on the larger theoretical issue usually phrased as an opposition between "essentialist" and "constructionist" views. Briefly, these terms denote the assumptions that some complex of behavior and preference that would now be termed "homosexual" (i.e., a continuous and preferential orientation to love with one's own sex) has existed throughout history, or, on the other hand, that both the idea and the reality of relatively distinct orientations to the same and the opposite sex are products of social development, and of recent origin. David L. Halperin, for example, contends not only that "the distinction between homosexuality and heterosexuality" is a recent construct but that its emergence coincides "with the emergence, in the same period (or in the centuries immediately preceding it), of some new sexual types. . . . From what I have been able to tell, these new sexual types, the homosexual and the heterosexual, do not represent merely new ways of classifying persons—that is, innovations in moral or judicial language—but new types of desire, new kinds of desiring human beings" (43). Discussions of these issues (as indeed this example shows) have been fraught with tensions between emphases on actual behavior or desires, official ideology, and popular attitudes. They have also been complicated by a focus on, and occasional cross-reference between, at least two distinct premodern societies and epochs (each with its own variations of time and place): Greece and Rome in the ancient world, and Europe in the medieval, Renaissance, and early modern eras. In the former, of course, some types of homosexual behavior were widely prevalent, and, possibly, there was no view of homosexuality as a distinct *kind* of behavior; in the latter, at least after about the twelfth century,[6] homosexuality or sodomy was officially regarded as completely antithetical to social norms and was defined, at least legally, as aberrant behavior rather than a type of person. With specific regard to early modern Europe, debates have opposed those who believe the period displayed shifting conceptions of homosexual behavior that did not view its practitioners as a distinct category of persons, and those who see evidence for self-conceptions and social views of homosexual behavior as a fairly stable predilection or identity. The further issue of whether most homosexual behavior may have been occasional, preferential, or exclusive has been less defined.

In a preface, naturally, I cannot argue a position on these issues; I can only explain my own assumptions. These are, roughly, "constructionist" with "essentialist" leanings; that is, though I agree that there has not been a single view of homosexuality or even a conception of homosexuality as a specific category throughout history, and that the incidence and types of homosexual behavior have varied widely as well, I suspect there has been less fluidity and more stability in the existence of visible or imputed homosexual types than constructionists sometimes assume. To cite one much-discussed literary example, when Chaucer's pilgrim-narrator notes the pardoner's lank hair, high voice, and beardless cheeks, and opines, "I trowe he were a geldyng or a mare" (1 [A]:691), he arguably thinks the pardoner may be either a eunuch or an effeminate male homosexual, a possibility he seems to view as involving a stable behavior or orientation, indeed one that is biologically based.[7] But despite my general suspicion that homosexuality as a "sexual type" (in Halperin's terms) may be stabler than some constructionists allow, I would not presume to offer any defined view on this point.

With regard to the period of my study, the late eighteenth and early nineteenth centuries, the historical record is clearer. Paradoxically, while the study of eighteenth-century homosexuality was pioneered by scholars with defined Foucauldian sympathies, much recent research on the eighteenth century has referred to "homosexuality," rather than "sodomy," and not only for reasons of convenience. A very extensive body of research has turned up substantial evidence of what would now be called male homosexual and lesbian self-conceptions, and awareness of homosexual and lesbian personality types by others, expressed in behavior, argot, hostile terminology, and the like. Hence, recent writers have pushed the conception of homosexual identity backward from Foucault's mid-nineteenth-century origin.[8] (Indeed, Halperin's elastic formula cited above, "or in the centuries immediately preceding," is little more than a recognition of recent scholarship that has found evidence of self-aware homosexual subjectivities in the eighteenth, seventeenth, and earlier centuries.)[9] Stephen O. Murray, for instance, summarizes a swatch of evidence that, he contends, "shows [a] conception of homosexual persons, a homosexual species even," before the nineteenth century (458; see 463–65 and passim). Emma Donoghue argues that the terms in use for lesbianism in the seventeenth and eighteenth centuries (including, if rarely, "Lesbian" itself) refer to "the emotions, desires, styles, tastes and behavioural tendencies that can make up an identity" (3; see 2–8, 21–23, 50–51). And Michel Rey notes that by the 1730s, Paris police usage was shifting from "sodomite" to "pédéraste," a term that, without connoting a preference for children, described "a man whose sexual desire is oriented exclusively toward other men" (188); the observation indicates contemporary belief in a settled homosexual state of mind, if not necessarily identity. Referring to early eighteenth-century satires, Jon Thomas Rowland usefully comments:

> Never, however, does sodomy signify *only* a physical act. It is always accompanied by something else—a style of dress, a mode of speech, a kind of politics, a manner of procreation, etc. That these tracts indicate considerable consensus about these things suggests that it is never *not* an orientation; in these tracts, at least, it is synonymous with "homosexual." (87)

Polemical and journalistic evidence for the period of my study leads to similar conclusions. A hostile pamphlet I cite later, *The Phoenix of Sodom, or the Vere Street Coterie,* refers to its subject this way:

> In contemplating this calamitous vice, a charitable disposition would lead us to believe that it is the effect of a dreadful malignant malady, that assumes such an irresistible dominion over the faculties, that neither religion, philosophy, or the fear of death, can resist. (17)

This writer assumes that homosexuality dominates one's being, and he likens it to the result of ongoing disease, a conception that removes it from the category of a choice to that of a condition—indeed, a medical condition, though this may not be meant literally. No expert but a pamphlet polemicist, the author is clearly reflecting notions widespread in public consciousness, during the period when Foucault feels homosexuality, in dominant discourse, was still only and exclusively "a type of sexual relations" rather than a "quality of sexual sensibility," and its practitioner, the "sodomite," a "temporary aberration" rather than "a species." In short, the pamphleteer views sodomy or homosexuality in a way Foucault says cannot yet have existed. In arguing against the "received opinion . . . that the prevalency of this passion has for its object effeminate beings only," moreover, and instancing instead its appearance in "an athletic Bargeman, an Herculean Coalheaver, and a deaf tyre Smith" (13), the writer shows familiarity with already-developed stereotypes and a desire to correct them, but in any case assumes that the "passion" is a lasting disposition, not an occasional act.

Journalistic usage shows similar conceptions. When a contemporary newspaper, *Bell's Weekly Messenger,* refers to the pillorying of "four miscreants of abominable propensities" (Jan. 20, 1811: 24), the term "propensities" implies that homosexual behavior is something one is inclined to throughout life or for a considerable time—a "singular nature" or "sexual sensibility" in Foucault's terms, rather than a "temporary aberration." The usage is notable, too, because as a euphemism employed in the press to avoid a more concrete description, it assumes readers will recognize its terms as appropriate and characteristic of the people denoted. At least in the limited venue of eighteenth- and early-nineteenth century England, the assumption that homosexual behavior was viewed as mere act rather than proclivity or identity is thoroughly exploded by historical evidence; hence my preference, with several others, for "homosexual" and "homosexuality" as terms for my topic.

Both empirical evidence and the terminological preferences based on it remain in flux. George E. Haggerty's finely argued *Men in Love: Masculinity and Sexuality in the Eighteenth Century* (1999) takes a resolutely Foucauldian view that avoids any use of "homosexual" as indicative of "ahistorical research into sexuality" (38; see also 14, 113). In place of such an umbrella word, Haggerty prefers terms referring to several distinct, if possibly overlapping, male identities (self-conceptions and categorizations by others), most relevantly "effeminate sodomites," fops, mollies (woman-identified or cross-dressing sodomites), and "men of feeling and other figures in which sensibility and sexuality are vividly interconnected" (19). Haggerty's arguments and evidence are worth the reader's full attention, and they offer an indirect challenge to my approach in this work: If Haggerty is right, my book and its title are not really *about* anything, except disparate types of behavior and feeling that I have linked out of present-day concerns. Equally, however, this study offers a test of Haggerty's hypothesis, which in no way accounts for Blake's seeming concern with male-male *and* female-female overt sexual relations and psychic attraction as a single issue, or a complex of closely related issues. If the reader finds evidence that Blake treated same-sex sexual relations and overtly sexual friendships in this way, then the view that linking these concerns is historically anachronistic in the eighteenth and early nineteenth centuries must be weakened.

On a related issue, several historians of homosexuality have argued that in Restoration times, if not later, penetrative sodomy was not seen as incompatible with heterosexual lewdness. Before 1700, according to Randolph Trumbach, "the sodomite was often pictured, and could be found, with his whore on one arm and his boy on the other." Trumbach generalizes that active (penetrating) sodomy "did not violate the gender code. . . . Sodomitical acts contravened the gender system only when they violated the patriarchal code, that is when adult men allowed themselves to be penetrated" ("Sodomitical Assaults" 408; "London's Sapphists" 113–14). Trumbach, Haggerty, and others have also traced literary treatments of libertine bisexualism and eroticized male friendship in works by Rochester, Dryden, Behn, Thomas Otway, Nathaniel Lee, and others.[10] Neither this literary evidence nor Trumbach's comments on sodomy and the gender system support broader inferences that sodomy was socially acceptable or was generally seen—particularly in plebeian and middle-class rather than court and literary milieux—as no worse than heterosexual licentiousness. Indeed, most careful writers avoid such assertions. Nevertheless it is easy to suppose that whatever was not seen as incompatible with masculinity must have been socially winked at, at least in elite circles. At least some scholars have tried to argue this case for the seventeenth century, and one or two have assumed that the same presumed indifference to penetrative sodomy existed as late as Blake's time.[11] To the arguments for seventeenth-century complaisance it can only be said that acknowledgment in some social circles does not mean acceptance in all, and that court cases and hostile polemics alike bespeak homosexuality's despised status in society at large (chapters 1, 4). For the period of my study, once more, the record is clearer: Blake's consideration of homosexuality takes place against a backdrop of uniform public execration of homosexual acts and persons, deeply closeted elite writing and behavior, and a clandestine plebeian life in the parks and public houses that was at once raucous and furtive, fraught with the steady danger of the pillory and gallows.

❄   ❄   ❄

Several intellectual, institutional, and personal debts should be recorded here. One work in a related field, Louis Crompton's now-classic *Byron and Greek Love* (1985), has had major impact on my study. Crompton provided the first modern account of the London antihomosexual persecutions of 1810–11, though without relating them to Blake; I expand on Crompton's account and correct it in details, but in no essential points (chapter 5), and I also utilize Crompton's discussion of Jeremy Bentham's writings on homosexuality (chapter 1). My debts to the many historical and cultural studies of eighteenth- and early nineteenth-century homosexuality published over the last twenty-five years appear throughout the book. The "Blake and the Book" conference at St. Mary's University College, Strawberry Hill, April 1998, allowed me to present an early version of the argument in chapter 5; I thank several participants for their comments, most especially Keri Davies, whose suggestions contributed importantly to the chapter. I thank several institutions for permission to reproduce Blake's artworks, and the Boston Museum of Fine Arts, the British Library, the British Museum, the Henry E. Huntington Library and Art Gallery, the Lenox Collection at the New York Public Library, the Lessing J. Rosenwald Collection at the Library of Congress, the Pierpont Morgan Library, and the Yale Center for British Art for access to Blake works in their collections. In a time when top-quality facsimiles of Blake's works are available in print and electronically, the bibliographic truism that nothing substitutes for direct inspection of the originals remains valid; to these institutions' hospitality I owe knowledge of the details of

Blake's art that would have been impossible or very difficult to glean from the best reproductions. Finally, Brian Culhane, Stuart Curran, Jackie Di-Salvo, G. A. Rosso, Ronald Tabor, Susan Weiner, and Joseph Wittreich all read and criticized early drafts, and David Worrall the completed manuscript; I owe special thanks to Tony Rosso for painstakingly reviewing the drafts of several chapters, and to Joe Wittreich for his early and consistent encouragement.

❉ ❉ ❉

Blake's texts are cited from David V. Erdman, ed., *Complete Poetry and Prose of William Blake* (abbreviated *E* when necessary); designs are cited from the listed facsimiles or reproductions. Dates are based on Joseph Viscomi's *Blake and the Idea of the Book* unless otherwise specified. Works are identified by short titles—*America,* not *America a Prophecy*—and by initials in citations and notes. Where page or plate numbers differ in cited editions, both numbers are given. In the final section of chapter 5, which often refers to *Milton*'s illustrations in relation to the text, references use the dual page numbers printed in *E* after plate 9, representing the order in *E* and in *IB* (corresponding to copy D) respectively. Full-page designs without text, not numbered in *E,* have only one number, corresponding to *IB*. By using the bracketed numbers, the reader may compare the positions of full-page designs and relevant texts—thus, plate 47, a full-page design, follows 40 [46] in *E*'s numbering. When necessary I include Essick and Viscomi's plate numbers in their facsimile of copy C, and in a few places I refer to versions of designs in copies AB, giving their numbers as well as the *E* or *IB* equivalents. (References to *Milton* elsewhere use only *E*'s main number.) Citations of *Jerusalem,* chapter 2, provide alternative numbers referring to Blake's two plate orders, e.g., 43/29; the first number refers to *E*'s text order (based on copies ACF), while the second corresponds to the Blake Trust facsimile of copy E, which has the alternative arrangement. Descriptions of coloring and details are ordinarily based on inspection of the original copies cited.

Abbreviations for Blake works:

A	*America a Prophecy*
Ah	*The Book of Ahania*
ARO	*All Religions Are One*
BL	*The Book of Los*
Eu	*Europe a Prophecy*
FR	*The French Revolution*

FZ	*The Four Zoas*
IM	"An Island in the Moon"
J	*Jerusalem the Emanation of the Giant Albion*
M	*Milton a Poem*
MHH	*The Marriage of Heaven and Hell*
NT	*Night Thoughts*
PS	*Poetical Sketches*
SL	*The Song of Los*
T	*The Book of Thel*
U	*The [First] Book of Urizen*
VDA	*Visions of the Daughters of Albion*

Abbreviations for Reference and Other Works:

BB	Bentley, *Blake Books*
BR	Bentley, *Blake Records*
BRS	Bentley, *Blake Records Supplement*
IB	Erdman, *Illuminated Blake*
PL	Milton, *Paradise Lost*
PR	Milton, *Paradise Regained*

Chapter One ✵

Eighteenth-Century Homosexuality and the Republican Tradition

> Jesus, from whose lips not a syllable favourable to ascetic self-denial is by any one of his biographers represented as ever having issued . . . in the field of sexual irregularity preserved an uninterrupted silence.
>
> —Jeremy Bentham, "Offences Against Taste" 497

In the text of page 78 of William Blake's manuscript epic-prophecy *The Four Zoas,* his chained rebel figure, Orc, is tempted by the tyrant Urizen to cease his opposition. Urizen offers Orc relief from his sufferings, a lure Orc easily scorns: "Thy Pity I contemn scatter thy snows elsewhere" (78:43). (Later he will succumb to other, subtler temptations.) The accompanying design shows a seemingly unrelated scene: A supine figure, inferentially Orc (his face, though roughly sketched, is Orc's), but without fetters, lies in a posture that might suggest either the pains of torture or sexual ecstasy (figure 1.1). The area above Orc's genitals has been heavily erased and penciled over, by Blake's or another hand, but within the shading can be seen a kneeling figure with head above Orc's groin. There are traces of what may be erect penises both between the kneeling figure's legs and above Orc's belly (the latter almost fully effaced). Most probably, then, the image shows two men in position for an act of fellation.

We are not sure at first how this design relates to the accompanying text, which does not directly mention homosexuality, or whether the action it shows should be viewed approvingly or negatively. On closer examination, it will turn out that the design's homosexual content is closely related to the passage's textual concerns—ruling-class hypocrisy, defiance and solidarity among the oppressed, possibilities of social utopia.[1] Other

2

Figure 1.1   William Blake. *The Four Zoas.* Page 78, detail. By permission of The British Library. Add 39764.

homosexual or sexually ambiguous designs and texts in works of Blake's middle and late periods share such thematic concerns. These references to homosexuality evince Blake's interest in the topic and his integration of it into his overall view of human liberation.

These uses of homosexuality evolve out of an earlier, masculinist outlook and aesthetic that nevertheless was roiled by contrary undercurrents, including a positive portrayal of some kinds of sexual perversion. In later work, starting roughly with *The Four Zoas* (ca. 1797–1807) and continuing in *Milton* (ca. 1804–21) and *Jerusalem* (ca. 1804–20), Blake revamps some of his earlier views, and his hatred of state cruelty, moral hypocrisy, and possessive male sexuality increasingly leads him to sympathize with and defend both female and male homosexuality. In these works, which are my major focus, Blake begins by figuring homosexuality positively in contexts of sexual and social repression, then incorporates a treatment of some homosexual relations as nonpossessive and equalitarian, at least compared to the possessive, sexually rigid, hypocritical forms of heterosexuality he links with "Moral Law" and the evils of economic exploitation and war. Simultaneously, Blake widens his focus from male homosexuality to include lesbian relations; indeed, his only relatively straightforward narration of a homosexual relationship, in *Jerusalem,* is of a lesbian involvement. In these poems, direct and coded references to male and female homosexuality become a compact, flexible way to refer to the brutality and hypocrisy of conventional morality, defiance of its strictures, and the possibility of alternative, mutualistic forms of love. In more directly political and social senses, homosexual relations become associated with such values as solidarity against social oppression, alternatives to private property, and prophetic inspiration. Finally, Blake's positive valuation of homosexuality contributes to a shift toward greater equity in his overall idea of relations among the sexes.

Blake's developing view of homosexuality—if I have grasped it correctly—runs counter to the thought of his time, though significantly not that of a few uncharacteristic thinkers or the eventual trend of liberal ideas; and it responds to events in the street. To understand Blake's development, we need to understand both these contexts. We need, then, to sketch the place of homosexuality in eighteenth- and early nineteenth-century London culture, including repression of homosexuals and their vilification in sexual polemic; the considerable contribution to antihomosexual ideology made by the republican tradition in letters, Blake's own tradition; and the alternatives possible within the thought of the time. These contexts provide a starting point for delimiting what Blake might have known about homosexuality and what cultural attitudes he might have absorbed and rejected in his own work.

Eighteenth-Century Homosexuality:
A Historical Sketch[2]

The last two decades have given us an increasingly full and nuanced knowledge of eighteenth- and early nineteenth-century homosexuality in Britain. We now know that London, like several other major European cities, supported an active sodomitical demimonde from the late seventeenth century at least through Blake's time. Scholars working from police records (a selective and class-biased but invaluable source) have found that the participants in this male homosexual milieu included single and married men belonging to a wide range of middle- and lowerclass occupations: alehouse keepers, fruitsellers, peruke-makers, servants, soldiers, schoolmasters, and many others, including, of course, male prostitutes. Besides such venues of opportunistic homosexuality as prisons, navy vessels, lodging houses, schools, and even churches, several kinds of locale furnished regular sites for homosexual assignations: public toilets, parks (late at night or early in the morning), deserted houses, public-houses. Some of the latter were ordinary establishments whose proprietors were unaware of or winked at the trade; others kept special rooms for it, and some entire establishments catered to homosexuals—the so-called molly houses. Men might repair to these deserted or safe sites after meeting in more open or mixed areas such as parks, latrines, and taverns, or in more or less well-known cruising areas, where, much like their present-day counterparts, they would make contact via coded language and gestures: "If one of them sits on a bench he pats the back of his hands; if you follow them, they put a white handkerchief through the skirts of their coat, and wave it," etc. (George Parker, *Views of Society and Manners* [etc.], 1781, qtd. in Trumbach, "Sodomites" 15). In the 1720s, as many as twenty "Houses of Resort" may have existed, and regular cruising areas included the coffee-houses by the Royal Exchange, Moorfields (where a particular path was known as Sodomites' Walk), public latrines in Lincoln's Inn and Covent Garden, St. Clement's churchyard, and the Birdcage Walk in St. James's Park.[3] Both in that decade and later, the masquerades held at Ranelagh Gardens and other sites provided opportunities for cross-dressing and homosexual assignations and a cover for the activities of female and male prostitutes, as well as for other violations of gender and class strictures.[4] By about 1810, the numbers of cruising spots and "houses" may have declined; one historian notes that "only St James's Park seems to have been still notorious as an out-of-doors picking-up spot," while the author of *The Phoenix of Sodom, or The Vere Street Coterie* (1813) could cite only four homosexual "houses"—in Blackman Street; near the Strand; near the obelisk in St.

George's Fields; and near Bishopsgate Street, "kept by a fellow known by the title of the Countess of Camomile" (Harvey 944; *Phoenix* 14).[5] Others came and went depending on police attention. The White Swan in Vere-street, discussed in a later chapter, may have been fairly typical—it was said to contain one room with four beds, another fitted like a women's dressing room, and a third where mock-marriages took place, besides the regular public and private rooms of a public-house (*Phoenix* 10; *Morning Chronicle,* Dec. 6, 1810: 3).

Being an active male homosexual was a dangerous business, bringing risks ranging from ostracism to execution. Proven sodomy was punishable by death. Since sodomy was legally defined to involve anal penetration (and sometimes emission), convictions were difficult to obtain, though not uncommon. Other homosexual acts were not legally prohibited as such. Men against whom sodomy could not be proved might therefore be charged with attempted sodomy or various misdemeanors for which standards of proof were lower. In 1760, for example, for having kissed and groped one James Fasset, a student aged sixteen, Richard Branson was convicted of attempted sodomy and sentenced to a year in jail and a £100 fine, then a very substantial sum; publication of the trial transcript in effect added a further sentence, public disgrace.[6] The predominant type of sex reported and prosecuted was anal, but oral sex was reported as well: In 1704 John Norton was accused of taking hold of John Coyney's privates, "putting them into his mouth and sucking them," as, in 1738, a Paris hustler offered his client that "if I wanted, I could consummate the act in his mouth" (Trumbach, "Birth" 136; Rey 184). Rey notes that such acts "appear to have been seen as depraved or very wanton, in any case extreme" (184).

While much repression was routine and individual, recorded only in the police and trial records that are our present-day sources, there were also repeated episodes of public repression, when numbers of victims were seized, tried, exposed in the pillory, and/or hanged. (Some committed suicide rather than face these punishments.) These episodes included raids on molly houses in 1707–09 and 1726–27, when two victims were hanged, and on taverns and other gathering places in 1763–65, 1776, and 1810 (the Vere-street persecution, discussed in chapter 5). Sometimes those raided offered resistance, and probably many more escaped than were apprehended.[7] Mob vengeance could step in where citizens felt the law too lenient. In the 1780s, when a group of upper-class alleged homosexuals were acquitted in Exeter, "the enraged multitude was so convinced of their guilt, that, without any respect to their rank, they burnt them in effigy" (*Phoenix* 27). Individual prosecutions are recorded in 1727, "nearly every week" from 1720 to 1740, then in 1763, 1772, 1775, and in a rising drumbeat in 1804, 1806, 1808, 1809, and 1810 (Norton 129–33, 170, 185–87).

Summing up the pervasiveness of legal repression in this period is difficult. As the dates just cited may indicate, major waves of persecution were not frequent. In the whole year 1798, for example, the London *Times*'s crime reports (covering London and the county assizes elsewhere) discuss only two trials involving homosexuality. In one, a Shropshire minister was successfully prosecuted for accusing three prominent local citizens of heterosexual infidelity, attempted sodomy, and actual sodomy in separate anonymous letters (*Times*, June 9, 1798: 3). In the other, worth detailing for what it shows about the law's workings, Edward Dawson, a gentleman, and John Hall, a soldier, were charged with "a certain detestable crime."

> *William Claverty* was called. He stated that on the morning of the 6th of March last, about one o'clock, in progress with the relief guard, he made the usual halt at a small distance from the centry-box, stationed near the Pay-office, but was not challenged by the centinel. In consequence of this, he stepped quickly forward; saw *Hall*, the prisoner, standing in the box, with his back towards the street. About this instant he saw Dawson run out of the box.—[The witness here stated some circumstances, which we omit for obvious reasons.]— He pursued him, and overtaking him at about 12 or 13 yards distance, he seized him by the breast, and brought him back prisoner to the guard.

Further testimony showed an effort to bribe Claverty and other incriminating particulars. The account continues:

> Here LORD KENYON addressed the Gentlemen of the Jury. He reminded them of the kind of evidence the law required to constitute proof of the commission of the abominable crime of which the prisoners at the bar stood charged. In the present case, most certainly, the evidence did not bear out the charge laid in the indictment; but, in his mind, enough had been stated to authorise a belief that either the act had been committed before, or was about to be committed at the time the witness, Claverty, approached the sentry-box. This, however, was not evidence on which the prisoners could legally be found guilty of the felony, and therefore his Lordship thought the Gentlemen of the Jury must acquit them.
>   The Jury found a verdict.—*Not Guilty.* (*Times*, April 24, 1798: 3)

In this and other instances, a draconic law was applied with reasonable fairness within its own terms. Still, evidence to convict *was* available often enough that twenty-nine persons were hanged for sodomy between 1805 and 1820, including six in 1806 alone (Harvey 947). Several prosecuted in that year belonged to the same homosexual circle in the town of Warrington, whose members "regularly assembled . . . on Monday and Friday evenings; and . . . they called one another brother." Five of the circle were sentenced to death, including one of the town's richest citizens, Isaac Hitchin (or Hitchen), but he and another were "respited during his Majesty's pleasure," and apparently later reprieved; three were hanged (*Bell's Weekly Messenger,* Aug. 31, 1806: 276; Sept. 21, 1806: 300; *Annual Register* 1806: 438).[8] In the navy, as well, courts martial imposed death sentences for sodomy in 1797, 1800, 1802, 1805, and 1815–16—thirteen times in nineteen years (Harvey 940). Overall, executions were not constant, but they were not rare either, at least in London and Middlesex. Though there had been only two in this venue from 1749 to 1796, eleven, or one every couple of years, took place in the next twenty years—the crucial years in my study of Blake—before their frequency fell again after 1816 (Harvey, Appendix 2, 948).

The infrequent general crackdowns no doubt had, and were meant to have, a deterrent effect, striking fear into a broader homosexual population. And by providing grist for hostile satires and polemics such as *The Women-Hater's Lamentation* (1707), *Hell upon Earth: or the Town in an Uproar* (1729), and *Satan's Harvest Home* (1749), they helped keep such behavior unthinkable, or at least indefensible. Commentaries such as that in the Reverend John Allen's fast-day sermon *The Destruction of Sodom improved, as a Warning to Great-Britain* (1756) were, one supposes, fairly common. In considering Sodom's fate, Allen asked,

> Who can help thinking—of MIDNIGHT MASQUERADES; secret assignations for GAMING; ROUTS, RIOTS, and other diversions of strange names . . . lastly, of the *unnatural* vices, which are more practised than sober people can well conceive of; vices, till lately, strangers to our colder climate, and which are the abomination of God and man[?] (26–27)

In a similar way, for genteel readers, elite homosexuality furnished matter for satire, pornography, and polemic by Pope, Smollett, Cleland, Churchill, Cowper, and others. Among the upper classes, too, less likely to face trial than teachers or clerks, ostracism served as a means of repression. Some cases were famous, notably that of William Beckford, the author of *Vathek* (1786), who was forced to leave England in 1785 after the exposure of his involvement with sixteen-year-old William Courtenay. Beckford spent most of the next eleven years abroad, and even later he was long shunned by members of his own class.[9]

Like that of male homosexuals, the rich and varied world of eighteenth- and early nineteenth-century lesbians is now being illuminated by cultural historians and literary scholars. Supplementing and partly disputing the pioneering work of Lillian Faderman, Emma Donoghue has argued for a self-aware lesbian tradition throughout the "long eighteenth century," in forms ranging from friendship to sex and under overlapping self-conceptions ranging from "a concept of sex acts between women to a concept of lesbian identity" (10, 20). More cautiously, work in progress by Susan S. Lanser argues that a sapphic identity emerged in stages throughout the century, first as an externally imposed category and ultimately as a "sapphic subjectivity . . . a self-differentiation according to sexual object choice" ("Sapphic Subjects"). Lesbianism was not subject to the same legal repression that has provided grist for students of the sodomitical culture. Lesbian acts were not covered by any law; what seems to be the only prominent law case of the period involving lesbianism occurred when, in 1810, two Scots school-keepers, Marianne Woods and Jane Pirie, sued Dame Helen Cumming Gordon, a local notable, for destroying their reputations and livelihood with allegations of lesbianism. Pirie and Woods were eventually upheld, though the case dragged on until 1820 without their being able to collect. Of twenty pages of precedents introduced by defense lawyers to support the plausibility of Gordon's accusations, none involved English or Scottish cases.[10] Nevertheless, lesbianism was well known in the culture, as Donoghue and others have demonstrated through linguistic, scientific, biographic, and literary reference. Contemporary sources refer to lesbians under labels with distinct though sometimes overlapping connotations, such as tribades, hermaphrodites, Sapphists, and even, in 1726, "Lesbians." "Tommies," apparently a correlative to the male "mollies," became current somewhat later in the century.[11]

Lesbian (or possibly lesbian) biographies take varied forms. Several instances are known in which women masqueraded for part of their lives as men—notably the actress Charlotte Charke, who, though twice married, maintained a loving domestic relationship with a woman for at least seven years in mid-life. In other cases women lived in ordinary middle- or upper-class milieux, while maintaining a fairly open primary emotional interest in women. Anne Conway Damer (1749–1828), for example, married and widowed young, was well known as a sapphist by her early thirties. (She was the subject of "A Sapphic Epistle from Jack Cavendish to the Honourable and Most Beautiful Mrs. D****," 1782.) Damer escaped open censure, though not private gossip, and always had her defenders. In still other cases, such as that of the "Ladies of Llangollen," discussed in chapter 6, women cohabited for decades in a situation that could be successfully presented as (and perhaps sometimes did constitute) "romantic friendship." As Donoghue notes, this socially approved category was also an ambiguous one: "The same pair of women could be idealised as romantic friends by one observer and suspected of unnatural acts by another, or even in some cases idealised and suspected by the same person" (143).[12] Discussions of lesbianism under the quasi-scientific label of hermaphrodism, erotic narrations of lesbianism in literature and pornography, most often written by males, and instances of noted women living together all have some importance in Blake's treatment of women's homosexuality.

In the activity of London's streets and taverns and its intermittent scandals, then, as well as in literature, broadsheets, and scientific speculation, Blake's culture offered abundant opportunities for forming an impression of the male homosexual underworld, and more limited avenues for an awareness of lesbianism. Yet the culture offered nothing like a publicly articulated defense of homosexuality, even by a small minority, on which Blake could have drawn for a positive view. Indeed, one of the remarkable aspects of eighteenth- and early nineteenth-century homosexuality—especially that of men but also that of women—is that it existed in a virtual double world, universally known but closed to discussion. Homosexuality was *literally* "not to be spoken of among Christians." The "circumstances, which we omit for obvious reasons" of the *Times* law report mentioned earlier recur over and over. In 1815, for instance, the *Morning Chronicle* reported the execution of "A hoary miscreant, a workhouse pauper" for "a crime at which nature shudders, not a syllable of the evidence on which we can state" (qtd. by Harvey 942). Scientific and medical literature either avoided discussing male homosexuality and lesbianism at all or resorted to euphemism or passages in French or Latin (Porter and Hall 3–4, 39, 102–103); nearly all the precedents supplied by the defense in Woods-Pirie *v.* Gordon were in these languages. The cliche that these vices were un-English, "till lately, strangers to our colder climate" *(The Destruction of Sodom improved),* must have been supported by the strict silence imposed on any discussion of them in Britain. The results were paradoxical: While references to unnaturalness or the impossibility of giving particulars denoted homosexuality with utter transparency, open debate about homosexuality as a practice or a philosophical or moral issue was all but nonexistent. In a period replete with clerical, pamphlet, satiric, and journalistic condemnations, historians cite only one apparent philosophic justification, Thomas Cannon's *Ancient and Modern Pederasty investigated and exemplified* (1749), which John Cleland described in a letter as "evidently in defence of *Sodomy*" (qtd. in Sabor 201), but this pamphlet is now probably lost. My initial hypothesis for this chapter was that Blake (with Bentham and Shelley, discussed below) must have represented a more general, though decidedly minority, view expressed in some way in print; this does not seem to be true.[13] Homosexuality was known as a fact, understood with varying tolerance and malignity by men and women in society, hinted at or lampooned in literature. Yet there was *not* a practical heterodoxy beneath the culture's overt disapproval; this was a thoroughly suppressive time that exacted enormous costs from nonconformists in act or thought.

Homosexuality and the Republican Tradition

Eighteenth-century literary culture shared the general social intolerance of homosexuality, and Blake's republican tradition in letters did so with a vengeance. Literary treatments of the topic in general either took up a posture of condemnation (even as a mask) or were so encoded and/or subtly nuanced that their homosexual content could be and often was denied. Negative references ranged from the titillating and pornographic, such as the anonymous *Love-Letters Between a certain late Nobleman And the famous Mr. Wilson* (1723, 1745) and lesbian and sodomitic scenes in Cleland's *Memoirs of a Woman of Pleasure* (1749), through the worldly, negative satire of homosexual episodes in Smollett's *Roderick Random* (1748), to the unrestrained invective of Pope's sneer at Lord John Hervey, the effeminate "painted child of dirt, that stinks and stings":

> Now high, now low, now Master up, now Miss,
> And he himself one vile Antithesis.
> Amphibious thing! that acting either part,
> The trifling head, or the corrupted heart,
> Fop at the toilet, flatt'rer at the board,
> Now trips a Lady, and now struts a Lord.
> ("Epistle to Dr. Arbuthnot" 310, 324–29)[14]

Alongside such hate-filled texts, some writers produced works in which we can now read a homoerotic sensibility, and several recent studies have explored the modes of expression and vicissitudes of such writing. Robert F. Gleckner's *Gray Agonistes* (1997), for example, extending earlier work by Jean H. Hagstrum, has shown how Thomas Gray was psychically and poetically crushed under the combined weight of his indebtedness to Milton and his life-shaping, unacknowledged love for Richard West: "[T]o attempt to be Milton and to fail is not . . . heroism at all but rather utter failure to be *a* poet; and to love another man in an age when ostracism and possibly severe legal punishment could result from public discovery and exposure, and to *write* of that relationship would be to court personal infamy, not merely poetic or personal failure" (6).[15] Jon Thomas Rowland's *"Swords in Myrtle Dress'd"* (1998) focuses on both antisodomitic and homoerotic writings. Rowland traces the polemics over Lord Hervey's effeminacy (including but going beyond Pope's attack) and the content of and responses to Charles Churchill's antihomosexual satires (discussed below). These sections frame studies of Mark Akenside's poetry, particularly *The Pleasures of Imagination* (1744), in whose arcadian landscape, Rowland says, "You never read of a path, a sight, a sound . . . without being immediately distracted to the foot, the eye, the ear of some young male. What attracts him makes *him* attractive, till *he* becomes the object—the pleased the *pleasing*" (117). But, Rowland shows, Akenside's revisions after 1757, responding both to his own growing political conservatism and to criticisms by Smollett, produced an "obviously . . . masculinized" work, in which "small verbal revisions remove the suggestion of sexuality and even gender" (137, 139). Even in highly disguised forms, possibilities for homoerotic expression in literature were meager.

Two works from late in the century might seem to be partial exceptions: Beckford's *Vathek* (1786), with its lyric portrait of thirteen-year-old prince Gulchenrouz, "the most delicate and lovely creature in the world," with "sweet voice" and "the bashfulness of a fawn" (115–17), and Richard Payne Knight's *Discourse on the Worship of Priapus* (1786), an illustrated investigation of pagan phallicism. Beckford's persecution, as well as his later commission to Benjamin West for a monumental series of paintings based on the Book of Revelation, might have made him a sympathetic figure for Blake.[16] Blake might also have approved the phallicism and implied anticlericalism of Knight's *Priapus,* which, though privately circulated, may have been known to him since some of its priapean emblems resemble Blake's own designs.[17] Knight and Beckford, however, avoid directly challenging antihomosexual feelings. Knight attacks the "violence and heat" of religious intolerance and urges the relativity of morals: Though even "the form itself, under which the God was represented [in priapean cults] appeared to [Christians] a mockery," the worship could "appear just and reasonable to those who consider manners and customs as relative to the natural causes which produced them" (23, 27–28). Such an argument almost begs to be extended to homosexuality. Yet *Priapus* skirts the issue of ancient homosexuality, despite its author's own probable homosexuality. *Vathek,* as published and reprinted by Beckford, similarly avoids using the distinct customs and morals of Arab lands to suggest cultural differences about homosexuality. Gulchenrouz is described as heterosexual, and in *Vathek*'s only actual homosexual encounter he unwillingly receives the "thousand odious caresses" of a powerful older man, responding with "a gleam of indignation" amid his tears (129–30). In short, neither Knight nor Beckford could take an openly approving stance toward homosexuality, and neither was publicly read as doing so—and yet *Priapus* injured Knight's reputation and Hester Thrale Piozzi confided to her journal that Beckford's *"favourite Propensity* is all along visible I think; particularly in the luscious Descriptions given of Gulchenrouz" (qtd. in Lonsdale xxi). To the modern reader these remain tantalizing works, suggesting much more about the variability of sexual experience than they affirm. Knight and Beckford, however, had the worst of both worlds: They were *not* read as striking blows for tolerance yet were injured as though they had done so.[18]

If the general literary culture offered no models for a positive treatment of homosexuality, except by deeply concealed implication, the literary tradition with which Blake was most closely allied—that of public, politically reformative poetry, which I refer to as the republican poetic tradition—was unequivocally hostile to sodomy and its supposed ties to aristocratic decadence. This antihomosexual stance developed gradually and was not exclusive to the republican tradition but occurs in it in a specific way: as a link between social privilege and homosexual misconduct.[19] We can trace the rise of this amalgam in Milton; his treatment is important both because he helped shape the amalgam and bequeath it to later republican thought and, more specifically, because of Milton's outsized importance to Blake as a poetic and political forebear whose positive and negative legacies he continually reassessed.

Milton's early and middle works treat homosexuality among the sins of licentiousness and abuse, without special emphasis, but later works fuse general licentiousness, homosexuality, and ruling-class privilege under the signs of Sodom and another biblical metonymy for lust, the sons of Belial. This development is consistent with what Gregory W. Bredbeck has identified as an overall shift in rhetorical usage, in which "[e]arly [i.e., sixteenth-century] translations and glosses tend to figure the incidents [of Sodom and Gibeah, discussed below] as examples of general debauchery and sin . . . [but] [b]y the end of the seventeenth century, the process of increased sexual specification progressed to such a point that Sodom was specifically and only male sodomy" (215–16, 218).

In *De doctrina Christiana* (ca. 1658–60), for example, Milton classifies male homosexuality among violations of one's own or one's neighbor's chastity. Among examples of the latter, Milton instances the story of Sodom and the somewhat less familiar one of Gibeah—in which "the men of the city, certain sons of Belial," demand that a traveler be delivered to them "that we may know him," and are instead offered his concubine (Judg. 19:22).[20] Milton thus treats sodomy as a sin against oneself or others, but not as uniquely depraved or a sign of social decay. Sodom, in treatises of the 1640s and 1650s like *The Reason of Church-Government, An Apology Against a Pamphlet,* and *Eikonoklastes,* signifies general wickedness, spiritual blindness, and the like, without specific reference to sexual sodomy. The first of these pamphlets, for example, uses "Sodom" to denote the "riots of ungodly mis-rule that Prelaty hath wrought both in the Church of Christ, and in the state of this Kingdome" (*Prose Works* 1: 861). Similarly, in these and other works, the sons of Belial connote wickedness and drunkenness, corrupt church practices, and "unbridl'd and vagabond lust" (*The Doctrine and Discipline of Divorce, Prose Works* 2: 225).[21] In polemics, Milton was quick to accuse opponents of effeminacy and/or homosexuality but initially without pinpointing the latter as uniquely horrible. In the two *Defences,* for instance, Milton continually ridicules the supposed effeminacy of his target Salmasius, usually implying that he is ruled by women but sometimes, through jokes about his buttocks, that he practices passive homosexuality; and he accuses Charles I both of fondling women in public and of having "joined the [homosexual] Duke of Buckingham in every act of infamy" (*Prose Works* 4: 408).[22] These thrusts seem to find general unmanliness, libertinism, and homosexuality equally damning. Milton's early outline for a tragedy on Sodom, however, hints at the later fusion of sexual sodomy and social depravity. General debauchery is Milton's target, and yet its homosexual component is prominent, in references to the townsmen strolling "every one with mistresse, or Ganymed," and to the temple priests' unseemly interest in the angels (*Prose Works* 8: 558–59). Sexual sodomy seems both a synecdoche for lust in general and a particularly flagrant example of it.[23]

By Restoration times, homosexuality had emerged as the more explosive slur—as ironically shown by its use against Milton himself, together with Marvell, his supposed catamite, in Richard Leigh's polemic against Marvell's support of religious toleration:

> *O marvellous Fate. O Fate full of marvel;*
> *That* Nol's Latin Pay *two* Clerks *should deserve ill!*
> *Hiring a* Gelding *and* Milton *the* Stallion;
> *His* Latin *was gelt, and turn'd pure* Italian. (*The Transproser Rehears'd* 135)[24]

Paradise Lost (1667) partakes of this more pointed rhetoric, using homosexuality as a marker of depravity more than had Milton's prose works. Milton's reference to Belial in Book 1, with its unstated application to the Cavalier court, firmly implants the link between homosexuality and class decadence in the republican tradition:

> In Courts and Palaces he also Reigns
> And in Luxurious Cities . . .
> . . . .
>   And when Night
> Darkens the Streets, then wander forth the Sons
> Of *Belial,* flown with insolence and wine.
> Witness the Streets of *Sodom,* and that night
> In *Gibeah,* when the hospitable door
> Expos'd a Matron to avoid worse rape. (*PL* 1:497–98, 500–505)

In this version of the stories of Sodom and Gibeah, Milton includes and conflates two interpretive traditions. One identified the relevant sin as the violation of hospitality ("the hospitable door"), the other as homosexual conduct. While he draws on both, Milton's emphasis is on the "worse rape" (because homosexual) averted by exposing the Gibeah visitor's concubine, and implied as the Sodomites' intention. Further, departing from the biblical stories, in which the violators are the cities' citizens in general, Milton links homosexuality to the insolence of wealth and royalty, elements that already had led some Puritans to call Charles II's courtiers "sons of Belial."[25]

Paradise Regained, less explicitly, refers to homoerotic enticements in Jesus' banquet temptation, a scene important not only in its original context but because Blake would allude to and illustrate it (chapters 3, 4). Here Milton uses classical, vernacular, and pastoral-generic allusion to signify homoeroticism: The wine that Satan manifests is served by "Tall stripling youths rich-clad, of fairer hue / Than *Ganymede* or *Hylas*" (2:352–53). Milton's mythic reference, argues Bredbeck, would be transparent to contemporary readers, for whom the characters in question regularly denoted homosexual objects and actions (197–99). The implied homoeroticism becomes part of what Bette Charlene Werner terms a show of "excess . . . [t]he sumptuous display, the lavish service, and the multitudes of fair attendants" that "associate the scene . . . with the invitation to partake of the riches of the earthly kingdoms" (192).[26] At the same time, arguably, the homoerotic enticement should be seen as more disturbing and more disruptive of desirable gender norms than a heterosexual temptation, since Satan has already indicated to Belial that the Son is of too "exalted mind" for such bait—"Therefore with manlier objects we must try / His constancy" (2:206, 225–26); the pun on "manly" may be intentional. Thus while the banquet's lavishness would in any case denote love for things of this world, and specifically the empty love of luxury, the Ganymede-Hylas reference uses homosexuality as a specific sign of moral contagion.

Condemnation of homosexuality is less direct in this scene than in *Paradise Lost*. Bredbeck, in fact, argues that the banquet temptation "removes the overt condemnation ascribed to it [homoeroticism] by separating it from the tradition of Belial" (226). Further, as noted in my preface, several scholars assert that in Restoration times penetrative sodomy was seen as compatible with male gender norms, and some have inferred that the practice must have been tacitly condoned. The association of penetrative sodomy with general male lewdness would indeed help explain how Satan and Belial can progress from the thought of tempting Jesus with women to that of presenting him with "Ganymedes." Yet this very progression suggests that homosexuality was *not* seen simply as one kind of debauchery—or, at least, that different groups in society may have had differing views on this point. Milton's own usage in *Paradise Lost,* Leigh's lampoon of Milton and Marvell, and later antisodomitic satires against William III all argue that in some social circles sodomy was seen, in distinction to heterosexual libertinism, as particularly outrageous, ridiculous, or shameful—an "Unnatural Vice" as opposed to a "Natural Sin," as a defender of William said in denying the charge (*Satyr* b'). Moreover, these attacks show no difference between condemnation of passive and active roles. It is reasonable to suppose that the Ganymedes in *Paradise Regained* function to intensify, not merely complement, the suggestion of moral corruption. Though Milton's tone is softer than in *Paradise Lost* (partly because he is less explicit), homosexuality remains a marker both of unseemly wealth and ease and of particularly insidious temptation.[27]

Over the next century, Jacobite, Country, Whig, and Tory interests all used antihomosexual satire and polemic at various points against William III (as examined in a later chapter), Anne, and later Walpole; the attacks on Hervey and probably the *Love-Letters* belong to this tradition.[28] But the use of homosexuality as part of an attack on class and political privilege as such is peculiar to the radical and republican traditions. The satirist Charles Churchill, for example, closely associated with the oppositionist John Wilkes in 1763–64, devotes a whole poem, *The Times,* to this theme. Affecting to defend women's honor and the purity of boys, *The Times* paints sodomy as London's regnant vice: "Women are kept for nothing but the breed; / For pleasure we must have a Ganymede, / A fine, fresh Hylas, a delicious boy, / To serve our purposes of beastly joy" (331–34). Churchill's full purpose is to stigmatize the current administration and the nation's ruling circles, several of whose present and past members he targets in coded passages (476, 494, 638, and elsewhere). His attack on homosexuals is linked to earlier references to arrogant grandees who ignore the cries of widows and tradesmen they have ruined, knowing "Heaven can commence no legal action here" (72; 55–76); venality and state corruption (129–40); and the Earl of Bute's administration and the peace of 1763, which Wilkite opinion opposed (29–30, 197–200). The poem's plebeian stance is found not just in its subject matter but also in its use of a "plain" style marked by everyday language, infrequent inversions, and so on. Its ultimate source is probably Juvenal's Satire 2, which, in a similarly vigorous and colloquial way, denounces widespread homosexuality as a sign of the times ("even among the dead / Rome stands dishonoured") and the vice of a decadent elite, as visitors carry back "[u]pper-class Roman habits" to their homelands (81).

Churchill underscores the supposed connection of homosexuality, like the other vices he mentions, to class and political privilege:

> Go where we will, at every time and place,
> Sodom confronts, and stares us in the face;
> They ply in public at our very doors,
> And take the bread from much more honest whores.
> Those who are mean high paramours secure,
> And the rich guilty screen the guilty poor;
> The sin too proud to feel from reason awe,
> And those who practise it too great for law. (293–300)[29]

And Churchill uses the assumedly un-English origins of homosexuality—a platitude of the age—to attack naval-mercantile imperialism, the main target of those poets who opposed the regnant genre of Empire panegyric:[30]

> To different lands for different sins we roam,
> And, richly freighted, bring our cargo home,
> Nobly industrious to make vice appear
> In her full state, and perfect only here. (181–84)

Though various vices thus made their way to England from Holland, France, Spain, and Italy, it was "the soft luxurious East" from which England had learned "sins worse / Than all her plagues . . . / . . . / . . . which but to name, / Would call up in my cheeks the marks of shame" (255–64). We should note here the yoking of softness and luxury with homosexuality that also marks Milton's banquet temptation.[31]

Thomas Chatterton, unknown in his brief career but later idealized as "the marvelous boy," plebeian genius and martyr for artistic independence, returns to the homosexuality-privilege theme in a distinct but complementary way. Chatterton's antiroyal, antiministerial satire "The Whore of Babylon," written during the struggle to seat Wilkes in 1770 and published posthumously in 1803, uses the supposed present "Catamitish Age," when "Unnat'ral Crimes afford Seraphic Joys / And all the Objects of Desire are Boys," as an emblem of corrupt servility (558, 553–54). Contrasting his own refusal to look "With Awe upon the Chains of Favour" (564), Chatterton first insists on his independence, then denounces catamites and demonstratively avows his heterosexuality, and finally reverts to the attack on ministerial and administration corruption, mentioning Lord North and the Earl of Sandwich (leaders in the current administration), Lord Chief Justice Mansfield, Henry Luttrel (Wilkes's opponent), and others (531–76 passim). Though in fact none of these seems to have been known as a user of "catamites," proximity smears their "Vices" (565, 572) as at least similar in quality. Chatterton implies that if he were to become a metaphoric and/or actual catamite, he too could find official favor (549–64).[32] In both poets, then, hatred of homosexuality is integral to the republican opposition's attacks on corruption, privilege, and imperialism.[33]

Another poet with affinities to the republican tradition whose condemnations of sodomy might have come to Blake's attention is Cowper. Though he came from a long-established Whig family, Cowper's reformist sympathies were looser than Churchill's or Chatterton's; in earlier poems, he is pro-Empire, anti-American, and hostile to the "mob," and some of these sentiments persist in his most noted work, *The Task* (1784). Yet he attacked slavery throughout his poetic life, most notably in *The Task*, in which it is "human nature's broadest, foulest blot," by which man "finds his fellow guilty of a skin / Not colour'd like his own, and having pow'r / . . . / Chains him, and tasks him, and exacts his sweat / With stripes" (2:22, 12–13, 23–24).[34] In eighteenth-century terms a "Commonwealthman" who based his political thinking on the 1688 revolution and settlement,[35] Cowper came to see George III as a neo-Stuart, and in Book 5 of *The Task* apostrophized liberty, condemned the origins of monarchy in conquest, and praised "[t]he king who loves the law; respects his bounds / And reigns content within them . . . / . . . / Beyond that mark is treason" (446–47, 230–41, 332–41). With attacks elsewhere in its pages on legal oppression of the poor, the conquest of India, and the factory system, and praise of humble pleasures and the rural life, *The Task* was read as an encomium of liberty.[36] We know that Blake respected Cowper, for he told Hayley, "I have the happiness of seeing the Divine countenance in such men as Cowper and Milton more distinctly than in any prince or hero" (letter, May 28, 1804; *E* 750).[37]

Both in early satires and *The Task,* Cowper's liberalism was inflected by strong religious beliefs, love of leisured country life, and hatred of urban luxury and vice. These concerns fused with attacks on episcopal, legal, and governmental corruption to produce the link between oppression, corruption, and sodomy that we have noted before. Together with other examples of arrogance and irreligion, Cowper asks,

> Hast thou [England] within thee sin that in old time
> Brought fire from heav'n, the sex-abusing crime,
> Whose horrid perpetration stamps disgrace
> Baboons are free from, upon human race?

When Sodom was destroyed, he warns,

> Then nature injur'd, scandaliz'd, defil'd,
> Unveil'd her blushing cheek, look'd on and smil'd[.] ("Expostulation"
>   414–17, 424–25)[38]

In *The Task,* Cowper avoids explicit attacks on sodomy but links wealth with vice and Sodom in general terms to which many readers would add sodomy by inference. Thus he warns that "Profusion deluging a state with lusts / Of grossest nature and of worst effects, / Prepares it for its ruin"; and condemns London, "resort and mart of all the earth," which, "spotted with all crimes," is "more obnoxious at this hour, / Than Sodom in her day" (2:688–90; 3:835–47). Though not a major theme of the poem, such attacks do color it subtly. But in *Tirocinium,* a long poem on education published in the same volume with *The Task,* Cowper returns to direct defamation: Along with abuses of wealth, military adventurism, and other vices supposedly "bred at schools" (838), one can

> See womanhood despised, and manhood shamed
> With infamy too nauseous to be named . . . (827–28)

Cowper's use of the privilege-sodomy amalgam, though influenced by his religious orthodoxy and ruralism, is also an expression of his quasi-republicanism and shows how widespread the amalgam had become.[39]

Contemporary Intellectual Alternatives

Despite this animus against homosexuality in the general culture and in the political traditions Blake shared, we know independently of Blake that it was intellectually possible to arrive at a relatively positive view of homosexuality within the framework of late eighteenth- and early nineteenth-century thought—and to do so without being homosexual oneself, as Blake was not. As Louis Crompton has shown, Jeremy Bentham did just this in a series of lengthy draft notes and manuscripts produced intermittently between 1774 and 1825.[40] In rich detail, Crompton establishes that Bentham moved from a criticism of the harshness and hypocrisy of antihomosexual repression, in his earliest discussions, to an affirmation of homosexual attachments as simply a variant of human sexuality, in his latest. Much of Bentham's argument is crabbed and legalistic, though possessing broader implications. In a 1785 manuscript, for example, he takes up, in order, such issues as whether homosexual acts offend against the security of the individual, are debilitating, or retard population; in 1814–16 manuscripts, whether they injure the health or reputation of the "operator," and so on. Some of these arguments serve more broadly to introduce material on cultural plurality, for example, by observing that Greek warriors did not show debility ("Offences Against One's Self" 1: 393–94). Bentham also reproduces some of the period's prejudices. He accepts without question the harmfulness of masturbation, and attributes homosexuality to the effects of sexual separation (and, in English public schools, the sexually exciting effects of feather beds). But he views antihomosexual feeling as a harmful prejudice and strives for non-pejorative language to describe homosexuality, such as "improlific venery" or "the improlific [or "unprolific"] appetite" ("Offences Against One's Self" 2: 107; "Offences Against Taste" 490).

Aside from these specifics, Bentham's position rests on at least three core ideas. First, he argues that punishment of homosexuality stems from antipathy to pleasure and from the punishers' prejudices and is therefore wrong; this argument derives from Bentham's basic dedication to the pleasure principle. Second, an Enlightenment stress on rationality and the relativity of custom produces a serious argument for universal toleration ("Offences Against the Self" 2: 94–98; "Offences Against Taste" 493). Finally, in the 1814–16 manuscripts Bentham introduces—and later develops at much greater length—a distinction between Pauline anti-sexuality and a sexually openminded Jesus: "Jesus, from whose lips not a syllable favourable to ascetic self-denial is by any one of his biographers represented as ever having issued . . . Jesus has in the field of sexual irregularity preserved an uninterrupted silence" ("Offences Against Taste" 497). These core ideas, with distinct lines of derivation, are equally available to Blake. Crompton indeed notes the closeness of Bentham's Jesus to the heretical, antiauthoritarian Jesus in Blake's "The Everlasting Gospel."[41] The emotive sources of Bentham's stance, disgust at the hatred of pleasure and at imposing personal morals on others, are also close to Blake's championing of sexual gratification and his visceral rage at victimization and moral hypocrisy.

A second contemporary reconsideration of homosexuality, Percy Shelley's draft essay "A Discourse on the Manners of the Antient Greeks Relative to the Subject of Love" (1818), was originally written as a preface or part of a preface to his translation of Plato's *Symposium.* There is no doubt he meant it to have educative value on the topic of homosexuality. Yet, despite Shelley's youth and overall radicalism, his position is less daring intellectually than Bentham's. Shelley "explains" Greek homosexuality as a product of the oppressed condition of Greek women and even their lack of beauty (408–409, 412). And he cannot quite bring himself to believe that Greek males had physical sex with one another: In most instances the lover slaked his physical needs with his wife or a slave, or his thoughts were too exalted to need physical expression, while in other cases, perhaps, when in company with a partner of supreme physical loveliness, something happened analogous to "certain phenomena connected with sleep, at the age of puberty" (411). Despite this squeamishness, Shelley does stress the normality of male-male attraction in Greek society, refers to the homoeroticism of Shakespeare's sonnets, and defends modern homosexuality in a gingerly way by observing that male-male sexual contact, though "sufficiently detestable," is no worse than intercourse with a prostitute (412). Shelley, of course, may have softpedaled his ideas expecting that the *Symposium* would do most of his work. In a letter to Thomas Love Peacock, he noted adopting a "delicate caution which either I cannot or will not practice in other matters, but which here I acknowledge to be necessary"; but he added that he had no "serious thought of publishing either this discourse or the *Symposium,* at least till I return to England" (*Works* 7: 362).

Bentham and Shelley's drafts show what could not be published in England in Blake's time, despite a wealth of circumlocution and defensive formulations—and also what *could* be intellectually conceived. Bentham developed his ideas in complete secrecy, except for a draft proposal for future collaboration addressed to William Beckford in 1817, which may not have been sent; he never published his writings on the topic, perhaps fearing that the predictable odium would cancel any influence he might have on other matters (Crompton, *Byron* 270–73). Similarly, Shelley published neither his draft essay nor the *Symposium* translation in the remaining four years of his life; when they were published in 1840, only the first, more general portion of the essay was printed, and the translation was bowdlerized. There can be, then, no question of any influence of Bentham or Shelley's views on Blake; Blake could not have known of their commentaries. The value of their examples for my presentation is their demonstration that within contemporary thought about civil society, liberty, and religion, it was possible for independent thinkers to arrive at views of homosexuality antithetical to the dominant ones—ideas similar to those that Blake's later poetry manifests.

Chapter Two ✣

Blake and the Poetics of Masculinity

I'll lie beside thee on a'bank & view their wanton play
In lovely copulation bliss on bliss with Theotormon

—*Visions of the Daughters of Albion* 7:25–26

lake's early works show relatively few signs of his later sympathy
toward homosexual desire; rather, they display an aesthetic of assertive masculinity. But this quality is not consistent. In early
works (for my purposes, those before *The Four Zoas*), Blake often idealizes aggressive maleness. So far as he asserts that apocalypse may come
through an "improvement of sensual enjoyment" (*MHH* 14), the enjoyment is normally conceived as genital, heterosexual, and dependent on
male gratification. These works largely devalue sexual modes other than
male-dominant heterosexuality, including male and female homosexuality, and particularly masturbation, which functions as a kind of stand-in
for non-"prolific" sexuality in general. Yet despite these emphases, Blake
conceives, is aware of, writes about, and illustrates these other forms of
sexuality. And underneath their predominant poetics of masculinity, gingerly but discernibly broadened representations of both masturbation
and homosexuality provide a countercurrent running through these
works.

By "poetics of masculinity" I mean dramatic treatments and imagery
that view masculine heterosexual desire as implicitly superior to other
kinds of sexuality; celebrate female desire insofar as it provides delight
with and for the male; and construct an ostentatiously heterosexual,
male poetic persona. Such a poetics is common to many of the writers of
the period. Among those already mentioned, for example, it is found in

Cleland's erotica, in Churchill's use of the rake's vocabulary ("much more honest whores," etc.), and in Chatterton's poetic persona in satires and lyrics. Though this poetics is not specific to the republican tradition, that tradition shares in it with little criticism, and it is present in various ways in early Blake. Centrally, it is implicit in his conception of the "prolific" as a general category of thought and behavior (*MHH* 16).

In Blake studies the prolific is conventionally said to refer to "our buried energies, our waking appetites, our more than natural resources" (Bloom, *Apocalypse* 91); it is understood to comprise more than mere sexual energy and to be a characteristic of male or female. But like much in conventional Blake commentary, such formulas slide over the male-centeredness of one of Blake's key terms. It is no coincidence that the term's root meanings center on "[g]enerating or producing offspring" (*OED*, *prolific* 1; exempla from 1650); in the usage of the time, *prolific* and its derivatives are bound up with the idea of generation and, in some senses, male generation.[1] We should also recall that one of Bentham's terms for sodomy is "improlific venery" ("Offences Against One's Self" 2: 107); again, *prolific* means tending toward generation. In line with these uses, Blake's imagery for the prolific is primarily male and his conception has untrammeled male sexuality at its core. Further, its contrary, the "devourer," is characterized through feminine, passive imagery—"a sea [that] recieve[s] the excess of his delights" (*MHH* 16). While necessary to the "prolific," the "devourer" is highly negative, and the two are not to be reconciled. By a kind of reduplicative logic, whatever is nonprolific—such as homosexuality or masturbation—becomes associated with the devourer.

Yet the inner logic of this conception is contradictory. *Prolific* to Blake means energy *suppressed* in the social world, exemplified by "the Giants who formed this world into its sensual existence and now seem to live in it in chains" (*MHH* 16), and is present in the powerless and oppressed. In turn, by an easy extension of the basic metaphor, the "devourer" becomes a social exploiter. Thus, while the masculinist component of the idea of the "prolific" implies identification with strident maleness and with sexual victimization of those who practice "improlific" sexuality, the idea of the social repression of energy should imply identification with such persons as oppressed. In several early Blake works the negative idea of the oppressor as "devourer," a nonprolific drinker-up of the energy of the oppressed, coexists with the assertively masculinist conception of sex through a specific, somewhat strained formula: Orc, as suppressed male sexuality, is prolific, while Urizen, as nonprolific devourer, is a masturbator. But ultimately the idea of the powerful as devourer generates an awareness that other forms of sexuality besides ostentatious maleness may be "prolific." Blake's increasing dissection of the psychology of oppression and its links to social oppression extends to the point where other forms of sexuality reenter, as it were, by the back door. This chapter traces the first steps of this shift.

Besides the instability of Blake's metaphoric-symbolic vocabulary, other factors may have prompted him to extend and ultimately subvert his hypermasculinist view. No doubt, Blake's raw hatred of sex-hypocrisy and repression pushed him in this direction. To write the "indignant page" revealing that once "Love! sweet Love! was thought a crime" ("A Little Girl Lost" 2, 4) must lead, at least, to some sense that a William Beckford has been condemned by the same law as Ona. More speculatively, an Enlightenment universalism like Bentham's may have pressed Blake to extend his sexual liberationism—in effect arguing that if Orc's suppressed sexuality blazons forth the body's holiness and indicts social repression, then so may other buried sexualities. The period's fascination with syncretic religion, the customs of distant lands, and other instances of the diversity of human experience, and its conception of the universality of reason, could prompt an effort to imagine how one's opposites view the world. The young Rousseau's experience with an aggressive homosexual, for example, while not making him any more understanding of homosexuality, led to a limited awareness of how women may feel about male sexuality: "I know of no more hideous sight for a man in cold blood than such foul and obscene behaviour, nothing more revolting than a terrifying face on fire with the most brutal lust. I have never seen another man in that state; but if we appear like that to women, they must indeed be fascinated not to find us repulsive" (71–72). Despite his critique of reason, Blake shared this universalizing impulse, which is echoed in his belief that distinct religions "are derived from each Nations different reception of the Poetic Genius" (*ARO,* prop. 5, *E*1). At this point, after all, Blake views Voltaire and Rousseau as positive figures (*FR* 276, 282; *SL* 4:18). Finally, Blake's early works already show a fascination with perverse sexuality. Under the impact of the extension of identification already referred to, such an interest may lead to a sense of the equivalency of several kinds of perversion. Hence, as Blake's early works progress, universalism and awareness of perversity act together to alter his sexual conceptions—to act as homosexuality itself acts for E. M. Forster's *Maurice*: "an ingredient that puzzles him, wakes him up, torments him and finally saves him" ("Terminal Note," 250–51).

Orc's Fierce Embrace

Blake celebrates aggressive male sexuality most graphically in the Preludium to *America* (1793), a key scene in his early work and one he revisited later. Here Orc, the poet's figure of elemental opposition and revolutionary desire, bursts his chains and "assay[s] his fierce embrace" of Urthona's daughter, setting in motion the revolutionary outbreaks of Blake's time (1:10). As several commentators have noted, Blake presents the rape unproblematically: "Round the terrific loins he siez'd the panting struggling womb; / It joy'd" (2:3–4). In an influential critique of Blake's politics some years ago, David Aers blasted the "*un*-revolutionary and very traditional devotion to 'masculine' violence" in this scene. Aers discounts "the all-too-familiar male cant that the female really 'joy'd' in such violence"; he contends that the metaphors Orc uses to describe himself—lion, eagle, serpent, etc.—"figure domineering, predatory, violently coercive action. They exclude all mutuality, care, and reciprocity. . . . Out of such a process only disaster can emerge" ("Representations" 250–51). Indeed, though the point may be obvious, one should note that the daughter's *womb* "joy'd"; at the crucial moment she herself, as a person, disappears, though she speaks immediately after.

In attacking Blake for showing revolution as coercive rather than mutualistic, Aers ignores the possibility that Blake may be politically asserting precisely this point, but he is right to note Blake's affirmation of sexual coercion itself. Within his underlying plot metaphor in which Orc's rape impregnates earth with revolutionary desire, Blake reemphasizes the opening plates' idealized sexual aggression, in copy A of the poem, by making the flames around the monitory Orc on plate 10 lick up between his legs like a phallus. Blake returns to the directly sexual meaning of Orc's embrace in the text of plate 15, when the narrator states that Orc's flames awaken sexual heat generally, leaving females "naked and glowing with the lusts of youth" (15:22). We understand that the flames stand for the whole process of social revolution that includes the crumbling of political authority, rejection of priestly rule, etc. (15:6–10, 19–20). But they are also liberated male sexuality specifically, opening the "doors of marriage" (15:19). The belief that males' "fierce desire" (15:21) will liberate women's repressed sexuality seems to assume, as Aers puts it, that "women exist solely in the domain of masculine (Orcian) sexual desire" ("Representations" 251).

Nor is it only in this poem that Blake metaphorizes revolution as violent male sex—and, by implication, presents male sexual coercion as liberating and positive. The final section of *The Song of Los* (1795) offers another version of *America*'s "fierce embrace": Orc, taking the phallic forms of "a serpent of fiery flame" and "a pillar of fire above the Alps," calls the dead from their graves in a scene of both eschatologic and revolutionary apocalypse that is also a depiction of female orgasm:

> Forth from the dead dust rattling bones to bones
> Join: shaking convuls'd the shivring clay breathes
> . . . .
> The Grave shrieks with delight, & shakes
> Her hollow womb, & clasps the solid stem:
> Her bosom swells with wild desire (7:31–32, 35–37)

The resurrection imagery prefigures *The Four Zoas,* Night 9, where similar phrases show the poor violently smiting their oppressors. These images and Blake's metaphors for Orc draw on powerful biblical images of social reformation—the Israelites' pillar of fire, Ezekiel in the valley of dry bones envisioning the resurrection of "the whole house of Israel," and the fiery serpent of Hezekiah, which signified that "the firstborn of the poor shall feed, and the needy shall lie down in safety."[2] So the passage is far from a literal depiction of male or female sexuality. Yet, so far as it uses phallic imagery as part of its oracle of social renewal, that imagery once again assumes an assertive male sexuality that calls forth a voluptuary response.

Elsewhere in Blake's early work, the title page of *The Marriage of Heaven and Hell* offers an image of arguably indeterminate sexuality. Of the two central embracing figures, Erdman remarks, "neither [is] manifestly male" (*IB* 98). The one at left, seen from behind, appears typically female in its broad-hipped body contour, but the one at right, though its sharply etched leg muscles appear conventionally male, is also broad-hipped and has no defined genitalia on its frontally viewed pelvis. (Indeterminate markings might suggest a vagina in some copies and a penis in others.)[3] Similarly, while some of the other embracing couples in the illustration's subterranean field include evidently female figures, none shows an identifiable male. (In the couple above ground at left, one figure is conventionally clothed as female, but the presumed male may have no clothing at all.) The images, then, may be lesbian or heterosexual, though they cannot show male homosexuality. Plate 2 shows a tableau equally ambiguous in a distinct way: Figures on the ground near a large tree include a couple whose sex cannot be determined, while from the tree branches a figure usually seen as female hands down something— probably grapes—to a female below. The ambiguity involves the gesture with the grapes, which recurs in other Blake works. Some have viewed the tableau as a temptation scene recalling Eve's, but in other contexts, the grape gesture has been taken to signify sexual initiation; that interpretation would make this a lesbian image.[4]

But if these visual images offset the early Blake's frequently assertive masculinism by implying a possibly androgynous world of sensual enjoyment, much of the *Marriage*'s verbal text, especially the Proverbs of

Hell, paints Hell's delights in male-centered terms. Proverbs 22–24, for example, present implicitly male virtues—pride, lust, wrath—as God's blessings, each linked to an appropriate male beast: peacock, goat, lion. Proverb 25, finishing the set, offers as God's work woman's "nakedness," i.e., the aspect that provides sexual attractiveness for males. Other proverbs involve implied gender roles (proverb 30), replicate the gendered division between humanity and nature (68), or associate excess and containment with tacitly gendered images (fountain and cistern—35). Some, in turn, provide images of male weakness or incapacity complementing the many male-gendered images of energy and exuberance, as does proverb 6, "The cut worm forgives the plow." The overall idea here, probably, is the rightness and prerogative of "energy" (the plow); the worm's response may reflect acceptance of this prerogative or its own abjectness, or both. With its phallically flaccid worm, the proverb carries overtones of male vulnerability. Moreover, the line alludes distantly to Vergil's "purpureus veluti cum flos succisus arato / languescit moriens" (*Aeneid* 9.435–36), "as a brilliant flower cut by the plow droops in death," the simile used for Euryalus's death, and so suggests the erotics of martial death and of males betrayed by love for one another.[5] Still other proverbs place ostensibly nongendered content within a gendered context, as does proverb 67, "Sooner murder an infant in its cradle than nurse unacted desires." The negative pole of this proposition—formally negative for either sex—is presented as a female-centered activity, nursing; the negative action that is nevertheless not as bad as this pole is metaphorized as murdering a child, a violation of typically female roles. The implied meaning of the murder-nursing polarity is, for men, "don't act like a woman" (by nursing without acting), and, for women, "unsex thyself." (The proverb directly echoes *Macbeth* 1.7.56–59: "I would, while it was smiling in my face, / Have pluck'd my nipple from its boneless gums, / And dash'd the brains out, had I so sworn / As you have done to this.") Moreover, in the sexual area that is one of its meanings, the proverb's overt content matches its imagery: On the surface it urges anyone to act on his or her urges, but in the real social world this advice rationalizes an existing male ethics of sexual aggressiveness.

In verbal images, then, as distinct from some gender-fluid designs, "desire" in *Marriage* is weighted toward men's needs and desires. Helen P. Bruder reaches a similar conclusion: "[M]arginal and interlinear female figures offer wry comment on the masculinist manifesto that is unfolding. But they do no more than this, and indeed their visual presence does no more than to underline a verbal absence. The work contains no female pronoun, and no woman is encountered or mentioned in the text's travels" (*Daughters* 118–19).[6]

And this is the nub of Blake's early treatment of sexuality: Despite the generalized rhetoric of desire, women and men are both urged into a world of "experience" that is dominated by men, both in the gendered imagery of Blake's presentations and in social actuality.[7] The worst dangers of this situation are recognized, indeed emphasized: The most common sexual betrayal in the cautionary literature of the period, the rape or seduction and abandonment of an unsuspecting girl, is made the central situation of *Visions of the Daughters of Albion*, is alluded to in *America* (8:10–12), and is present as underlying threat in several of the *Songs*, notably "The Little Girl Lost."[8] But behind this awareness of victimization lies a conception in which male (heterosexual) sexuality is an absolute good in itself, while that of the female is affirmed so far as she gains satisfaction by providing pleasure for men.

Most of the few direct references to homosexuality in Blake's early work are consistent with the poetics of masculinity as outlined so far: They treat the subject satirically, show some anxiety about it, or subsume it to male heterosexuality in a tutelary role, permissively but dismissively. On the last page of the 1784 manuscript satire known as "An Island in the Moon,"[9] for instance, one character remarks, "[N]ow I think we should do as much good as we can when we are at Mr Femality's" (*E*465). The manuscript does not continue, and we never see Mr. Femality, but evidently he is an effeminate man or homosexual with a salon or literary evening. He has been seen as a reference to the cross-dressing French occultist and secret agent Chevalier d'Éon,[10] but might fit other personalities of the day, such as Walpole. Given "An Island's" general humorous stress on the pretense and emptiness of the social scene it describes, the reference can only be a negative satire and may be meant to put its stamp on the whole scene. But the satire is light-toned and not overtly hostile.

If "An Island" refers obliquely to male homosexuality or effeminacy, the opening plates of *Visions of the Daughters of Albion* metaphorize lesbianism, female autoeroticism, or both. There Blake presents lesbian involvement and/or fantasy in a positive light, but in a way subordinated to and preparatory to heterosexual initiation. In the poem's "Argument," trembling in "virgin fears" in her love for Theotormon, Oothoon "hid in Leutha's vale! / I plucked Leutha's flower, / And I rose up from the vale" (iii:3–6), only to encounter Bromion's rape. Below the text the initial scene, rather than the rape, is shown: A woman we take for Oothoon kneels before a pair of blossoms—marigolds (mentioned in plate 1) or May-flowers—from one of which an infant form springs up to kiss her, its left hand touching her breast. The scene is suffused in light that may come from a rising sun or from the flowers themselves.

The text narration of this scene recounts Oothoon's wandering, her hesitation to pick the "Marygold," and its reply:

> pluck thou my flower Oothoon the mild
> Another flower shall spring, because the soul of sweet delight
> Can never pass away. she ceas'd & closd her golden shrine.

> Then Oothoon pluck'd the flower saying, I pluck thee from thy bed
> Sweet flower. and put thee here to glow between my breasts
> And thus I turn my face to where my whole soul seeks. (1:8–13)

Nearly every interpreter has noted the flowers' sexual associations. Marigolds were emblems of fertility and marriage in contemporary texts and were also thought to emit light at dusk, while the May-flower was popularly supposed to protect fertility; S. Foster Damon notes that plucking a flower is "an ancient symbol for sexual experience" and views "Leutha's vale" as the female genitals (*Dictionary* 238, 265).[11] The illumination, in turn, shows the plucking of the flower as a sexual encounter. The infant/nymph springs up, touching Oothoon's breast rather than coming to rest there, and Oothoon—in a fashion appropriate to her later avowal of nonpossessive love—"kisses the joy as it flies," like the person living "in Eternitys sunrise" in Blake's epigram (*E*474; another version at 470), whose appositeness to the image has often been noted. If the infant/nymph, whose sex cannot be determined, is male, then the encounter is heterosexual, but if female, it is lesbian, and this possibility is also suggested by Leutha's gender in the text version and by the paired flowers below the two figures. Since Oothoon herself is an emblematic character, the image may refer to several kinds of actual experience in the lives of young girls, such as masturbation (with a male or female fantasy partner) or an actual lesbian tryst. But in any of these instances, as also if one views the scene as referring to general sexual awakening, the experience with Leutha is as transient as Leutha's touch: The autoerotic or homoerotic action is preparatory to heterosexual initiation, as Oothoon turns her "face to where my whole soul seeks" (1:13).

The presentation's ironies are substantial. The experience with Leutha provides a nonbinding, generous love Oothoon is never to know heterosexually, and its example partly inspires her plea for nonpossessive love in the "silver girls" passage discussed later. Yet the poem's dynamics leave little doubt that this experience is merely a stepping-stone to "real" love. This point is reinforced by the scene's similarity to contemporary treatments of lesbianism in such works as Cleland's *Memoirs of a Woman of Pleasure* (1749), in which the experienced prostitute Phoebe initiates

Fanny in lesbianism as a way of preparing her for the greater delights of heterosexuality (10–34 passim). Ultimately, Fanny passes beyond Phoebe's lesbianism, which offers "not even the shadow of what I wanted" (34); her experience is important but transitional, like Oothoon's. In partial contrast to this view, and assuming that the Leutha scene refers definitely to autoerotic and not lesbian activity, Helen Bruder argues that in it Blake grasps possibilities of autonomous female sexuality that he cannot maintain through the poem, because he is unable to endow Oothoon with the fully autonomous consciousness that would sustain such a choice (*Daughters* 73–79). However, Bruder overlooks or discounts the way genre conventions present female auto-eroticism and homosexuality as initiations into male-dominated sexuality.[12] The Leutha scene, in sum, is *less* an embodiment of women's autonomy than Bruder believes. Here and elsewhere in *Visions* (his practice would differ in later work) Blake seems to replicate conventional treatments of female masturbation and lesbianism, rather than parodying or inverting them.

In a few other places in early works Blake uses metaphors that suggest autoerotic or homosexual gratification as a prelude to, or immature substitute for, heterosexual action. In the Preludium to *America,* for example, Urthona's daughter is twice described in such terms:

> Invulnerable tho' naked, save where clouds roll round her loins,
> Their awful folds in the dark air; silent she stood as night . . .
> . . . .
> . . . she put aside her clouds & smiled her first-born smile (1:7–8; 2:4)

The clouds primarily embody the daughter's "shadowy" nature (1:1) and hint at her affinities with Urizenic "mystery" in Blake's later development of a version of this figure as Vala.[13] But the clouds also have a sexual quality: They surround her loins and roll their folds (transitively) around them, just as Orc imagines himself, as serpent, "folding / . . . round thy dark limbs" (1:15–16), and the daughter puts them aside in Orc's favor after her rape. Thus they are a cloud counterpart to Orc's snake form. Clouds are often masculine in early Blake—as in *Thel* 3 and *Europe* 14:15–19, where Antamon, a son of Enitharmon, floats cloudlike on "the bosomd air." But here the similarities between the clouds' formlessness and the daughter's "shadowy" and "nameless" qualities (1:1, 4) indicate that they may be either an aspect of her or a similar female principle. The sexual contact between daughter and clouds may be autoerotic or lesbian. Blake's language thus sets up a rather tight metaphoric structure: The "folding" of different entities round the daughter's limbs enacts a shift from immature autoeroticism or homosexuality to heterosexual expression through Orc's rape, a sexual conception consistent with Blake's early ideas of homosexuality and autoeroticism.

Blake's Oothoon and Sexual Perversity

Visions, widely recognized as a key poem in Blake's treatment of sexuality, is also a transition point in his "poetics of masculinity." The poem has prompted extensive debate, largely focused on whether it truly articulates ideas of women's equality and autonomy. This focus has identified critical moments of tension in the poem and opened up but not fully resolved crucial issues for any discussion of Blake and sexuality.

The central situation in *Visions* is Oothoon's addresses to its male characters following her rape by Bromion and rejection by Theotormon. With increasing scope and daring, she interrogates these characters and finally Urizen on the morality of women's status, the relations between sexuality, slavery, and economic possession, the sufficiency of sense experience, and women's sexual nature. Her final situation is ambiguous: Though attaining a measure of freedom in her spirit, she yet seems to remain immured with her tormentors and repeats her lament daily. Early commentators championed Oothoon's viewpoint as a "defence of free love" (Damon, *Philosophy* 106).[14] In 1972, Jane E. Peterson inaugurated the recent contention over the poem by arguing that Oothoon's perceptions and psychic development remain limited, and that she is immobilized, in the conclusion, by her inability to break psychically from Theotormon. As the quintessence of Oothoon's dependence, Peterson and several other writers have focused on her offer to Theotormon:

> [I'll] catch for thee girls of mild silver, or of furious gold;
> I'll lie beside thee on a bank & view their wanton play
> In lovely copulation bliss on bliss with Theotormon[.] (7:24–26)

The self-abnegation and inequity of this offer (no comparable demands are made on Theotormon) represent for Peterson as for several other writers a "perverted course of action, or lack of action" (263); in David Aers's forceful critique, "The libertarianism celebrated here actually reinforces the traditional culture of male discourse which Blake's poem sets out to undermine" ("Sex, Ideology and Society" 38). In an especially sweeping attack, Anne K. Mellor concludes that "[a]t the level of sexual politics . . . *[Visions]* must finally be seen as condoning the continuation of female slavery under a benevolent master" ("Sex, Violence, and Slavery" 369).[15]

Two recent writers have offered important counterstatements to this virtual consensus that *Visions'* celebration of female desire is backward and patriarchal. Harriet Kramer Linkin proposes that Blake meant to stress Oothoon's development rather than the overt content of her doctrines. For Linkin, Oothoon's psychic self-liberation, though incomplete, nevertheless embodies several "exponential leap[s] of awareness." Further, the design on the last text page, showing a female figure soaring outward above others crouched at the ocean's edge, encourages the reader to view the conclusion with "double vision," seeing Oothoon both static on the shore and advancing in prophetic flight. Ultimately, Linkin believes, Oothoon is a positive figure because of her "wonderful determination to awaken those around her," which is the "compelling responsibility of the true prophet" (189, 185, 192).

More recently, in an immeasurably enriching though finally limiting evaluation, Helen P. Bruder has argued that the poem "attempts to find a place for the unfettered expression of women's desires at a historical moment when the controlling discourses of patriarchy were attempting . . . to silence the voices of female eroticism" (*Daughters* 57).[16] Bruder singles out two aspects of the poem that express this effort: the references to autoeroticism in its first plates, mentioned above; and its celebration of female desire as such. Of the opening lines, "I loved Theotormon / And I was not ashamed" (iii:1–2), Bruder notes, "It is easy to neglect how radical the poem's first two lines are," in a culture in which "respectable women . . . were not allowed to speak about their desires" and "many male writers seem to have felt . . . something unspeakably destabilizing in women's erotic potential" (*Daughters* 74, 85, 60). Nevertheless, Bruder believes that the rest of the poem, with some exceptions, expresses the phallocentric ideology Blake is trying to protest: Oothoon "entirely loses her sexual vision as a result of Bromion's rape, and consequently capitulates to the value system of her oppressors. . . . [A]s the poem continues we see Oothoon's rhetoric slip slide away to the point of complete apostasy," ultimately because of limitations both in the discursive vocabulary available to Blake and in the external world, i.e., its lack of a vital, independent women's movement (78–79, 84–88). For Bruder, as for most other detractors, the hallmark of this slippage is the "silver girls" speech, a "harem fantasy" by an Oothoon who has become a "voyeur" and accepts "a profoundly unjust erotic economy" (82, 64).

Clearly the "silver girls" offer hits a nerve among readers most in tune with Blake's criticism of patriarchy, and it is worth asking if their negative responses refer only to the passage's implied ethic of servicing male sexuality. Three preliminary points may be made, partly recapitulating earlier discussions. First, Oothoon's offer to Theotormon should be read dramatically, not doctrinally. Rather than expressing either Blake's ideal of sexuality or Blake's critique of Oothoon's limited consciousness (the polarities assumed in much discussion),[17] it can be seen as a failed gambit to awaken Theotormon sexually in *some* way; it would then represent not Oothoon's ideal but a stage through which she hopes to lead Theotormon. Moreover, this gambit and Oothoon's pleas in general are an effort not to procure personal happiness—as nearly all negative criticisms assume—but to activate and enlighten both Theotormon and the Daughters. Oothoon is trying to push them away from the dead center of sexual repression that cements their toleration of religion, slavery, economic exploitation, and empiricist philosophy. This point is underlined by the tradition that the poem pays tribute to Mary Wollstonecraft, whose two major works as of 1793—*A Vindication of the Rights of Men* (1790), on the French Revolution, and *Vindication of the Rights of Woman* (1792)—were attempts to awaken the English people in general and English women in particular. The prophet or the political publicist is thinking first of all of the public good, whether or not we agree that this should be the case. Finally, while Oothoon's offer does assume the primacy of the male in sexual relationships, early commentators like H. M. Margoliouth (95) were nonetheless right to see it as counterposing an idea of nonpossessiveness to the acquisitiveness and possessiveness exposed in the poem's analyses of slavery, political economy, and marriage (1:20–2:2; 5:10–16; 7:17). Indeed, the opposition between possession and sharing, both psychic-sexual and political-economic, is the unifying theme of the entire poem. Neither the limitations of this nonpossessive vision nor, for that matter, the indifference of early commentators to its implied sexual subordination should blind us to its genuine embodiment of an ideal of mutuality. But it will remain for Blake to broach, elsewhere, the possibility of male renunciation of sexual acquisitiveness and male joy in women's sexual fulfillment.

But these comments are evidently too cerebral. Apparently there is something profoundly jolting about a celebration of female desire that ends in imagined voyeurism, provoking critics to employ terms such as "voyeur" and "perverted" as epithets rather than descriptions (Bruder, *Daughters* 82; Peterson 263). This jarring quality, I suggest, is not just subservience to the male, but also the implications that Oothoon takes sexual delight in watching someone else perform and, less directly, that she herself may shrink from sex with others. Blake, in other words, here dramatizes and celebrates sexual perversion, more openly than anywhere else in his early writings.

Blake unquestionably knew what Oothoon's comments implied, for he built on a tradition of female voyeurism in such works as Cleland's

Memoirs of a Woman of Pleasure (e.g., 29–33). Specifically, Oothoon means to watch Theotormon and the "girls" have sex, and to take sexual pleasure herself in doing so (perhaps while masturbating)—as implied by her recumbent posture and the phrase "bliss on bliss," which applies to herself as well as to Theotormon and the "girls."[18] We are here in the area of W. J. T. Mitchell's "dangerous Blake," particularly the second of his three categories, "Blake's obscenity" (413–14). Most commentators have preferred either to explain away the speech's evident endorsement of perverse sexuality or to condemn it as self-oppressing. But the perversion expressed here can work in the opposite direction as well: It raises the possibility of sexual gratification other than through heterosexual intercourse. Even if this idea is first broached in a male-dominated heterosexual context, once it has been voiced no defined line can block a reevaluation of masturbation or homosexuality. The approval of perverse sexuality here opens up other forms of perversion for examination, ultimately undercutting Blake's restrictive masculinism and broadening the affirmation of sexuality in his works.

There can be no doubt of the importance of this opening to perversion. In general, the eighteenth century provided few approved outlets for perverse fantasy, but these exercised considerable power over its imagination. Most notable, perhaps, was the masquerade, frequently condemned by moralists, which flourished in London through most of the century before disappearing in the period when *Visions* was written; Blake alludes to it in "An Island in the Moon" and remembers it in *Jerusalem,* decades later.[19] Without idealizing the masquerade as a site of free personal and sexual interaction, we can still see that it provided ways of acting out fantasies of class fluidity, gender reversal, domination and subordination, and the like. More generally, everyone has fantasies going beyond recognized sexuality, involving homosexuality, onanism, dominance and subordination, sadism, masochism, voyeurism, raping and being raped, and much else. To take just one pertinent eighteenth-century example, Rousseau testifies that through his whole life he was sexually aroused only by fantasies of submission to a woman, involving punishment and, apparently, spanking: "I never dared to reveal my strange taste, but at least I got some pleasure from situations which pandered to the thought of it. To fall on my knees before a masterful mistress, to obey her commands, to have to beg for her forgiveness, have been to me the most delicate of pleasures. . . . [But] I have never, during the whole course of my life, been able to force myself, even in moments of extreme intimacy, to confess my peculiarities and implore her to grant the one favour which was lacking" (27–28). Oothoon's "silver girls" speech thus has a double aspect. Narrowly—more than most critical discussions have realized—it captures the psychology of sexual injury, showing a possible response to the horrific experience Oothoon has endured; someone sexually brutalized *may* subsequently avoid direct sexual encounters and achieve orgasm by watching (or fantasizing) others' sexual acts, including by the person who has rejected him or her. More broadly, the speech opens up the world of perverse sexuality that everyone, in Blake's time and ours, shares to some extent.[20] In this way, paradoxically, it is *less* limiting than a more abstractly satisfactory affirmation of equal sexual relations, which could—though it would not have to—leave the various perversions outside its range of acceptance.

Visions does idealize an unequal male-centered sexuality, and this aspect weakens but does not vitiate both its plea for nonpossessive love and its limited opening to perverse sexuality. The reasons for this idealization, however, seem not to lie so much in the limits of the available vocabularies of female desire or in the absence of an active women's movement in the 1790s, important as these are, but rather in Blake's limitation of mature sexuality in "experience" to genital heterosexuality, and his conception of alternative sexualities as mere waystations or impediments in the transition to this state. In other words, Blake's treatment of perversity jostles up against his overall sexual conceptions. In the world of the *Visions,* and other early Blake works, women's possible alternatives to hierarchized heterosexual relations—virginity, masturbation, lesbianism and/or female companionship—are ruled out or viewed as antecedents to mature sexuality, while the equivalent possibilities for men are only hinted at, or attacked. Abstractly, perhaps, this limitation might be compatible with a commitment to genuine equality in heterosexual love. But in practice, the opposite seems true: Failure to recognize deviant sexuality, or its trivialization as a stage in maturation, closes the door to a full recognition of heterosexual equality. This situation makes the "silver girls" speech extraordinarily important, because it not only dramatizes an unequal heterosexual relation, but also marks the first point in Blake where mature sexuality takes an evidently approved perverse form. Once Blake takes this step a powerful though slow-acting logic pushes toward recognition and validation of other types of perverse sexuality, and then to an incomplete revision of his idealization of the male.

Spanking the Monkey

Part of this contradictory dynamic is played out in Blake's early treatment of masturbation. In its own right and as a figure for "nonprolific" sexuality and behavior generally, masturbation plays an important, negatively charged role in several of Blake's early works. Blake's references have not generally been seen in their proper light: as extending but also limiting his exploration of sexuality. Interpreters have often tacitly endorsed Blake's view of the practice as an abuse. Thus, Damon refers to Oothoon's denouncing such evils as "the bondage of marriage . . . and the self-abuse of the solitary," and Mellor to her attacks on "the public injustice of prostitution . . . and the private abuse of masturbation" (*Dictionary* 308; "Sex, Violence, and Slavery" 366); Jane E. Peterson, referring to the "silver girls" speech in a passage partly quoted earlier, complains that Oothoon denounces masturbation "only to suggest, in a self-exulting context, an equally perverted course of action" (263). Contrary to these writers' conventional view of the matter, Blake's condemnation of masturbation is as much a deformation in his liberatory poetics as his masculinist treatment of women. In fact, Blake's willingness to countenance sexual perversion in the "silver girls" speech marks his view of masturbation as regressive, not the other way round. However, Blake's handling of this topic undergoes a subtle but important shift in *Ahania*, with analogues in other early works.

Oothoon's long speech of accusation against Urizen in *Visions*, to which these writers refer, links masturbation with both psychic and social evils. Oothoon first contrasts infant sexuality, both in the literal sense and in Blake's usual figurative meaning of "infant" as innocent and unashamed, to the "subtil modesty!" that traps "virgin joy" with "nets" found under the "night pillow"—establishing a link between repression of nighttime sexuality and hypocritical antisexuality in general (6:7, 11). Then the pillow that hides the nets becomes the pillow of a masturbating boy, and the actions of boy and girl masturbators become the fountainheads (so to speak) of antisexual religion:

> The virgin
> That pines for man; shall awaken her womb to enormous joys
> In the secret shadows of her chamber; the youth shut up from
> The lustful joy. shall forget to generate. & create an amorous image
> In the shadows of his curtains and in the folds of his silent pillow.
> Are not these the places of religion? the rewards of continence?
> The self enjoyings of self denial? (7:3–9)

When, in the next section of Oothoon's speech, she makes her "silver girls" offer to Theotormon, masturbation is implicitly counterposed to the "generous love" she champions, and virtually equated to Theotormon's "self-love that envies all!" (7:29, 21).

Blake's images have at least two possible contemporary literary sources. Rousseau's *Confessions* describe how "my restless temperament had at last made itself felt. . . . [I] learned that dangerous means of cheating Nature, which leads in young men of my temperament to various kinds of excesses, that eventually imperil their health, their strength, and sometimes their lives. This vice, which shame and timidity find so convenient, has a particular attraction for lively imaginations. It allows them to dispose, so to speak, of the whole female sex at their will . . ." (108–109). Rousseau's description, emphasizing how he "kissed my bed . . . my curtains, all the furniture of my room, since they belonged to her" (his fantasized lover, his patron Mme de Warens), may partly suggest Blake's "curtains" and "pillow" (108). The word "shadows," used twice in Oothoon's remarks, also echoes the lesbian scenes in Cleland, noted above as a possible subtext for Oothoon's dalliance with Leutha. Not only does homosexuality fail to provide Fanny with "the shadow of what I wanted," but when Phoebe uses Fanny's hand to masturbate, she "procure[s] herself rather the shadow than the substance of any pleasure" (34). Masturbation is shadow not substance also in Blake's text, which thus sets up a complex amalgam: If Cleland's novel indeed lies in the background of *Visions,* both masturbation and homosexuality (the latter not directly mentioned here) are mere "shadows" of sexuality. Both are linked to the night pillows of denied desire, with their concealed "nets," and thus both to the daytime evils of enslaved sexuality, repressive religion, economic exploitation, war, and slavery generated from Urizen's "nets" or webs (1:20–22, 5:3–32).

Blake explores this idea in two related parts of *The [First] Book of Urizen* (1794) and its companion *The Book of Ahania* (1795). In chapter 4 [b] of *Urizen,* Los's creation of time conditions the formation of Urizen's body.[21] As the "eternal Prophet" forges rivets and pours solder "dividing / The horrible night into watches" (10:9–10),

> [2. . . .] Urizen (so his eternal name)
> His prolific delight obscurd more & more
> In dark secresy hiding in surgeing
> Sulphureous fluid his phantasies.
> . . . .
> 3. The eternal mind bounded began to roll
> Eddies of wrath ceaseless round & round,
> And the sulphureous foam surgeing thick
> Settled, a lake, bright, & shining clear:
> White as the snow on the mountains cold.
> . . . .
> 5. Restless turnd the immortal inchain'd
> Heaving dolorous! anguish'd! unbearable
> Till a roof shaggy wild inclos'd
> In an orb, his fountain of thought. (10:11–14, 19–23, 31–34)

Especially with *Visions'* virgin in "secret shadows" and youth "shut up from / The lustful joy" as background, Urizen's "obscur[ing]" his delight "In dark secresy" suggests a masturbation scene, and this idea is confirmed by the "sulphureous" fluid that hides his fantasies and the white lake formed by his thick, surging foam.[22] And we know the overall quality of his fantasies: Since he has obscured his "prolific" delight, he has become one of the devourers. Hence, Urizen's masturbation reflects his nature as a devourer or perhaps constitutes him as one.

But this is not all. Urizen's masturbation also constitutes his *world*— his body and his social character result from it. In verse 3, responding to Los's continued forging of time, but also continuing the action in verse 2, Urizen's mind begins to roll, either creating eddies of wrath (the verb omitted by syncope) or rolling them round transitively, and this circular motion (self-reflexive, and so like masturbation) churns the fluid of verse 1 into foam, which in turn settles as the lake. (Urizen, like Onan, has spilled his seed on the ground, though the ground does not yet exist, but because he is a giant it forms a lake. Blake is having a good time.) As he continues to roll or turn (31), his circular motion forms the roof of his skull in the circular shape of an orb. As an orb is also the symbol of royalty, one of Urizen's attributes, his *social rule* has taken form, not just his skull; and since his "fountain" of thought is shut in, this process is the same as, or parallel to, the obscuring of his prolific delight in masturbatory fantasy. As the narrative continues, Urizen's "slumber" allows or causes his spine to form, and ribs to freeze "Over all his nerves of joy" (35, 41). But of course slumber follows orgasm, and "dark secresy" obscuring prolific delight (13) is equivalent to ribs freezing over nerves of joy (41). So masturbation has created, or is a figure for, the processes that have shaped Urizen's body and his social role.

Reading backward—justifiedly in this self-recursive poem[23]—we find that Urizen's onanism encompasses other aspects of his world. On plate 4 (present only in copies A-C), Urizen desires a "solid without fluctuation," and also declares that he has written into his books "The secrets of dark contemplation / . . . / With terrible monsters Sin-bred" (4:11, 26–28). On first reading, we take these as abstract desires and contemplations. But since Urizen's orb *is* a "solid without fluctuation" (a spherical shape) and "phantasies" dreamt in "dark secresy" *are* dark contemplations, retrospectively the human fear of change and sense of sin also appear, or are metaphorized, as products of Urizen's masturbation. As "improlific" sexuality, it generates an unprolific world.

Ahania extends the suggestion that Urizen's autoerotic sexuality creates his social existence, but its treatment of the topic is ambiguous, at some points seeming to jibe with the poem's overall argument on sexuality and at others to run counter to it. The poem as a whole pinpoints the role of sexual division in the foundations of society and treats sexual inhibition as an evil. After Fuzon's emasculating blow "dividing" Urizen's loins in chapter 1, for example, Ahania appears as a materialization of Urizen's "parted soul," or divided sexuality (2:29–32). In chapter 2, as a further consequence of Urizen's genital injury, his "dire Contemplations" form "Eggs of unnatural production," one of which, grown into a serpent, pushes "With his horns" at the level of Urizen's knees until Urizen smites it and shapes the bow of his oppressive law from its ribs (3:5–25). The phallic snake butting at Urizen's legs seems to allude to attempted homosexual entry. This sequence implies that rejection of homosexuality becomes part of an overall antisexuality that is one basis for tyrannic rule—though it also suggests that homosexuality forms from sexual injury.

Despite this emphasis on the evils of suppressing sexual impulse, in another major sequence *Ahania* continues the treatment of Urizenic existence as autoerotic, in a tableau similar to the one in *Urizen*. This scene occurs as part of a genealogy of the hero's weapons, one of several parodies of epic convention in this poem. The genealogy—of Urizen's "arrows of pestilence" (4:9, 37)—turns out to be that of Urizenic creation as a whole. Again we see a white lake (4:14). Though the details about fantasies and fluids are not repeated, the scene is clearly a variant on that in *Urizen*—it takes place in the same time period of Urizen's preexistence, the "infinite ages of Eternity" (4:12), involves some of the same imagery, and likewise ends in the formation of Urizen's body. But we do not need these parallels to see that *Ahania*'s scene, too, is autoerotic: The lake is formed from Urizen's melted "Nerves of Joy" as he lies alone in his "slumbers of abstraction" (4:13, 11). The aftermath of this process is the important feature of this account. Once the lake appears, "Effluvia" condense above it in "noxious clouds," also called "clouds of disease," while the lake surface, "scurfd o'er" by pain, forms "hurtling bones" that the clouds perch round like vultures, "shape on shape, / Winged screaming in blood & torment" (4:17–26). Los now captures the bones in nets, while some of the "shapes" formed from the clouds become muscles, glands, and organs of sex and hunger, but "Most remain'd on the tormented void: / Urizens army of horrors"—called his "self-begotten armies" in *Urizen* (*Ah* 4:34–35; *U* 5:16). Urizen's "white lake," then, is the source both of his body and of the winged shapes variously called "army of horrors" or "arrows of pestilence"—evils formed from distorted sexuality that, as the poem returns to its main time frame, torment the "living Corse" of his adversary Fuzon on the tree of mystery (4:6, 36).

These works' presentation of masturbation or autoerotic thought as sources of social "pestilence" seems to be in part metaphoric and in part representational, though still figurative. We learn in *Visions* that slavery, exploitation, the evils of marriage, empiricism, and sex-repressive religion are all aspects of Urizen. In *Urizen,* abstract reasoning, fear of change, and the sense of sin are added to the list, and we learn as well that the fundamental cause of all these—in other words, of Urizen's formation—is his separation from the Eternals, "Self-closd, all-repelling" (3:3), though both Los and the Eternals are deeply implicated in this process. We know, too, from Urizen's appearances here and in Blake's other early works, that his separation has two aspects: He is separate from the common existence in general—the life of the Eternals, with their acceptance of change and death—and also separate from it on a social level as ruling classes or elites. For this multifaceted separateness autoeroticism serves as a metaphor, one particularly disturbing to eighteenth-century minds, and is present even in *Urizen's* opening description, where the separating "horror" is called a "shadow . . . / . . . unprolific!" (3:1–2), echoing the "shadows" of the masturbators' rooms in *Visions* 7. Simultaneously, in a more representational way, if not arguing that masturbation literally creates class, social, and religious oppression, Blake is quite serious that these result in part from sexual repression and that masturbation is a manifestation of this repression, an expression of repressed and therefore deformed desire.[24] Presenting the white lake as the material source of Urizen's "horrors," then, is not just a use of metaphor. The image figuratively represents the idea that repressing and distorting desire does create social repression, and expresses what Blake sees as the interwoven dynamics of psychic and social repression.

Given these emphases, it is all the more remarkable that in several passages in these early works, including *Ahania's* closing chapter, Blake moves away from his view of masturbation as source or figure for social repression and presents it in qualifiedly positive ways. Two instances occur in *Europe.* These pick up *Visions'* thread of autoerotic suggestion but are more ambiguous, merely hinting at sexual meaning and lacking the unmistakable animus of the *Visions* passage. The first is the illustration of plate 4 (Dörrbecker pl. 6 [7]), in which a female figure, usually seen as Enitharmon, lifts, lowers, or adjusts a veil or coverlet over a sleeping youth, probably Orc, whose head is bathed in a flaming halo. The association of Orc's flames with his sexuality, and the embracing and postcoital figures above his sleeping form, suggest that Orc is fast in a sexual dream. In this page's text, Enitharmon calls to Orc, "Arise . . . / . . . / For now thou art bound; / And I may see thee in the hour of bliss . . ." (4:10–14); Orc does rise, and Enitharmon "down descend[s] into his red light" (4:15–17). The text episode implies that Orc becomes "bound" to Enitharmon by his sexuality in a dynamic stasis that lasts through her eighteen-hundred-year dream of history. In the design, however, Orc remains asleep and the veil keeps Enitharmon from descending to him (though, as D. W. Dörrbecker points out, Blake's ambiguous perspective leaves us in no doubt that she can see him [184]). Here, the sexual quality of Orc's dream—autoerotic so far as he is enmeshed in his own sexuality rather than Enitharmon's—acts protectively, since we understand that to unite with Enitharmon would be a negative occurrence in Blake's overall narrative. Of course, the design could simply show the moment before Orc wakes, and this possibility should make us remember the difficulty of assigning unambiguous meaning to Blake's designs. Nonetheless, Orc's inaction in the design is somewhat more positive than his action in the text, or that of the boy creating "an amorous image" in *Visions* (7:6).[25]

Later in *Europe*, Enitharmon again calls to her children to join her. Despite various reproaches the children are unresponsive, and the episode ends with Orc's appearance as revolutionary son/sun above France's vineyards (14:37–15:2). Of interest here is Enitharmon's rebuke to one of the sons, Antamon, for ignoring both her and his consort (Leutha, from *Visions*): "Where is the youthful Antamon. prince of the pearly dew, / . . . / Alone I see thee crystal form, / Floting upon the bosomd air: / With lineaments of gratified desire" (14:15–19). "Pearly dew" suggests semen, as many interpreters have noted, and in an overall way Antamon reworks the unnamed Cloud of *Thel*, whose role was to inseminate the dew (*Thel* 3:13–16); Damon considers both to symbolize "the male seed" (*Dictionary* 24), though such identifications should be taken as only suggestive. Here too Antamon acts like a cloud, floating on the "bosomd" air, and though "Alone," he exhibits "gratified desire." The implied autoeroticism is relatively positive in context: The children's refusal of the roles Enitharmon selects for them is, if not necessarily liberatory, still better than their obedience would be—it is part of the dissolution of Enitharmon's rule. Both here and in the earlier illustration of Orc, then, Blake shows autoeroticism in a quasi-positive light, at least as an alternative to Enitharmon's sway.[26]

Finally, *Ahania*'s closing chapter departs from all the episodes considered so far by presenting what seem to be fecund, "prolific" qualities through androgynous, partly masturbatory imagery. In this section, Ahania mourns the primal harmony that she believes once existed between her and Urizen. Ahania presents herself both as cloud and as dew (4:50, 5:13), images Blake has used before in varying sexual senses. In *Thel* the cloud was male and the dew female (3:5, 13), while in *Europe* Antamon's "pearly dew" was male, as just discussed; here cloud and dew combine androgynously. The fecund sexuality Ahania imagines in the past is also androgynous: After Urizen's embraces she found "bosoms of milk in my chambers / Fill'd with eternal seed," that is, breasts that are also testicles (5:20–21). She recalls Urizen and his activities androgynously as well:

> 12: Then thou with thy lap full of seed
> With thy hand full of generous fire
> Walked forth from the clouds of morning
> On the virgins of springing joy,
> On the human soul to cast
> The seed of eternal science.
>
> 13: The sweat poured down thy temples
> To Ahania return'd in evening
> The moisture awoke to birth
> My mothers-joys, sleeping in bliss. (5:29–38)

In Ahania's memory, Urizen's sexual actions with her and his role as agricultural sower merge. Urizen's lap is full of seed, like a pregnant woman's (or a sloppy masturbator's), while his hand holds phallic fire. Seed, of course, is a common term for semen, so that Urizen's lap appears like a womb; botanically, seed is the fertilized and ripened ovule of a plant, which Urizen seems to carry for sowing. The combined sexual and agricultural contexts give both elements of this fused image some weight. In either sense Urizen seems to have been fertilized by Ahania as much as— or more than—she by him; in an earlier reference to their mingling, it is impossible to say for sure whether she or he falls from her clouds onto his harvests (5:7–14). Urizen's hand, in turn, contains fire, either a male equivalent of the seed or the form in which it appears after being taken in the hand, and the fire then becomes seed that he sows in the field. Urizen's action is both agricultural and masturbatory—in both aspects, he gathers seed in his hand. Moreover, the sweat from his temples, i.e., from his day in the fields or his masturbation, awakens Ahania's "mothers-joys" of maternity and sexuality. Overall, the androgynous generation of seed in Urizen's lap and hand and its quasi-masturbatory distribution are recalled as the basis for harmonious mutual sexuality. If male-centered, this is also a positive image of fecund masturbation.

We must certainly be cautious about taking this image of harmony at face value. Once again Blake has imagined sexual harmony in a thoroughly male-centered way, typified by Ahania's regret that she cannot now "kiss the place / Whereon his bright feet have trod" (4:70–71).[27] Moreover, even Ahania's male-oriented idea of androgyny may be only a fantasy: Is she doing anything more than nostalgically reprocessing the same masturbation scene (or some version of it) that already produced (with Los's help) the "army of horrors"? As with other Blakean evocations of primal harmony, such as those in *The Four Zoas,* there is no evidence that the scenes Ahania recalls occurred objectively; such scenes are always "remembered" by the characters, not described by the narrator. However, through such memories the characters conceptualize possibilities they believe they possess, projecting them onto an imagined past; thus, although mythic, these images are not necessarily delusory. Alternatively, happy images of Urizen's gentle mastery may suggest a self-enslaving mentality, and it is possible that Blake means them this way. In this case the implied critique of Ahania's illusions would also reaffirm Blake's narrow-minded view of masturbation. But Blake does not present such a critique clearly, and there are no textual markers that would indicate an ironized treatment—the text contains no defined suggestions of the limitations of Ahania's conception of harmony. Blake's text, then, presents a male-dominant sexual harmony as a positive alternative to Urizen's world, but it also shows a mutually collaborative, fecund masturbation as a variant or alternative to earlier suggestions that an autoerotic distortion of sexuality helped create that world.

After these early works, Blake does not return to his negative editorializing or his use of masturbation as a token of Urizenic creation. The scene of Urizen's formation in *The Four Zoas,* which copies much of its wording from *Urizen,* retains the "sulphureous foam" and white lake but drops the references to Urizen obscuring his "prolific delight" and "hiding in surgeing / Sulphureous fluid his phantasies"; nor does it trace the lake to melted "Nerves of Joy," as in *Ahania.* In context, the foam and lake appear as results of Los's binding Urizen's mind into circular motion. And *Milton*'s version of the same scene omits the lake and foam as well. (See *FZ* 54:1–3; *U* 10:12–14; *Ah* 4:13; *M* 3:6–27, copies CD.) Later works do include pictorial images of women masturbating, in contexts involving lesbian contact or flirtation, and they picture male homosexual contact and all-male sexual arousal as well (see chapters 3, 5). The disappearance of Blake's adverse portrayals of male masturbation, at a time when he was increasingly exploring homosexuality, suggests that he no longer found such portrayals consonant with his sense of sexual multiplicity, even if he was not ready to describe male masturbation positively.

Blake's negative accounts of masturbation were, of course, in line with the thought of his time. Bentham, as noted in chapter 1, professed to consider the practice "incontestably pernicious," enervating, conducive to impotence, and far more "mischievous" than homosexuality itself ("Offences Against One's Self" 2: 101–102). Such phrases mirrored popular and learned prejudice. The anonymous tract *Onania:*

or, the Heinous Sin of Self-Pollution, and All its Frightful Consequences,
in Both Sexes consider'd, &c. With Spiritual and Physical Advice to those
who have already injur'd themselves by this abominable Practice, which
appeared in 1710 and was in its sixteenth edition in 1737, warned that
the practice hindered growth in both sexes, caused disorders of the
penis and testes, fainting fits, epilepsies, consumptions, "nightly and
excessive Seminal Emissions; a Weakness in the *Penis,* and a loss of
Erection" in men (13), and in women hysteric fits, consumptions, "and
at length a total Ineptitude to the Act of Generation itself" (15). Such
claims were not regarded as quackery.[28] As Roy Porter and Lesley Hall
observe in *The Facts of Life,* their study of English sex-education literature, "From early in the [eighteenth] century there was a torrent of
medical and moral opposition to masturbation, directed primarily
against young people. Such opposition came largely from those generally hostile to sexual liberalism, but it also arose from medical men and
educators otherwise enlightened in their outlook" (29). Masturbation
was "portrayed in the advice and warning literature as entirely pernicious" (96). In an example particularly instructive because it occurred
within Blake's republican milieu, the politically radical medical writer
Thomas Beddoes was certain that masturbation caused disease and
weakness and had led to Jonathan Swift's mental decline (Porter and
Hall 102). Blake's initial warnings about masturbation, then, were
hardly unique. What is unique is the typically Blakean way in which
he linked condemnation of masturbation to advocacy of sexual promis-
cuity and an attack on religion, and, additionally, the broadening of his
treatment in *Ahania* to find androgynous and masturbatory sources for
the "prolific."

Positive Images of Male Passivity and Homosexuality

In a few places Blake's early works suggest positive views of male passivity or homosexuality. Besides *Ahania*'s suggestion that Urizen's bow
partly manifests denied homosexuality, already mentioned, three other
instances indicate the complexity of Blake's approach to sexuality even in
early works. The first is the design for *America* 6, showing a beautiful
naked youth sitting spraddle-legged on a grave mound, looking with
wonder into the sky. His wonder seems to come from his own resurrection and from hearing Orc's prophecy of universal liberation, both detailed in the text. The boy's body is drawn with sharp details and his
genitals are carefully outlined, with pubic hair suggested by a leaflike
patch. Though there is nothing homosexual as such about this design, it
is an image of intense, and intensely vulnerable, male beauty—the boy,

genitals exposed, would be helpless before any oppressor. The design, indeed, forms part of a sequence with others, especially those of Urizen and the militant Orc on plates 8 and 10, which indicate the opposition the boy faces and the strength needed to combat it.[29] But the image is remarkable for its combination of male erotics with vulnerability or passivity, qualities often gendered feminine and disparaged in males, and at odds with the aggressive male sexuality emphasized elsewhere in *America*. Contrary to the way he frequently idealizes masculine roughness and aggression—e.g., "Let man wear the fell of the lion" (proverb 30, *MHH* 8)—here Blake provides a nonaggressive gender equivalent for the text's political promise, "the Lion & Wolf shall cease" (6:15).

If this image returns to and revises Blake's negative valuation of male weakness elsewhere, part of the "Africa" section of *The Song of Los* implies a criticism of the accompanying moral code, though it does not mention homosexuality directly. In this section, the poem's narrative voice (supposed to be Los's in the poem's title and prelude verse) details the historical consequences of Mosaic law, classical and hermetic philosophy, and, apparently, Jesus' acceptance of an ethic of sexual restraint. One result is that

> The human race began to wither, for the healthy built
> Secluded places, fearing the joys of Love
> And the disease'd only propagated:
> So Antamon call'd up Leutha from her valleys of delight:
> And to Mahomet a loose Bible gave.
> But in the North, to Odin, Sotha gave a Code of War[.] (3:25–30)

Blake's terms are gnomic and carry more than one possible meaning. The "secluded places" literally are "Churches: Hospitals: Castles: Palaces" (4:1), places of religious antisexuality, warrior and kingly rule, and either bodily sickness or charitable and religious isolation (the hospitals; see *OED, hospital* sb. 1.2). They are also regions of the earth, as human culture diversifies from what Blake takes as its African origins. The "loose Bible" fairly clearly refers to the Qur'án or Islamic codes. With the Norse religion but in an opposed way (note "But"), it appears as a reaction against Christianity. Blake explicitly identifies Norse beliefs with war; in contemporary discourse, Islam was known for sexual permissiveness (or "looseness," a contemporary meaning) in general, and tolerance of sodomy in particular—"the Arabs, indeed, make very light of the offence," *The Phoenix of Sodom* complained (25).[30] The passage, then, appears to present the warlike Norse religion and what were thought to be sexually accommodating Islamic beliefs as counterposed reactions to Christianity, to the apparent advantage of the latter.[31]

Finally, Blake may depict homosexual activity directly on one early plate, *America* 15, whose design seemingly shows women "naked and glowing with the lusts of youth" in response to Orc's fires (15:20–22). Of the women shown in various poses and combinations at page bottom and in the left margin, the central group at bottom shows three (identifiable as women by body contour, long hair, and the breasts of the one at right) in an interlocking embrace. In one copy (M, Yale Center for British Art) the figure at right turns her face to us with an expression of either passion or distress. Most commentators have euphemized the lesbian implications of this tableau—it has been said to show "a cluster of three [women], self-involved," who may be hiding a child, or "three sisters [who] embrace" (*IB* 154, Dörrbecker 67). But if the figures indeed glow with lusts, the lusts are for one another. Moreover, unlike the scene shown in the "Argument" to *Visions,* the embrace is not a prelude to any heterosexual involvement but is taken on its own terms. The design in effect presents an alternative outcome to the verbal description, in which the reader tends to assume that the females will go on to seek Orc or Orcs, and it counterbalances the insistent subservience to the male found in the "Preludium," suggesting instead a female sexuality not dependent on male satisfaction.[32] While these implications remain minor counterpoints in *America,* the motif of this design and the use of visual images to suggest more woman-centered possibilities than those described verbally will both recur in *The Four Zoas.*

Chapter Three ❈

Homosexuality, Resistance, and Apocalypse: *The Four Zoas*

feeding thyself
With visions of sweet bliss far other than this burning clime
Sure thou art bathd in rivers of delight on verdant fields

—*The Four Zoas* 78:34–36

T*he Four Zoas* marks a crucial point in Blake's development. Begun in 1796–97 and continued over the next decade, though never put into finished form, this epic-prophecy cast as a dream-vision in nine nights is a universal history that also comes to grips with a key aspect of contemporary history: the failures of the French Revolution and the English radical reform movement from the 1770s through the 1790s. Through salient events involving Orc, Blake amends his initial scheme of human renewal through elemental rebellion and unfettered desire. In political terms, he recognizes the need for a social movement based on historical-prophetic awareness and contemporary fraternity. The resulting perspective does not repudiate social rebellion but accepts the need for enlarged understanding and eventually, in *Jerusalem,* mutuality and love to guide the people.

In sexual terms as well, Blake retains his belief in the liberation of desire. But in *The Four Zoas,* this idea no longer refers to unchecked male heterosexual desire. While homosexuality is not directly mentioned in the text and never becomes a major topic, an important visual image depicts male homosexuality as a form of resistance to Urizen or simply an alternative to his strictures. Other text and visual episodes refer to sexual bimorphism and polymorphism. Moreover, the poem's text and designs contain a criticism of predatory masculinity that revises what I have called Blake's poetics of masculinity. Lesbianism, too, emerges as a topic of some designs in a way that partly offsets misogynistic implications in the text. Despite the text's preoccupation with what male characters feel as women's domineering and predatory impulses, a series of visual images presents lesbianism as an alternative to male domination, even a component of apocalypse.

The expression of sexual ideas in *The Four Zoas* is extraordinarily complex, partly because it often occurs through the interaction of text and image. As often remarked, illuminations in Blake's works frequently do not directly illustrate the text; they may present similar ideas in a distinct conceptual form or go off at an angle, contradicting or departing altogether from a poem's words. Blake's designs also commonly admit counterposed interpretations: an image that seems hopeful to one commentator is despairing to another, and so on. These generalities are particularly true in *The Four Zoas*. Aspects of the relations of the sexes may appear in one light in the text and quite another in designs; designs may give a sexual meaning to seemingly nonsexual text descriptions or provide an alternative meaning unrelated to the narrative. Often, a sexually conventional way of reading a design coexists with a less conventional way, creating a kind of dialogue between different ways of regarding the acts or scene in question. Further, most of the poem's drawings are unfinished, and some have sexual details obliterated. Finally, a sizable number of designs—unlike those in any printed Blake work—graphically depict illicit sexual acts, grotesquely formed body parts, and the like—masturbation, fellation, winged penises, giant phalluses, many-breasted dragon women, and more. The common view of these images is that they portray degraded sexuality; even as perceptive a viewer as Jean H. Hagstrum feels that they show "the horrors of sexual tortuosity" in "grotesque and repulsive distortion" ("Arrows" 120, 141). Yet, detached from the supposition that sexual perversity and gender polymorphism must be negative (or that Blake must have felt they were), the images that show these phenomena are not necessarily horrific, and reading Blake's drawings together with associated texts allows the possibility that some of them may depict alternatives to the texts' sexual wars. Overall, despite the ambiguity inherent in Blake's pictorial approach and in this poem's unfinished state, the designs add to the text's criticism of aggressive masculinity and complicate its seeming masculinism by showing male and female homosexuality in an ambiguous, possibly positive light.

Orc, Homosexuality, and Heroic Resistance

The image with which I began my discussion (figure 1.1, chapter 1), on page 78 of *The Four Zoas,* is the poem's only direct illustration of male homosexuality. It occurs at a moment of high tension, in Night 7a, following Orc's birth and binding and Urizen's search through his dens for the imprisoned boy, whose howls have shattered his own bonds (Nights 5, 6).[1] Urizen's ultimately successful subversion of Orc in the two texts of Night 7 is the poem's key turn, causing Orc to lose prophetic wrath and divide into chained boy and ravening serpent. Politically and historically, the episode refers, among other meanings, to the subversion of the French Revolution through temptations of power, resulting in inter-imperialist war and the collapse of hopes for social transformation. From this point Blake begins recasting his paradigm of liberation. So while the homosexual drawing is a visual detail within just one episode of *The Four Zoas,* that episode is central to the poem's meaning.

The drawing, we recall, shows a male, assumedly Orc because of his presence in this page's text, receiving or about to receive oral sex from a lightly sketched kneeling figure, now almost blacked over but visible in outline. Orc's face is very lightly sketched but retains the bell cheeks characteristic of other representations (e.g., *America* 1). On direct visual inspection, the outline and mass of the kneeling figure's head and body are rather clear, despite medium-heavy pencil shading. No facial features are discernible. A shaftlike figure projects downward on the inner side of the figure's thigh in the location of an erect penis, and a much-obscured tubular outline can be traced above Orc's belly in the position of his own erect penis (implying that the kneeling figure is directing his attention to Orc's testicles). In the original manuscript (the effects are less clear in reproduction), the shape above Orc's belly is rather distinct at first glance, even though the shading strokes, longitudinal with respect to the supine body, are not distinguishable from possible underlying pencil lines; there appears to be erasure beneath the shading (noted by Butlin 1: 285). Slightly wavy or erose heavier pencil marks form the longitudinal edges of this shape, and a distinct gap in the shading forms its end. These features are most consistent with shading marks reproducing erased pencil impressions, in the manner of a shaded pencil-tracing through paper; but the gap at the end may result from a kink in the paper. While the shape cannot be identified with certainty, clearly something was sketched there before erasure and shading.[2]

In the text, Urizen, trying to undermine Orc's resistance, taunts him on his seeming indifference to suffering:

> [T]hou reposest . . . feeding thyself
> With visions of sweet bliss far other than this burning clime
> Sure thou are bathd in visions of delight on verdant fields
> Walking in joy in bright Expanses sleeping on bright clouds

> With visions of delight so lovely that they urge thy rage
> Tenfold with fierce desire to rend thy chain & howl in fury
> And dim oblivion of all woe & desperate repose
> Or is thy joy founded on torment which others bear for thee
>   (78:34–41)

The republican tradition's link between sodomy and upper-class power may seem to suggest that the visual scene shows Urizen's fantasy of Orc's submission. In this view, the consciousness of lust repressed in Urizen's speech would reappear as a visualized fantasy in which the kneeling figure enacts Urizen's desire. Urizen would represent, for example, Churchill's grandee "too great for law," Orc his "delicious boy / To serve our purposes of beastly joy," playing the catamite role Chatterton refused (see chapter 1).[3] Complicating this interpretation, however, is the existence of subtexts for Orc's opposition—rather than his submission—that involve male loyalty and devotion.

Orc's defiance of Urizen, Martin Bidney has shown, alludes to an emblematic scene of political defiance: the resistance of the Aztec prince Guatimozin or Cuauhtémoc, Montezuma's nephew and the major hero of Aztec struggle against Spain, to Cortés's torture. The incident was well known in Blake's lifetime through William Robertson's *History of the Americas,* originally published in 1777. In particular, Bidney contends, Urizen's uncomprehending gibe about "repos[ing] . . . / . . . on verdant fields" echoes Guatimozin's scornful dismissal of his own sufferings: "Am I now reposing on a bed of flowers?" (Robertson 2: 127; Bidney 196). As Bidney shows, the identification is supported by secondary echoes in Blake's text and by the wide familiarity of Robertson's work—it went through many editions, was read by Keats at school and later, and the Guatimozin incident, in particular, was mentioned by both Mary and Percy Shelley (195 and nn).[4] Bidney's detective work deepens our understanding of Orc's opposition; Guatimozin's resistance to imperial conquest and his defiance of tyranny provide historical referents for roles Orc has had since Blake's *America.*

But Guatimozin's is a story not merely about heroic suffering but about male comradeship: Guatimozin is tortured "together with his chief favourite," and at the crucial moment:

> His fellow-sufferer, overcome by the violence of the anguish, turned a dejected eye towards his master, which seemed to implore his permission to reveal all that he knew. But the high-spirited prince, darting on him a look of authority mingled with scorn, checked his weakness by asking, "Am I now reposing on a bed of flowers?" Overawed by the reproach, he persevered in his dutiful

silence, and expired. Cortes, ashamed of a scene so horrid, rescued the royal victim . . . and prolonged a life reserved for new indignities and sufferings. (Robertson 2: 126–27)

The "favourite"—the term could connote simple patronage or an emotional relationship—is steeled by Guatimozin's fortitude and Guatimozin, inferably, is heartened by the "favourite's" willingness to bear torture for him—a response Blake's Urizen seems to recognize dimly in his query, "Or is thy joy founded on torment which others bear for thee" (78:41).[5] For eighteenth-century readers, the story as told by Robertson would also carry an echo of such classical sacrifices as Nisus's for Euryalus—itself strongly eroticized, though this dimension may often not have been recognized. The story therefore had strong implications of male-male devotion, with homoerotic undertones, though the directly sexual inflection of the page 78 drawing is Blake's addition.

The Guatimozin story had a contemporary antislavery analogue as well, in one episode of John Gabriel Stedman's 1796 *Narrative* of his military service against revolting slaves in Surinam, for which Blake engraved illustrations from Stedman's watercolors in 1792–93. Stedman's account of the stoicism of a slave hung by a hook piercing his ribs (illustrated by Blake) includes an incident in which the slave reproaches a second prisoner: "Notwithstanding all this he never complained, and even upbraided a negro for crying while he was flogged below the gallows, by calling out to him—You man?—*Da [boy] fasy?* Are you a man? you behave like a boy. Shortly after which [the second prisoner] was knocked on the head by the commiserating sentry" (1: 109).[6] Though unstated, the second slave's silence after the rebuke seems implicit in this account too. There are thus several powerful referents for Orc's contempt for suffering, and all include some element of male-male emulation, with Robertson's including specific details that Blake seems to have echoed verbally.

In addition, the drawing and text refer, as so often in Blake, to a Miltonic original. Orc's temptations in Night 7a combine elements of Jesus' in *Paradise Regained.*[7] This first scene, in which Urizen taunts Orc with an implied promise to ease his sufferings, has affinities to Jesus' trial of wealth and sexual laxity (see chapter 1): like Milton's Satan, Urizen unsuccessfully appeals to bodily impulse before turning to more insidious ethical and intellectual temptations. But for Milton, sexual desire and particularly homoerotic attraction are potential subverters of Jesus' will, which he must reject; in Blake's narration male homoerotic solidarity and sexual attraction become, thanks to their references to a male culture of antityrannic resistance, analogues for Orc's defiance of Urizen's wiles.

Blake's illustration thus gains multiple resonances. It may, in part, represent Urizen's fantasy. But the fantasy cannot simply be of homosexual aggression; Urizen's own words, "thou reposest . . . *feeding thyself* / With visions" (my emphasis) indicate that he is imagining the way in which Orc maintains his indifference to Urizen's power. The sketch may represent Urizen's fantasy of Orc's own homosexual reveries as the basis of his defiance or a further fantasy in which Urizen substitutes for Orc's imagined homosexual partner. But in either case, it must show Urizen's jealousy of pleasure he feels Orc capable of having or imagining. Nor can the drawing be viewed only though the single lens of Urizenic projection. To the extent that it is related to Orc's defiance and its literary subtexts, especially the Guatimozin story, Blake's depiction of homosexual conduct in the drawing appears as a sexualized version of the "favourite's" devotion, and the relations of other warrior pairs. It therefore gains independent force as a portrayal in sexual terms of solidarity and sustaining devotion. Further, it associates the fellator's role with these positive qualities. Within the ordinary dynamics of male sexuality, indeed, giving orgasm to another male appears as a denial of self, a sacrifice of direct sexual release to take pleasure in the release of another. Hence, in psychic terms the drawing appears as an analogue for the mutual solidarity that allows victims to withstand their tortures, and in a broader way it presents a sexualized form of that mutual giving of self for another which Blake elsewhere prizes so highly (e.g., *J* 96:20–21).

Finally, besides drawing out a nonexplicit suggestion in the main narrative, Blake's drawing may function independently of the narrative as well—and in a markedly powerful way. As an illustrator, as noted above, Blake often departed from direct depiction to comment on, present an analogue for, or draw out a suggested idea in the text. In illustrating Gray's poems and Edward Young's *Night Thoughts,* for example, he would star a line in the text and produce a visual analogue for that line, without necessarily paying much attention to the line's immediate context.[8] In *The Four Zoas,* with the Gray and Young illustrations fresh in his memory, and using some of the latter as templates in his own poem,[9] Blake sometimes follows an equally free procedure.[10] Pages 39–41, for example, describe a dream of Ahania in which Vala walks with Albion "in dreams of soft deluding slumber"; Vala's consort Luvah appears above them in a cloud as "the sorrow of Man & the balmy drops fell down" (39:16, 41:1). On page 41, Blake apparently illustrates the latter line by showing a woman on her back reaching up to masturbate a massive penis from which, inferably, balmy drops do fall.[11] Since the text episode focuses on the creation of religion as a projection of sexual guilt, Blake may have meant to show the hidden sexual content of Ahania's dream or the sexual content of religious abstractions in general. But, on the contrary, the design may show an alternative, guilt-free way in which balmy drops can fall.

Something similar may happen on page 78. Besides or instead of specifically illustrating Urizen's fantasy or imagining a sexual analogue for Orc's resistance, the tableau may simply show one way in which a male may feed himself with visions of delight and/or bathe in rivers of delight. In this case, the drawing would still show an alternative to Urizenic repression, since it is illustrating Urizen's words. But the alternative would be to sexual rather than political repression; the drawing would show "rivers of delight" Urizen cannot enjoy and would condemn if he became conscious of them. The image, that is, would evoke and attack Urizen's function as enforcer of sexual repression, otherwise unmentioned in the narrative at this point. Further, and more remarkably, the image would seem to refer as much to the fantasy or act of the partner performing oral sex, for whom the other's semen would be like a river, as to the experience or fantasy of his partner. The image, that is, does not present oral sex merely from the perspective of the "masculine" partner, whose role is sometimes thought to have been compatible with pre-nineteenth century gender norms, but from that of the fellator as well. While we still cannot be certain the depiction carries positive value, showing such an act as an implicit rejection of Urizen's law departs substantially from Blake's early idealizing of aggressive heterosexual masculinity as both sexual behavior and political metaphor.

Though *The Four Zoas* contains no other literal depictions of sodomitic scenes, at least one text sequence suggests that repression of homosexuality may be a component of Urizen's rule and/or a "Urizenic" psychic structure. At the end of Night 5, Urizen utters a powerful lament for lost possibilities of harmony that he associates with a prior Eden. Among other points, he rues his own fall, in which he dragged down Urthona and Luvah; and, addressing "beauteous Luvah" (64:29), he grieves for the time

> When thou didst bear the golden cup at the immortal tables
> Thy children smote their fiery wings crownd with the gold of heaven
> Thy pure feet stepd on the steps divine. too pure for other feet
> And thy fair locks shadowd thine eyes from the divine effulgence . . .
>   (64:31–65:2)

In the references to Luvah's fairness and his role as cupbearer, Eugenie Freed hears an echo of the "stripling youths . . . of fairer hue / Than *Ganymede*" in Milton's banquet scene, as well as Ganymede's homosexual associations (55, 136 n. 95; *PR* 2:352–53). Freed takes the lament to refer to the transition from guiltless sexuality in "Eden" to guilt and degradation in the "fallen" world; Urizen's nostalgia for the lost "immortal tables" may also signify the sexually rigid psyche's exclusion of its homosexual portion, seen here as a quality of Luvah (partly disguised by the reference to Luvah's children). If so, the lament complements the suggestion on page 78 of a sexuality Urizen cannot comprehend; it also anticipates similar suggestions later in the poem and about Satan in *Milton,* as well as Blake's creation in *Jerusalem* of a masculine "emanation" for France, one of Luvah's identities (see chapters 4, 6).

Elsewhere in *The Four Zoas,* Blake executes other images showing sexual ambiguity or polymorphism, whose thematic impact is hard to assess.[12] A notable example, on page 26, features four highly bizarre winged creatures (figure 3.1): from bottom to top of the page, a multibreasted female dragon; a form with semidivided legs, prominent vulva, and fish tail, surmounted by a scrotum and phallic neck terminating in a bird's head; a scrotum and penis (partly erased), with legs dangling below, embraced by a partly hidden figure; and a seemingly female figure with butterflylike wings, bloblike limbs, and enlarged breasts and belly, the latter divided by a darkish line so that it also looks a little like a scrotum. The second and third figures are reminiscent of priapean emblems reproduced by Richard Payne Knight (see chapter 1). The third evidently involves some sort of phallic perversity. It cannot be determined whether the hidden figure (male, with short hair) is obscured by his own enormously enlarged penis, or is riding on an independently flying penis, but in either case he is hugging and perhaps kissing it. This figure, then, prefigures the oral-genital sexual contact shown in literal terms on page 78, suggesting either fellation or self-fellation. If one attempts to view the four figures as a sequence, they can be seen as progressing either toward greater sexual differentiation, from the top to the bottom of the page, or toward greater hermaphrodism or androgyny, from bottom to top. Most interpreters assume the first perspective, seeing the ensemble as showing Vala's evolution from "Earth-worm" to "Dragon winged bright & poisonous" (26:8–13); progression toward increasing definition and differentiation may seem a natural sequence to find in the figures.[13] But the drawings may also—or instead—show an alternative to this sequence. If one reads upward, the images might show Vala's further development from dragon to "weeping Infant" (27:2), or, more simply, a reversal of the increasing differentiation in the text. The woman's arching dragon neck becomes the bird's arching phallic neck, the latter becomes an actual phallus embraced by its rider, and finally the phallus becomes a body incorporating suggestions of female and male

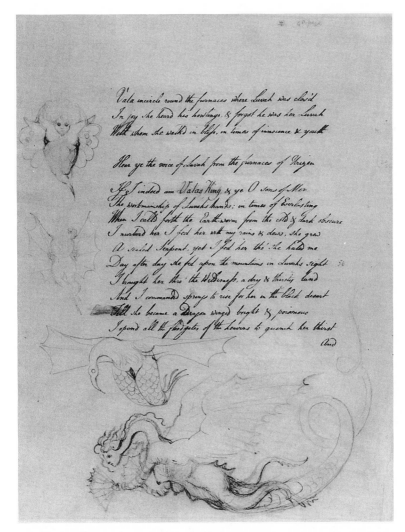

Figure 3.1   William Blake. *The Four Zoas.* Page 26. By permission of The British Library. Add 39764.

sexual parts. In this case the picture's valence is entirely different: Instead of culminating in the predatory bottom figure (to which the eye is unquestionably first drawn), the series of transformations ends in the rather harmless biomorphic blob at the top. Though either way of ordering the figures is possible, the second makes pictorial and symbolic sense: The lower figures are flying toward the left margin in which the upper two appear, the third is clearly rising, and the butterfly (at the top) appears as an emblem of metamorphosis in eighteenth-century usage, including Blake's (see Rose). If the images are viewed this way, they show an alternative to Vala's malevolent initial development in the text. Blake may be following his frequent procedure of varying the text, showing a progression from sexual differentiation toward polymorphism, with the third figure—merging with its own or someone else's penis—as one stage in the blurring and fusing of sexual identities.

A final, verbal depiction of sexual indeterminacy occurs in a text fragment separate from the main narration, which describes how two hermaphroditic youths appear, to the astonishment of various immortals:

> Male formd the demon mild athletic force his shoulders spread
> And his bright feet firm as a brazen altar. but. the parts
> To love devoted. female, all astonishd stood the hosts
> Of heaven, while Tharmas with wingd speed flew to the sandy shore
> . . . .
> With printless feet scorning the concave of the joyful sky
> Female her form bright as the summer but the parts of love
> Male & her brow radiant as day. darted a lovely scorn
> Tharmas beheld from his high rocks . . . (141:11–14, 17–20, *E*845)

The fragment may be unrelated to anything else in the text—no male-female hermaphrodites are described elsewhere—but it could also be related to a trio of short scenes on the reverse of the same sheet, depicting Tharmas and Enion's copulation. In one of these scenes Tharmas appears to impregnate Enion, but an apparently alternative version describes an inverted fertilization: The "seed of life & death" pours from Enion and "in the womb of Tharmas rush the rivers of Enions pain / Trembling he lay swelld with the deluge" (142:8–10). These scenes may narratively precede those on the front side of the page, which begin as Tharmas rises "from dewy tears" (141:1) and views the "demon," and they provide a logical antecedent for the "Male formd" child's birth. (The female's origins, however, are not explained.) This possibility is significant because if the fragments are related, they seem to provide an alternative account of Los and Enitharmon's births, which in the main text occur when Enion copulates with Tharmas's Spectre—herself becoming "Half Woman & half Spectre"—and brings them forth (7:10, 8:2). In sum, the draft episode definitely shows the advent of a pair of hermaphroditic beings and may narrate a substitute, hermaphroditic genealogy and physiognomy for Los and Enitharmon.[14]

Though ultimately not used in the poem, these fragments have several important features. First, the descriptions are relatively uncondemning. Blake is quite capable of describing his beings as "horrible" or "A monster," terms applied in the main narrative to Tharmas's Spectre and the transformed Enion (7:8, 13); he avoids such phrases here. Descriptive phrases for the male—"demon mild," "athletic force," "firm as a brazen altar"—would normally carry positive connotations in Blake, though the female's combination of radiance and scorn is, in Blake's usual vocabulary, a tipoff to a potentially negative role. ("Demon" is usually a positive description in Blake; it is frequently applied to Orc, but also to the young Los in *The Four Zoas.*) The assembled spectators, including Urizen, Urthona (Los's form in "Eternity"), and others, are distressed, and "Pitying they viewd the new born demon. for they could not love" (141:9); but this response seems to show their incapacity for sympathy as much as the boy and girl's monstrosity. Second, if the boy and girl are meant as Los and Enitharmon, Blake may have devised the episode to dramatize the couple's radical incompatibility. (They spend most of the poem's first seven Nights in constant sexual struggles.) If so, Blake would be linking the conventional idea of hermaphrodism as unnatural to that of Los and Enitharmon's mutual cruelty and jealousy; but in the event, he decided to present these emotions as part of an ordinary heterosexual union, with no use of metaphoric or symbolic hermaphrodism. Finally, the absence of the words "hermaphrodite" or "hermaphroditic" is itself noteworthy. Later in *The Four Zoas* and in other works Blake does use these terms, usually in negative senses; however, they do not signify hermaphrodism in the ordinary physical or gender senses but rather political and cultural occurrences and even, paradoxically, gender determinacy (see chapter 6). By not using these terms here and ultimately not using the text description of the two beings, Blake leaves himself free to develop this idiosyncratic sense of hermaphrodism elsewhere; in designs, both in this poem and in *Milton,* he continues to present some images of physical hermaphrodism without necessarily negative connotations.

Critique of the Poetics of Masculinity

In Urizen's taunt against Orc we notice the phrase "fierce desire," reminiscent of Orc's "fierce embrace" in *America* (1:10). Though the desire is for freedom, the sexual overtones of Urizen's language point to the connections Blake has always shown between Orcian rebellion and sexual desire. Clearly, up to this point in the poem, Orc retains his fiery sexuality, and so far as Orc remains a positive figure, Blake maintains his own belief in it. But

Blake now reexamines the locus of this sexuality in aggressive heterosexuality. Besides showing male homosexual and/or sexually polymorphous images, some text sequences and designs in *The Four Zoas* level an attack against Blake's earlier "poetics of masculinity," especially its political aspects.

This critique emerges partly from the larger narrative action surrounding page 78. As Night 7a proceeds, Orc submits to Urizen following a second temptation and divides, one of his aspects becoming a serpent and the other remaining human, imprisoned "in the deeps" (98 [90]:46). This second temptation continues the thread of allusion to *Paradise Regained,* combining aspects of Milton's trials of earthly power and philosophic wisdom: Urizen offers Orc power over the poor and knowledge of the arts of war (79:20–80:21). Complementing the visual suggestion on page 78 that homosexuality may be a force for, or analogue to, antityrannic resistance, the text narration criticizes the aggressive heterosexuality that earlier works showed as a positive force. While it centers on worldly power, this temptation also manipulates Orc's sexual desire for his mother, Enitharmon, and Oedipal jealousy of Los, his father—"By gratified desire by strong devouring appetite she fills / Los with ambitious fury that his race shall all devour," Urizen suggestively tells Orc (80:25–26). Following this last provocation, Orc weakens, loses his defiant wrath, and begins to assume snake form (80:27–48). This sequence of events implies a critique of heterosexual male sexual possessiveness as a corrupting weakness. Though never directly illustrated, Orc's serpent form, "A Self consuming dark devourer rising into the heavens" (80:48), is clearly a transmogrification of the erect penises in the page 78 illustration; but it is one that results from the release of heterosexual possessiveness and, perhaps, the repression of homosexual desire. Orc's inflamed male sexuality, then, along with political temptations, is a vehicle for collaboration with and submission to tyrannic power and a source of Orc's serpent aspect that colludes with Urizen in the murderous wars of Night 8.

Blake also presents a critique of untrammeled male sexuality in the alternative account of Orc's transformation in Night 7b. This version provides a direct revision of Orc's "fierce embrace" of Urthona's daughter in *America* (1–2). Repeating and varying *America*'s words, Blake makes a sexual temptation by the "nameless shadowy Vortex," or Vala, acting as a conduit for Urizen's "arts," the prelude to Orc's snake transformation:

> With sighs & howling & deep sobs that he might lose his rage
> And with it lose himself in meekness she embracd his fire
> . . . .
> So Orc rolld round his clouds upon the deeps of dark Urthona

Knowing the arts of Urizen were Pity & Meek affection
And that by these arts the Serpent form exuded from his limbs
Silent as despairing love & strong as Jealousy
Jealous that she was Vala now become Urizens harlot
And the Harlot of Los & the deluded harlot of the Kings of Earth
His soul was gnawn in sunder
The hairy shoulders rend the links free are the wrists of fire . . .
    (91:4–5, 10–17)

In *America,* we remember, the impulse to seize and master the female was partly a metaphor for social revolution and partly a direct representation of sexual rebellion; in both aspects it appeared positive and fructifying. Here this same impulse leads Orc to take snake form, lose his oppositional power, and emerge as Urizen's destructive partner and rival. This impulse is still both sexual and political—it encompasses Orc's jealousy of Los, his desire for Vala (consort of Luvah, Orc's ur-form), and his hatred of her prostitution to tyrannic power. But the impulse is no longer liberatory. Blake's revision is two-sided. It presents the female as temptress and a source of male weakness; in this respect Blake merely varies his earlier treatments of gender. But Blake's revision also shows the impulse to male sexual mastery as a weakness that betrays the male into complicity with repressive violence in the larger world, and as destructive of one's own identity: "The form of Orc was gone he reard his serpent bulk among / The stars of Urizen in Power rending the form of life" (93:25–26).[15] In this respect Blake's treatment sharply departs from his earlier emphasis on the positive, awakening function of aggressive male sexuality.

In both versions of the Night 7 story, then, male heterosexual competition, domination, and violence (implied or explicit) help to subvert Orc's resistance to tyranny. In contrast, in the first temptation episode, the "visions of delight" Urizen imputes to Orc (78:38), figured as male comradeship or love in the Guatimozin story and as male oral-genital contact in the accompanying drawing, provide the strength to withstand Urizen. These elements, however, are present only in historical subtext and visual analogue; in the text, Orc has no companion, and his lack of supporting comradeship may in part condition his eventual submission.

Other visual images in the poem continue the critique of aggressive male sexuality, though without specific homosexual reference. Those for pages 4 and 88 [96] (figs. 3.2, 3.3) show complementary aspects of male phallicism. In the former, a huge serpent emerges from a chaotic sea, coils through the bottom of the page, and rises up the left margin; its head is shaped like that of a penis, sharpened to an arrowhead form, and on the creature's flank an angrily frowning, fully grown cupid figure aims an arrow from a drawn bow. As the presence of a cupid indicates, this image views male phallicism in its sexual aspect. The image is appropriate to page 4, which narrates the marital division of Tharmas and Enion, the beginning of the "torments of Love & Jealousy" mentioned in its revised subtitle (*FZ* 1 and textual note, *E*818). But while the written text gives primacy to Tharmas's voice, allowing him both to speak first and to reply to Enion with the poignant "I wish & feel & weep & groan Ah terrible terrible" (4:45; 4:7–5:4), the design focuses on phallic aggression through the scowling cupid and the repetition of its arrows in the arrowhead form of the serpent-penis's head. The visual image also suggests that the serpent rising from the sea, Tharmas's element, is a form of Tharmas's Spectre, which Enion weaves from his dissolved form and which appears later in the text "in masculine strength . . . / Reard up," though in human form (6:4–5; 5:13–6:8). The design counters the preeminence of Tharmas's perspective in the written text and suggests that crude phallic power generates aggression and cruelty.

In the design for page 88 [96], three kneeling figures bow down before a massive penis with testicles; as distinct from that for page 4, this design focuses on religious-political aspects of predatory maleness. The text of this page shows collusion between war and religion: "The day for war the night for secret religion in [Urizen's] temple" (88 [96]:18). The design makes clear that underneath its mystified forms, the "secret religion" is phallic fetishism. As the page 4 design suggested that aggressive masculinity is linked to sexual cruelty, this image illustrates its connection to war and oppression.[16]

Interpreters have often discussed how Blake links war with distorted sexuality. Most, however, have assumed that he simply attacks the restraint and rechanneling of male desire. In *The Four Zoas,* Blake is far more critical of male phallicism. Those who criticize Blake for a male-centered sexual ideology have missed his attack on that ideology in parts of *The Four Zoas;* a kind of interpretive circular reasoning, abetted by failure to perceive homosexual subtexts, leads to the assumption that heterosexual phallicism must retain the positive connotations it had in earlier works, even if the images that now present it are blatantly predatory or abjectly adoring toward warfare. But just as *America*'s paradigm of social liberation comes under attack in *The Four Zoas*—an attack that focuses on its weakness in the face of Urizen's temptation, not on the destructiveness of social radicalism—so too does Blake revise and deepen his understanding of sexual liberation, rejecting the idealization of phallic aggression that once formed its core.[17]

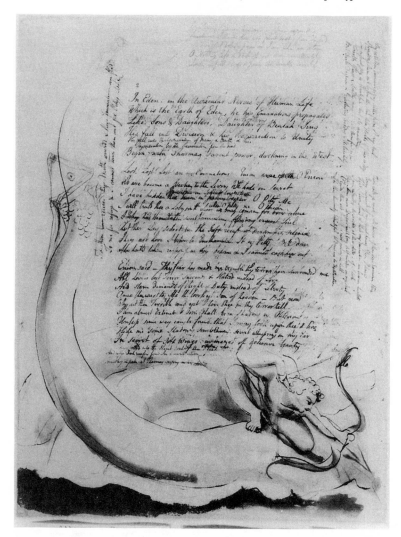

Figure 3.2 William Blake. *The Four Zoas*. Page 4. By permission of The British Library. Add 39764.

Lesbianism as Haven and as a Portion of Apocalypse

Many drawings for *The Four Zoas* show a fascination with lesbianism, including its supposed manifestation through physical hermaphrodism. Some of these images have no obvious thematic significance beyond evincing interest in all types of sexuality; others present rich, sometimes

Figure 3.3   William Blake. *The Four Zoas*. Page 88 [96]. By permission of The British Library. Add 39764.

contradictory thematic meanings. While their precise import is often ambiguous, some seem to explore lesbian alternatives to predatory masculinity, and others appear to present lesbian meanings for Blake's projected apocalyptic culmination of history.

These drawings occur in a verbal text that in many respects expresses rampant misogyny. Destructive sexual competitions abound in *The Four*

Zoas. They are usually seen through the eyes of male characters and are felt by them as violations of women's proper role—as when the Fallen Man, appearing to Enitharmon in dream, complains that women no longer exist for man's "sport & amusement" but to "drink up all his Powers" (10:25). This idea is echoed in an apparently redemptive context by "Eternal Men" at the harvest feast of Night 9, who shudder to see a separate female form, "Not born for the sport and amusement of Man but born to drink up all his powers / They wept to see their shadows they said to one another this is Sin / This is the Generative world" (133:7–9). Tharmas, and later the awakened Eternal Man, also argue that in Eden females die or sleep with the seasons while "Males immortal live renewd by female deaths," phrasing that joins Blake's habitual figuring of nature as female with ideas of the females' dependency on males and the males' superior, even predatory, relation to them (5:1–3; 122:12–15). The conception that an independent female will is evil, or at least a product of "fallen" existence, seems firmly established in later Blake: It is expressed by the narrators of *The Four Zoas* and *Jerusalem,* by Blake in his own voice in *A Vision of the Last Judgment,* and twice by Los in *Jerusalem* (*FZ* 30:48; *E*562; *J* 30/34:31, 56:43, 86:61).

Though such pronouncements, general or universal in form, have often been taken as statements of Blakean doctrine,[18] on closer examination some appear as expressions of the characters' limited views. Yet the line between these two possibilities is by no means clear. The comments about Eden—once they are understood to be statements by male characters—bear an evident symmetry with those about women's intentions: As females are charged by males with wanting to "drink up" their powers, so males state that females properly die to renew them. Both statements evince a power-lust characteristic of sexual competition, though presumably the males from whom we hear them are not fully aware of this. But the accusations about females wishing to "drink up" men's powers may actually be projections of the males' own desires to cannibalize females, disguised as memories of a fantasized earlier state in which females existed only for men's pleasure. At the least, the accusations reflect fear of women's independent existence and sexuality, and in one case the narrative itself makes this clear. Though the "Eternal Men" who appear in the harvest sequence of Night 9 are apparently superior beings, their labeling of women's existence and sex as "Sin" is a fairly clear Blakean marker of their own error; and their application of this term to the "Generative world" prompts another of the Eternals to deliver the "Man is a Worm" speech, whose purpose (notwithstanding its virtual erasure of women from discussion) is to justify generative existence as a sustaining force and a path back to "Eternity" (133:11–26).[19]

Blake's apparent condemnation of female will is also problematic, despite this idea's several repetitions. "Look back into the Church Paul! Look! Three Women around / The Cross! O Albion why didst thou a Female Will Create?" bursts out Los in *Jerusalem,* only to have Jerusalem expose his light-mindedness six pages later when she calls herself Jesus' "Magdalen," one of the three women Los has denounced (56:42–43, 62:14).

Both *The Four Zoas* and *Jerusalem,* then, suggest the limited and selfserving quality of their characters' misogynist appeals in several instances; where the narratives seem to label females as dominators or devourers, they may instead show how men in the throes of sexual wars perceive women.[20] Still, not all the comments I have noted are easily explained in this way. The belief that females in Eden die to renew males, though first spoken by Tharmas in his marriage quarrel with Enion, is echoed by the Eternal Man in what appears a key doctrinal context, when he is explaining Jerusalem's advent to the reformed Urizen (122:12–15);[21] his comment that females in the renewed world "shall learn obedience" echoes Blake's own that "There is no such thing in Eternity as a Female Will" (*FZ* 122:13; *E*562). (Yet we have seen that Eternal Men may be mistaken; the Eternal Man's viewpoints are called into question by the poem's closing sequence, in which the redemption the characters seem to have been fashioning is postponed [137:5–138:19].) The nub is that often it is not possible to be sure whether Blake is simply describing the views of his male characters or is identifying with and sharing them. And in an overall way, *The Four Zoas* seems to affirm the higher status of the faculties Blake metaphorizes as male, such as imagination and intellect, and the proper primacy in Eden of the beings that embody them.

The balance shifts when we turn from words to images. Just as the designs of *The Four Zoas* offer a critical view of aggressive phallicism that extends that in the verbal text, so they present the primary counterbalance to the male-supremacist viewpoints in the text, in particular through several fairly open depictions of lesbianism. Among others, these images include two that show women with enlarged clitorises, resembling small penises (pages 22 [20], 32; figs. 3.4, 3.5). In the first, a supine woman with prominent breasts and vulva displays a penislike clitoris, while a much larger, sketchily rendered face, apparently joined to a serpentine body indicated by a few curving lines, smiles down on her. The second, a tableau of as many as nine figures, some now erased, includes a woman, facing the viewer, who holds a penislike clitoris in her right hand; a second figure faces her, back to the viewer, but with its legs reversed so that knees and feet face outward and with what seems to be a tiny penis or a clitoris in the resulting pelvis-buttocks. Two other illustrations show evidently lesbian scenes without anatomical peculiarities (pages 110 [106], 118; figs. 3.6, 3.7). In one a male figure lies supine with a very faintly outlined erect penis (discernible in reproduction and a little clearer in the original); behind his head a naked woman masturbates as a second reaches through her legs from behind. In the other, three women are mutually entwined in erotic interplay.

Though they have not generally been seen as lesbian, these images in fact draw on specific eighteenth-century views of lesbianism. Using examples from 1671 to the mid–1700s, Emma Donoghue shows that women who engaged in lesbian practices were often thought to have a "female member," imagined "as either a prolapsed vagina or an enlarged clitoris" (4; see also 35). In scientific and anecdotal literature, it was unclear whether the enlargement led to desire for other women, or the desire to the practice and hence to enlargement. In either case Giles Jacob's *A Treatise of Hermaphrodites* (1718) classified as "Masculine Females" the "many Lascivious Women [who] divert themselves one with another at this time in the City [London]" (qtd. in Donoghue 46). While some writers thought it "not probable [that hermaphrodites] are truly of both Sexes," others produced classifications ranging from men with some female parts, through women with large clitorises, to "perfect" hermaphrodites.[22] Donoghue notes that "ideas about giant clitorises were not experimental notions on the borders of medicine; they became part of the common stock of knowledge handed down through the medical mainstream" (39). So a considerable tradition identified lesbians as what Donoghue calls "double-sexed" (27), and the designs on pages 22 [20] and 32 seem clearly to draw on it.

Mutual genital rubbing, or "tribadism," and joint masturbation were also parts of the period's conception of lesbian practices. "I began, Sir, the Folly [of masturbation] at 11 Years of Age, was taught it by my Mother's Chamber-Maid," a well-off girl declared in one purported account, " . . . and so intimate were we in the Sin, that we took all Opportunities of committing it, and invented all the Ways we were capable of to heighten the Titillation, and gratify our sinful Lusts the more. . . . We, in short, shamefully pleasured one another, as well as each ourselves" (*Supplement* to *Onania* 125–26).[23] The brothel scene in Cleland's *Memoirs of a Woman of Pleasure,* in a 1766 edition, included an illustration of the act, performed from the front.[24] Lesbian masturbation and tribadism seem clear points of reference for the designs on pages 110 [106] and 118 of *The Four Zoas.*

Magno and Erdman, lacking reference to these contexts, identify the female organs in the first and second designs as penises; they also identify the

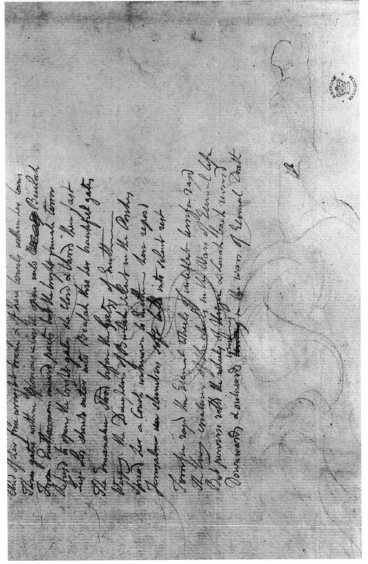

Figure 3.4 William Blake. *The Four Zoas.* Page 22 [20], detail. By permission of The British Library. Add 39764.

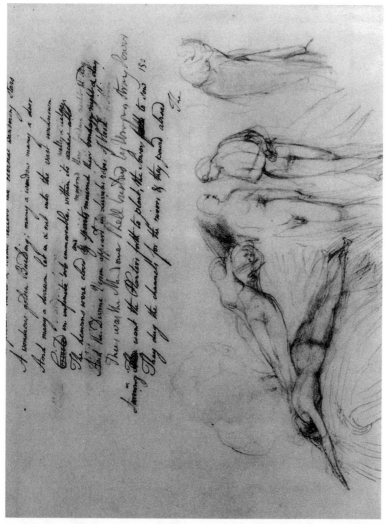

Figure 3.5   William Blake. *The Four Zoas.* Page 32, detail. By permission of The British Library. Add 39764.

large smiling face on page 22 [20] and the front-and-back figure on page 32 as male (37–38, 42–43), heterosexualizing the drawings. But the curvilinear representation of the first and the head with rounded features and hair tied back in the second suggest female figures. The front-back reversal of this figure itself, in fact, suggests a kind of metaphoric hermaphrodism.

70

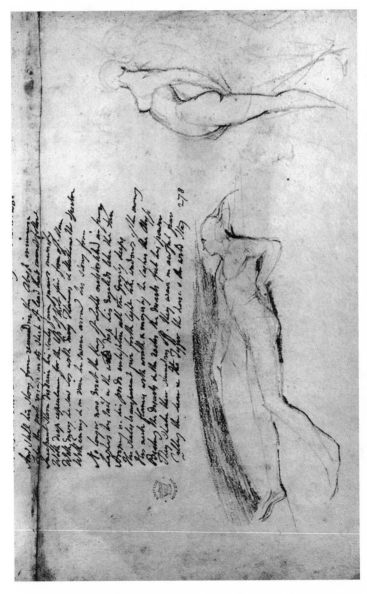

Figure 3.6   William Blake. *The Four Zoas.* Page 110 [106], detail. By permission of The British Library. Add 39764.

Figure 3.7 William Blake. *The Four Zoas.* Page 118, detail. By permission of The British Library. Add 39764.

Magno and Erdman also see the "penises" as foreign to the female figures. They argue that page 22 [20] continues a design of a cupid shooting at a woman's vagina on page 21 [19] (recto to this page's verso), and that it shows "the arrowhead (a pink-colored penis)" embedded in the female's vulva. On page 32, the female figure's "penis" is "planted in her vulva like the one on page 22 [20]" (37, 42). Magno and Erdman do recognize that the women in the other two scenes are engaging in sex, though they avoid the term "lesbian." But they heterosexualize the masturbation image in a subtler way, arguing that though the two females disregard the male, whom Magno and Erdman identify as Urizen, "his power over them is evident from their behavior" (83). Evidently, for two women to masturbate together shows Urizen's power, but it is not clear why.[25] In the context of contemporary ways of understanding lesbianism, however, the lesbian reference of Blake's drawings is rather obvious.

These figures are hard to interpret, partly because their connections with events in Blake's text are even more enigmatic than usual. The scene on page 22 [20], which we now recognize as one of lesbian arousal rather than male penetration, may relate to Enitharmon's refusal, in the text, to let Los "enter into Beulah thro her beautiful gates" (22 [20]:7); in this case the large face would probably be a fantasy figure, since Enitharmon has no preferred female companion in the text. Alternatively but less probably, the design could show Jerusalem reposing on "a couch unknown to Enitharmon" (line 10) under the Daughters of Beulah's protection; in this case the large face could be either Enitharmon's, coveting Jerusalem, or that of the Daughters collectively, guarding her. In a similarly indeterminate way, the pair of coquetting figures on page 32 could relate to Vala's refusal of Luvah's love in the text (31:18–32:2), showing a lesbian flirtation imagined or actually occurring in preference—though the other figures in the scene have no obvious relation to the text. On page 110 [106], the text describes Urizen's metamorphosis into a dragon as he "[e]mbrace[s] / The Shadow[y] Female." As this occurs, his human shape becomes a "form of Senseless Stone" in "the Abyss immense" (110 [106]:23–24, 32, 35).[26] The design, which suggests an erotic dream once we notice the man's erection, could show either an analogue of or a variation on the text. Possibly the image shows the dream itself—the sexually aroused sleeping Urizen dreams of lesbian masturbation, while the waking Urizen unites with the Shadowy Female in dragon form. Alternatively, the design could show what happens in reality during the dream: While the text represents Urizen's dream of embracing the Shadowy Female, she actually cavorts with another woman. Finally, the trio on page 118, early in the apocalyptic ninth night, could be Rahab, Tirzah, and Vala, female spirits who play malefic roles in the second half of the poem. Rahab and Tirzah are mentioned on this page, seemingly facing apocalyptic ruin as they "wail aloud in the wild flames they give themselves up to Consummation" (118:7); inferably, Vala is in the same peril. Alternatively, a later passage indicates that these characters' perdition may be avoidable: "Error can never be redeemd in all Eternity / But Sin Even Rahab is redeemd in blood & fury & jealousy" (120:48–49). But neither of these dire descriptions corresponds directly to the "apparently enjoyable tangle" (Butlin 1: 291) in the drawing.

These designs' attitude to lesbianism can be viewed as negative if (for example) one sees Enitharmon and Vala's refusals of male attentions as destructive manifestations of "female will," or Rahab and her friends' erotic entwining as showing obliviousness to their impending doom (or as showing the evils for which they are to be punished). But other meanings emerge once we consider what these designs have in common: All show an awareness of lesbian relations as an alternative to heterosexual gratification. Such an alternative need not be read as negative; it may represent a way of avoiding what Blake is now presenting as a destructively aggressive masculinity. These senses emerge when the designs are placed in their narrative contexts, both visual and verbal.

The first scene, as noted earlier, follows one on the previous page in which a cupid shoots an arrow at a female figure's vagina. That drawing shows the predatory aspects of male heterosexuality, and throughout Night 1 the poem has shown a mutually destructive sexual war. Often told from male characters' viewpoints, the narrative still makes the sexes' joint responsibility clear: "She [Enitharmon] drave the Females all away from Los / And Los drave all the Males from her away" (9:30–31). So contextualized, the refusal of male sexuality in this drawing is at least not more negative than the male sexual aggression on the previous page or page 4, and may represent a preferable alternative.

The context of the drawing on page 32 also suggests possible positive readings within a cosmic-historical framework. The image comes amid a text sequence that moves from Vala's enslavement to Urizen's creation of a geometric universe of oppression. On the previous page Urizen sees Vala "mourning among the Brick kilns compelld / To labour night & day among the fires" (31:1–2), and her ensuing lament, evoking biblical slavery, suggests the real basis of Urizen's creation: "infinitely beautiful the wondrous work arose / In sorrow & care" (32:7–8). This narrative context suggests a broader reference than just Vala's and Luvah's personal relations for the illustrative tableau, with its exhausted figures, its sprouting grain or strewn straw beneath one prone woman, its several amorous negotiations, and even its poorly defined shape at the right that may show either an embracing couple or a large penis-shaped natural form. This scene may occur at the brick kilns, as the straw suggests, or may show a respite from them and from Urizen's abstractions: The scene shows human emotions and (perhaps) natural fecundity, contrasting with both the slavery of the brick kilns and the sterility of Urizen's geometric creation.[27] In this light the central lesbian interchange appears as one among several human erotic possibilities—all female-centered—counterpointing the female slavery and the implicitly masculine abstract sterility of the text scenes.

Similarly, the larger context of page 110 [106]—Urizen's assumption of dragon form, a stage in Night 8's seemingly endless, inescapable war, which is the European war of Blake's time as well as all the wars of history—suggests several radical meanings for that page's image. Just before assuming dragon form, Urizen experiences a "numming stupor" that he feels as a "female death," a "deadly dull delusion" that rouses "horrors of Eternal death" (lines 19–21). If the illustration shows what its sleeping, human Urizen is dreaming, its content may represent the "death" that Urizen in the text has felt creeping on him. The implication, not present in the text alone, is that the dragon-Urizen of war and extreme oppression takes form partly through repressive denial of homosexuality, specifically lesbianism. Alternatively, as suggested above, the text may give the content of Urizen's dream—after all, the dragon in the text is a form of the drawing's erect penis. In this case, while the "dream" is a destructive social reality that persists through history, the lesbian figures imply that the actual women behind Urizen escape his total control. Moreover, since page 32 reminds us that Blake's designs need not directly illustrate his texts, we can also see the page 110 [106] drawing not as directly presenting some version of the text material but simply as showing a variation on it: While sexualized war and destruction rage on in the text, in the drawing a male figure with an erection, in an erotic dream or stupor, is balanced by two females in active amorous play. Under any of these interpretations, the drawing's lesbian action is at least not negative, once we recognize that the text's union between Urizen and the Shadowy Female signifies a historical-cultural calamity.

Finally, the last of these drawings becomes a rather delightful free variation on the text. In contrast to the narrative implication that Rahab and Tirzah will burn in flames of punishment, or be redeemed "in blood & fury & jealousy" (120:49), we recall that flames signify sexual desire and that "consummation" has a specific sexual meaning.[28] For these three women, whether or not they include Rahab and the others, apocalyptic consummation may also be sexual consummation, an idea usually associated with the *Marriage* rather than *The Four Zoas* but inescapable once the double senses of "flames" and "consummation" are recognized. The association with apocalypse becomes stronger in context. Pages 117–118 are the opening pages of Night 9, whose subject is the Last Judgment.

Both the text of page 118 and the previous page's illustration depict this event. The latter, one of the *Night Thoughts* engravings, shows a pair of (probably) female angels bearing a praying male figure upward toward a third female angel, evidently in the resurrection of the dead. Resurrection has powerful social-revolutionary meanings in Blake's text; yet the *Night Thoughts* image itself is relatively conventional both in religious terms, portraying the Last Judgment as an ascent to heaven, and in a sexual sense, showing the females supporting and aiding the male. The image on page 118, once more featuring three female figures but without a male, upends theological *and* gender conventions, showing a scene of autonomous female delight and a sexual "consummation."[29] The drawing, then, includes both a repressive and a liberatory meaning: The sufferings in the text, whether of condemnation or redemption, may punish the lesbianism of the drawing or the drawing may illustrate, through lesbian activity, a second, sexual meaning for apocalypse. If the image finally contains no clearcut directive for choosing between these meanings, nonetheless its context and our understanding of Blake's illustrative procedures open up a second, sexually catholic reading alongside the restrictive one the design first seemed to imply. The same is true for the other lesbian designs considered here.

Lesbianism and male homosexuality overall seem to function in *The Four Zoas* in slightly different ways, each of which Blake will develop further in later works. The page 78 drawing seems to attach political values of solidarity and self-sacrifice against tyranny to homosexual interchange. In addition, in tandem with the text and with other illustrations, the drawing presents homosexuality as an alternative to possessive male sexuality. Despite Orc's submission to Urizen in the narrative, these elements retain their thematic importance, and they return in later sympathetic depictions of homosexual victimization and of male-to-male transmission of prophetic vocation. The lesbian depictions in turn may simply show various forms of perverse female sexuality, all based on rejection of "normal" heterosexual relations. But in view of *The Four Zoas'* emphasis on the mutual harassment involved in these relations, the rejection can also be seen as an alternative to the "torments of Love & Jealousy." Blake here seems to move very far from his assumption, in earlier works such as *Visions,* that negotiating the shoals of male possessiveness and rejection is the only way for women to enter "experience"; his portrait of conventional male sexuality is darker, and his awareness of alternatives to it is greater. Finally, lesbian relations also appear in an anagogic framework, as a portion of the mutual delights of apocalyptic renewal. These senses of lesbianism as alternative to possessive male sexuality and as an opening to human mutuality will also return in later works.

Chapter Four ✳

History, Homosexuality, and Milton's Legacy

> he [Satan] drove
> Me from his inmost Brain & the doors clos'd with thunders sound
>
> —*Milton* 12:47–48

Blake continued his exploration of homosexuality in episodes of his long poem *Milton* and in some of the many designs illustrating Milton's poetry that he produced after 1800. As in *The Four Zoas,* these episodes and individual designs, though intermittent, are crucial to Blake's meaning, particularly in their reference to Milton's historical, doctrinal, and poetic legacy. With his shift in and after *The Four Zoas* from elemental resistance toward historical awareness and conscious mutuality as the bases for social upheaval and reform, Blake turns once more to the figure of Milton as an emblem of the revolutionary, prophetic responsibilities of poetry and of the poet as public tribune transforming the consciousness of the nation. A criticism and revision of the historical Milton's shortcomings is integral to this revival.

Blake's relationship to Milton in both *Milton* and his Milton designs has been much debated. Did Blake continue to "correct" Milton in polemical fashion, as in *The Marriage of Heaven and Hell?* Or did he gradually accept and emphasize the positive side of Milton's legacy and so finally approach him "not in a spirit of contention but in one of collaboration and celebration" (Wittreich, *Angel* 139)? The most thoughtful discussions discern a gradual shift from the earliest Milton illustrations to the latest, with the poem *Milton* falling partway along the continuum. Here Milton appears as tribune and liberator, one of whose acts in the poem is to admit and rectify his own errors. Unless Blake was being exceptionally indirect, he must have felt that Milton indeed held such a potential for the present age and that the core of Milton's beliefs permitted such a correction. Yet even in the later designs, within the celebratory spirit Wittreich notes, there is room for revision and cross-statement in several areas: Milton's theology (his conception of the elect), his class politics (including also the idea of the elect), and finally his sexual politics, including, as one thread, his and the republican poetic tradition's conception of homosexuality.[1]

In *Paradise Lost,* as already noted, Milton identified Belial with monarchy and luxury, his sons with the inhabitants of Sodom and Gomorrah, and their predominant sin as homosexual rape. The same identification of homosexuality with power and decadence recurs, in a different inflection, in *Paradise Regained.* In *Milton* and elsewhere, Blake refuses Milton's amalgam. In his annotations to Lavater's *Aphorisms,* which he apparently read soon after publication in 1788, Blake defined Sodom's sin as "Pride fullness of bread & *abundance of Idleness,"* quoting Ezekiel 16:49 (*E* 594). Blake surely was aware of the Sodomites' intention to "know" the visiting angels (Gen. 19:5), but makes no reference to it. To some extent Ezekiel was a standard text for references to Sodom, yet this verse was often quoted along with the following one, "[they] committed abomination before me" (50); the sermon quoted in an earlier chapter, *The Destruction of Sodom improved, as a Warning to Great-Britain,* probably stated the obvious in glossing, "among the rest [was] the abomination which has ever since taken its name from this vile place" (4). By quoting only the first verse, Blake avoids this identification. In *Jerusalem,* Blake refers to Sodom and Gomorrah twice, in contexts that focus on commerce and empire, human sacrifice, and what he calls Moral Law, but not sexuality. In the first, the cities are mid-destinations in the spread of the Polypus's fibers from Bristol "round the Earth, thro Gaul & Italy / And Greece . . . into Judea / To Sodom & Gomorrha: thence to India, China & Japan" (67:38–40); the place names fuse the routes of Roman and English imperialist expansion. Later, the two cities appear (89:27) within a long description of the Covering Cherub or Antichrist, among references to "Druid Temples . . . with Victims Sacrifice" and to "Generalizing Gods" (lines 32, 30); the latter phrase would include the abstractions of Moral Law, upending the conventional meaning of the cities. Blake's meanings cannot, of course, be known with finality. By introducing Sodom where Lavater refers only to "indolence," for example, he may tacitly assume the reference to "abomination," or he may be commenting that Sodom's sin was idleness and *not* homosexuality. Similarly, in anatomizing the Polypus, he may mean to place sexual sodomy among the evils of imperialism, as Churchill had (chapter 1), or, on the contrary, to associate the sites of conquest with Sodom and Gomorrah's arrogance before God. It is striking, however, that none of his few references to Sodom mentions its sexual meaning, even through euphemism.

Finally, in *Milton,* the ninth of the twelve false gods seen within "Miltons Shadow who is the Covering Cherub" is "Belial of Sodom & Gomorrha, obscure Demon of Bribes / And secret Assasinations," a description that identifies Belial, more pointedly than Milton had, not just with wealth but with corrupt worldly power, yet omits any sexual reference (37:44, 30–31). The twelve gods generally, also called the "Twelve Spectre Sons of the Druid Albion" (line 34), are presiding spirits of the England of war and oppression that was Milton's ambiguous historical legacy. They are located within Milton's "Shadow," the Covering Cherub. (This complex Blakean idea refers both to false doctrine and to sexual mystification; in another aspect, it is Antichrist, the institutions and practices that embody these falsehoods.) Belial's inclusion indicates that Milton's idea of Belial is among the historical Milton's errors, which his returned spirit is striving to cast off; Blake, then, identifies Belial, like Sodom, with social evils and not with homosexual conduct.

Blake's correction of Milton does not depend on omission alone. Homosexuality becomes Blake's topic in a relatively direct way in one section of *Milton,* the "Bard's Song," and through pictorial innuendo in several of his Milton illustrations, produced at intervals between 1801 and 1816 or later. (Veiled allusions also occur in passages added to *Milton* in 1811 or later, after the first two copies, A and B, were printed. My next chapter discusses public events in 1810–11 that may have influenced these additions and accompanying changes in the poem's visual plates, so I avoid discussing these passages and plates here.)[2] Tying these discussions together is the idea expressed negatively in this chapter's epigraph: The construction of both English masculinity and the English state depended on the repression of homosexuality; this repression produces distortion and aggression in the individual and the state, and overcoming it is necessary to the sexual integration that Blake sees as central to human renovation. Blake also hints at an alternative, positive conception of homosexuality and sexual amalgamation that can be the source of heroic deeds and that is ultimately identified with Jesus, conceptions I explore in later chapters.

History and Homosexuality in Milton's Bard's Song

The Bard's Song, comprising *Milton*'s first third, is sung in heaven to Milton before his descent to our sublunary world. The song's main sections comprise a narrative of a mythic time in which Satan challenges

Los's son Palamabron for control of his harrow and falls from his station into a coma-like state that also appears as rule over our own world. This narrative contains fairly explicit and, on the surface, quite negative references to homosexuality, which are an important part of the bard's account of Satan's rise. These references form part of a larger mythic history of the solidification of the English political-religious system after Milton. As a parallel thread equal in importance, they offer a critique of the moral-sexual foundations of this system by attacking Moral Law, criticizing guilt over sexuality and homosexuality, and showing repression of homosexuality as one cornerstone of Satan's rule.

To establish the Bard's Song's view of homosexuality, especially in the face of countervailing interpretations, requires a considerable detour into its broader focus. The song as a whole has often been read as a partly autobiographical narrative revolving around Blake's artistic struggles and/or as an elaboration of the relations of mental faculties. The first view has taken Satan as Blake's patron William Hayley, who persuaded Blake to settle near him and work under his direction at Felpham, Sussex, from 1800 to 1803, the only time the Blakes lived outside London. Besides trying to usurp Blake's artistic function, Hayley is supposed to have evinced sexual interest in Catherine Blake and, unconsciously, Blake himself, who are assumed to be Elynittria and Palamabron in the narrative.[3] The biographical interpretations are both wrong and beside the point, since Blake's relations with Hayley—or even his concern with artistic vocation, the apparent application of the Hayley story—are only a secondary focus of the Bard's Song. Furthermore, while giving some attention to the song's homosexual material, paradoxically these accounts downgrade its significance by treating it as a biographical datum incorporated adventitiously rather than as part of an analysis of the bases of English social and religious oppression.

Views of the Bard's Song that approach it as an allegory of mental faculties, like those that view it biographically, tend to discount its historical aspects or treat them cursorily. Peter Otto's chapter on *Milton* in *Constructive Vision and Visionary Deconstruction* (1991), one of the most thoughtful studies along these lines, provides full accounts of the poem's harvest imagery, the shifting relations among the psychic aspects the characters are assumed to embody, and the three "classes" Blake discusses, the Elect, Redeemed, and Reprobate. Yet Otto's references to Blake's historical material are rather brief and occasionally arbitrary,[4] and he apparently views the historical actors only as instances of the interaction of the three classes, which exist throughout time. Otto believes the classes exist "on the levels of the individual, the group, and the collective" (43–44), but he treats this last dimension so abstractly that it is all but

undetectable. In addition, Otto's and similar readings leave the homosexual strand in the Bard's Song out of account altogether.

Neither biographical nor symbolic approaches account for the speci-
ficity Blake provides about the song's occasion and effect. It is sung just
as Milton has been in heaven for "One hundred years" (2:17), that is, in
1774, at the opening of the revolutionary period of the late eighteenth
century. According to the poem, Milton descends at a *particular* moment, even if the "moment" lasts (as this historical moment did) until
the poem's composition nearly forty years later. Logically, the song that
prompts the descent should refer in large part to what has occurred during the hundred years, not solely to interactions that can take place at
any time. Moreover, the song sparks Milton's "unexampled deed," his descent to "Eternal Death," or the terrain of struggle in this world, in the
conviction that "The Nations still / Follow after the detestable Gods of
Priam; in pomp / Of warlike selfhood . . . / . . . / I will go down to the
sepulcher to see if morning breaks" (2:21, 14:14–21). Milton, then, is
moved by the song and continuing war on earth to return to find
whether resurrection and apocalypse are possible. The rest of the poem
concerns several interrelated tasks of preparation for the apocalyptic upheaval foreshadowed in its last pages. Summed up in a series of episodes
just before the conclusion, they include overcoming the divisions among
the zoas, or human faculties and populations (Milton's strife with the
zoas on the Brooks of Arnon); overcoming the division of the sexes (Milton's order to Ololon to "Obey" his command of self-annihilation); and
recreating a poetry of faith and inspiration (40:4–8; 28–37; 41:3–28). As
the recovery of poetic vocation is but one of these tasks, it cannot be the
main topic of the Bard's Song. And it is plain what the main topic *must*
be: the events on earth, specifically in England, since Milton's time that
make his return imperative.

Paradoxically, the main obstacle to an accurate historical reading of
the Bard's Song has been the one attempted by Blake's preeminent historical interpreter, David V. Erdman, which is all but incoherent. Erdman assumes without justification that *Milton*'s historical material was
originally contained in an "early draft" for the supposedly lost twelve-
book *Milton,* leaving only "remnants" in the finished poem. (The title
page contains the designation "in 12 Books," incompletely altered to "2"
in copies A and B.) Erdman proposes that the Bard's Song refers to the
English civil war as an "object lesson" for present events, and takes Satan
as both Cromwell and Napoleon—which would mean, however, that
Milton returns to earth to correct the errors of the English and French
revolutions but not to settle accounts with English tyranny. Suggesting
that Palamabron is Parliament in the civil war, Erdman sees Palamabron's

brother Rintrah as both Pitt, who opposed English radicalism, and the Commonwealth army, which was its spearhead. He sees Leutha as a "spiritual form of Marie Antoinette," urging Satan/Napoleon to continue the war with England, but finds no civil war equivalent for her at all. And he is unable to explain Blake's specific statement that "James calls for fires in Golgonooza" (5:40), seeing it as a reference to the London fire of 1666 but supposing that it illogically refers to James I rather than Charles II. Though Erdman makes some excellent suggestions, particularly the identifications of Palamabron as Parliament and perhaps of Rintrah as the Commonwealth army, this historical interpretation has not satisfied many readers.[5]

In line with some of Erdman's emphases, but contrary to his specific analysis, I argue that Satan in the Bard's Song primarily means the English state, including the monarchy and state church, and that Blake both examines this "Satan's" general character and traces its foundations in the struggles of the Commonwealth, Restoration, revolution, and settlement periods. The aim of his presentation is to understand the past errors that led to Satan's rule. This purpose is made urgent by the new period of struggles from the 1770s to the 1790s; their resumption, after a hiatus, in 1807–11,[6] the probable years when much of *Milton* was composed; and the new "interregnum" begun by King George's mental decline and the declaration of regency in 1810–11—hence the specific, concentrated historical references on plate 5, which dates from those years or later. The presentation focuses both on the political and social consolidation of the English ruling system and on the solidification of the Moral Law—thematic strands that sometimes lend overlapping meanings to the same narrative events. Within this overall pattern, the homosexual material in the Bard's Song refers specifically to the Williamite period, while also forming a critique of antihomosexualism and sexual guilt and their place in the creation of Moral Law.

The extraordinary scope that Blake gave to the idea of Satan is evident elsewhere, notably in a late passage of *The Four Zoas* focusing on a mythic version of the English-French interimperialist war. There Satan, as an entity prosecuting the war, appears as "multitudes of tyrant Men in union blasphemous / Against the divine image. Congregated Assemblies of wicked men" (Night 8, 104:29–30; E 378). Satan therefore is a collective entity, and since the "divine image" is for Blake the "Human Form Divine"—the human body, and particularly the male body—Satan represents collective entities that destroy and degrade the human body in war. Hence, among other meanings, Satan is the English Parliament, army, and state. In *Milton,* Satan's scope is as vast or vaster. The bard tells how Satan's Spectre "raging furious descended into its Space," among "the rocks of Albions Temples, [where] Satans Druid sons / Offer the Human Victims throughout all the Earth, and Albions / Dread Tomb immortal on his Rock, overshadowd the whole Earth" (9:52, 11:7–9). There, later in the narration, Leutha (parodying Milton's Sin) bears Death as well as Rahab (13:40–41). The analogues with the *Four Zoas* passage just cited should be clear: The "rocks of Albions Temples" are those of London, equivalent to the Druid triliths we see in the illustrations to other plates; Satan's Druid sons offering sacrifices throughout the earth, like the blasphemy of *The Four Zoas'* "Assemblies of wicked men," point to England's imperial wars from the 1660s through Blake's present day. In an overall way, then, the Bard's Song traces the origins of the present system of imperialism and religious-political tyranny, especially its solidification since Milton's time. Politically, to trace this process is equivalent to asking how and why a monarchic imperialist system arose in place of the first attempt at an English commonwealth, and one facet of Blake's explanation deserves particular mention. The bard blames "Satans extreme / Mildness," a quality emphasized over and over in the Song (7:12–13; see also 7:4, 7:21, 9:19), and equivalent to Urizen's "soft mild arts" in *The Four Zoas* (80:9; see also 80:37)—those qualities of deception and ingratiating appeal that have characterized the English state system and allowed it to exist with popular support, at least since the 1660s. Blake, then, investigates the foundations of the English ruling system of his day, including its popular foundations, and follows these back to the civil war and Restoration periods. The English state's deceptive "mildness," corresponding in scope and importance to *Milton's* concern with Britain's ruin and possible redemption, is a more resonant meaning for this quality than Hayley's unsatisfactory patronage.

Within this schema, several more specific episodes can be identified; it will be convenient to look at the general historical material before the song's homosexual aspects. The identifications will necessarily be tentative, both because of the reconditeness of Blake's references and because of one of their fundamental qualities: Blake does not write historical allegory but a mythic history. Events are not shown through a consistent "keyed" symbolism but are reference points within a free narrative that supplies an underlying truth or essence of the history referred to. Its events take place in a mythic sphere coinciding in part with earthly locales and history. The "Great Solemn Assembly" of plates 8–9, for example, is conducted by "all Eden," but is held in "Palamabrons tent / Among Albions Druids & Bards, in the caves beneath Albions / Death Couch, in the caverns of death, in the corner of the Atlantic" (9:1–3)—several different ways of naming the houses of Parliament, in London, in the British Isles. Freedom from strict allegory means that Blake's narrative may include details that carry no specific referents but do convey important meanings. Examples might include Michael's weariness in the struggle prior to the assembly (8:37), a detail that fits with the confusion and loss of élan in the later Commonwealth period, and Satan's rage at Palamabron in the assembly (plate 9), which can refer to events of several historical episodes.

Complicating this interpretive puzzle even more, Satan will be found to refer to several British monarchs rather than one; Satan is indeed a "state" rather than an individual (*M* 32:10–29), though not in the abstract way that much commentary has assumed.[7] This "state" controls "those combind by Satans Tyranny first in the blood of War / And Sacrifice &, next, in Chains of imprisonment" (32:16–17). Specific monarchs represent this "state" in distinct historical episodes that Blake alludes to—not in chronological order—in different parts of the song: James II and perhaps Charles I in the episode of Satan and the "artillery" and "arrows" (plate 5); Charles I and II in the narrative of the harrow and the Great Solemn Assembly (plates 7–9, 11); William and Anne in the episodes of Satan, Leutha, and Elynittria (plates 11–13).

James, the bard tells his audience, "calls for fires in Golgonooza," or London (5:40). While Damon notes Blake's allusion to the tradition that Catholics set the fire of 1666 (*Dictionary* 204), the reference is more specific: In January 1681, Parliament resolved, "[I]t is the opinion of this house, that the city was burned in the year 1666 by the papists" (Hume 12: 138).[8] Coming as part of the three-year "exclusion crisis" (1678–81) aimed at barring the Catholic James's future succession to the throne, the resolution effectively did blame the fire on James. Blake's use of the accusation aligns him with the parliamentary opposition of those years and indicates that the James episode alludes to the long succession battle stretching from 1678 through James's accession and his deposition in 1688. This was a time mythologized in the republican tradition; Sir Algernon Sidney and Lord William Russell, executed for alleged involvement in the Rye House Plot of 1683 against Charles II and James, were names resonant in republican culture a century later. But these years saw both success and failure: James's opponents won the revolution of 1688, averting what Whigs of the time saw as a threat of absolutism and papal tyranny, yet their victory only ushered in new struggles with King William. But for the moment the perceived threat was nipped. In the crucial military episode, in November 1688, after William had landed at Exeter, James's general and adviser Lord John Churchill (later Earl and Duke of Marlborough) urged the king, camped at Salisbury, to take the offensive; James dithered, refused, and retreated to London, never to regain the military initiative: "Satan fainted beneath the artillery" (*M* 5:2). Churchill went over to William even before James's retreat. Meanwhile James's daughter, Princess Anne (later queen), and her husband, Prince George of Denmark, abandoned James's banner for William's, and it was soon intimated that Churchill's wife Sarah, Anne's closest companion (and rumored lover), had engineered this desertion. Anne's abandonment was a second, crucial political and personal blow that helped precipitate James's flight to France in December: "Satan fainted beneath the arrows of Elynittria" (5:43).[9]

Identifying James as Satan fits Blake's reference to the fires on this same plate and the historical details just mentioned. If, with Erdman, we take Palamabron as Parliament, then his consort Elynittria may seem wrong for the fused roles of Sarah Churchill and Anne; but both can be seen as acting in the parliamentary cause in this instance, and hence as Palamabron's female equivalent. Other references on this plate are more cryptic, particularly "Charles calls on Milton for Atonement. Cromwell is ready" (5:39). The call for atonement jibes with the emphasis in plate 5 on Moral Law and with the English kings' roles as heads of the church and members of the Elect, for whom atonement is a central doctrine. Possibly the reference is to Charles II, seeking Milton's political submission, but the sequence Charles, Cromwell, James (lines 39–40) suggests Charles I. Perhaps, then, the lines refer to Milton's political writings: Charles's supposed memoir, *Eikon Basilike,* in effect asked atonement for the regicide, while Milton's justifications in *Eikonoklastes* and the first and second *Defence of the English People* helped solidify Cromwell's position. If so, the five lines 5:39–43, from Charles to the arrows of Elynittria, have an epic sweep, covering the period from 1650 to 1688. But in any case Satan's fainting and James's retreat and flight match well.

The second major episode of the Bard's Song recounts Satan's plea to wield Palamabron's harrow, Los's initial decision favoring him, the Great Solemn Assembly called by Palamabron, and its consequences (7–11)— key events through which Satan receives control over a "Space" equivalent to the sublunary world. The episode is lengthy and complex, and my present purposes do not require a full account of its details. On the other hand, understanding its historical meaning requires reference to the characters' overall symbolic identities, as well as their possible historical roles. Rintrah as plowman, Palamabron as master of the harrow, and Satan as miller (3:41–4:2, copies CD), as often discussed, play symbolic roles of turning the soil, breaking it up and burying the seed, and grinding the grain.[10] While all are necessary, these functions are differentiated: Plowing and harrowing are productive processes of human labor, as are

Los's smithing and Enitharmon's weaving; though milling is necessary to production, the miller has traditionally been seen as an exploiter. Blake discusses these roles in *A Descriptive Catalogue of Pictures* (1809), written while *Milton* was still in gestation and its symbolism salient in his mind:

> The Plowman is simplicity itself, with wisdom and strength for its sta-
> mina. . . . The Plowman of Chaucer is Hercules in his supreme eternal state,
> divested of his spectrous shadow; which is the Miller, a terrible fellow, such as
> exists in all times and places, for the trial of men, to astonish every neigh-
> bourhood, with brutal strength and courage, to get rich and powerful to curb
> the pride of Man. (21–22; *E* 536)

These meanings make the miller a social-political figure for exploiting classes and political tyrants, so that miller-Satan's identity with the generated Urizen (10:1–2, copies CD) makes fundamental sense. In turn, Los as smith must also be a figure for human labor as well as for imagination (the identification traditional in Blake interpretation). If we now return to the central segment of the Bard's Song, we see that the miller's initial usurpation of the harrow with Los's backing has two overlapping meanings. In the whole sweep of human history it signifies the rise of exploiting and ruling classes over productive labor; in English history it appears as the rise of tyranny and exploitation—events the Commonwealth tradition associated with Stuart absolutism and the struggles against it—abetted by failures of historical imagination and of resistance by the common people, Los's roles. Most specifically, the usurpation would refer to the period when Charles I prorogued Parliament and ruled alone, from 1628 to the pre-revolutionary crisis of 1641. However, this segment of the Bard's Song also establishes the broader basis for Satan's rule, its "mildness," which was most characteristic of the later monarchy, so that the sequence has a dual focus.

As the episode continues, Los's repentance ushers in a heroic but also chaotic and confused struggle, in which the "Genii of the Mills," at Los's call, "Wildly . . . follow'd Los and Rintrah" against Satan (8:11–45). Though the details are exceptionally unclear (I believe intentionally), in historical terms these events may mythologize the political and military battles against Charles and the future Charles II during the civil war and Commonwealth. Finally, the debate at Palamabron's Great Solemn Assembly (8:46–11:27) would refer to the Convention Parliament of 1660, which offered Charles II the throne, and to Restoration politics generally. While again much of this episode is murky,[11] it is clear that Satan defends himself by denouncing Palamabron, and the assembly's judgment seems to leave Satan's position unchallenged:

He created Seven deadly Sins drawing out his infernal scroll,
Of Moral laws and cruel punishments upon the clouds of Jehovah
To pervert the Divine voice in its entrance to the earth
With thunder of war & trumpets sound . . . (9:21–24)

Finally, as Satan grows "Opake against the Divine Vision" a "World of deeper Ulro was open'd, in the midst / Of the Assembly" (9:31, 34–35). In a simultaneous fall and triumph, Satan comes to "repos[e] . . . / . . . on the seven mou[n]tains of Rome / . . . Rome Babylon & Tyre" (9:49–51). While these locales indicate the sway of tyranny and empire throughout time, a later passage places Satan's "Mills" amid "the rocks of Albions Temples" (11:6–7), showing that his reign also occurs within English history. The upshot of this sufficiently confusing narrative is that Satan's attempts to destroy Palamabron are checked (9:43–45) but his power remains intact, processes analogous to the struggles between king and Parliament in the post-Restoration period and beyond, up to the revolution and settlement of 1688–89.

Plates 7–11, then, present in an extended way the same time-span shown in a compressed way at the end of plate 5; but they focus on the events of the 1630s through the 1660s rather than on 1688. The remaining period in an account of the foundations of the English state system of Blake's time would be the reigns of William and Mary (1689–1702), leading to the Act of Settlement (1701) and Anne's accession (1702). These latter events gave permanence to the Protestant succession, cemented Parliament's role in delimiting royal powers, and were crucial in what J. H. Plumb calls the "growth of political stability" in England from 1675 to 1725. I take Blake's political stance to be contrary to the general Whig view that they continued and added to the achievements of 1688–89. The Bard's Song suggests that despite the importance of William's defeating "Satan" in 1688, William's defense of royal power was a resurgence of "Satan" in a more subtle form, while the settlement itself consolidated a fused form of "Satanic" monarchic rule with parliamentary backing, buttressed by such institutions as the English church, in particular its broad-church or latitudinarian wing,[12] and ruling-class universities. The final portion of the Bard's Song, covering Leutha's relations with Satan and Elynittria, has affinities with this history and also brings Blake's critique of antisexuality to the fore.

Blake's account falls into two parts. In the first, Leutha takes on herself Satan's "Sin" (11:30) while retelling part of the harrow story. We know Leutha as a female sexual spirit who has appeared variously as the partner of Oothoon's awakening and as Antamon's consort (*VDA* iii, 1; *Eu* 14; *SL* 3). Here she is identified only as a "Daughter of Beulah" but calls Satan her "Parent power" and functions as a parody of Milton's Sin (11:28, 36; *PL* 2:760). According to her account, "I loved Palamabron & I sought to approach his Tent, / But beautiful Elynittria with her silver arrows repelld me" (11:37–38), whereupon:

> . . . entering the doors of Satans brain night after night
> Like sweet perfumes I stupified the masculine perceptions
> And kept only the feminine awake. hence rose his soft
> Delusory love to Palamabron: admiration join'd with envy
> Cupidity unconquerable! my fault . . . (12:4–8)

A distinct version of the harrow story follows, during which Leutha springs "out of the breast of Satan," maddening the horses who pull the harrow, hides again in his brain, reemerges only to cause mutiny among the "Gnomes of the Harrow," and hides once more (12:10, 36, 38, 40–41). At length Elynittria connives with Satan to isolate Leutha, and

> . . . in selfish holiness demanding purity
> Being most impure, self-condemn'd to eternal tears, he [Satan] drove
> Me from his inmost Brain & the doors clos'd with thunders sound
> (12:46–48)

After Leutha's account of these events, the bard tells the sequel. Among other events, Elynittria lays down her weapons, soothes Leutha,

> & brought her to Palamabrons bed
> In moments new created for delusion, interwoven round about,
> In dreams she bore the shadowy Spectre of Sleep, & namd him
> Death.
> In dreams she bore Rahab the mother of Tirzah & her sisters
> In Lambeths vales; in Cambridge & in Oxford, places of Thought
> Intricate labyrinths of Times and Spaces unknown, that Leutha lived
> In Palamabrons Tent, and Oothoon was her charming guard.
> (13:38–44)[13]

This sequel, which I consider first (out of historical order), brings the overall political-social history to a close. (It also has a mythocosmic thread that I shall ignore, a version of the narrative of the "seven eyes of God" that appears elsewhere in Blake.) Most interpreters have seen Elynittria's leading Leutha "to Palamabrons bed" as a sign of reconciliation in line with Blake's later politics of forgiveness; they have missed his firm insistence that Elynittria's action and its consequences take place in "moments new created for delusion" (line 39). Forgiveness here is *not* positive; on the contrary, Leutha's coupling creates Death and then "Rahab the mother of Tirzah & her sisters" (lines 40–41), malevolent entities in the present-day world to which Milton will descend.

If Elynittria's assistance to Leutha is indeed a reconciliation between the female counterpart of Palamabron (whom I have been viewing, with Erdman, as Parliament) and Satan's female portion, then in a general way these events correspond in English history to the Act of Settlement and Anne's reign. The settlement chipped away at the royal prerogative, determined the Protestant line of succession to follow Anne's reign, and furthered the political detente with Parliament that had eluded William. The settlement and Anne's accession, with other actions of the 1701–1702 Parliament, also paved the way for the War of the Spanish Succession (1701–13), England's first modern imperialist war. During much of the war English politics were dominated by an alliance between Anne and pro-war Whigs led by John Churchill, now Duke of Marlborough, whose wife was then Anne's closest companion and adviser: Elynittria led Leutha to Palamabron's tent.[14] The births of Rahab and Tirzah and Leutha's lying-in "in Cambridge & in Oxford, places of Thought / Intricate labyrinths of Times and Spaces unknown" (lines 42–43), covered in a rush as the Bard's Song moves to its conclusion, carry meanings that can be supplied from other uses in the poem and from eighteenth-century social contexts. Rahab later appears as "Religion hidden in War," and she and Tirzah send their sons and daughters to tempt Milton to assume supreme power on earth (40:20, 19:28–20:6). Cambridge and Oxford have their contemporary identities. Roughly, then, these lines speak of a system of war and tyranny interwoven with state religion and buttressed by ruling-class education. Notably, if Leutha is the mother of these evils, Palamabron or Parliament is their father. With the creation of sin, death, and delusive religion and philosophy through the sexual union of Leutha and Palamabron, or crown and Parliament, the bard completes his tale of the formation of the post-Miltonic world.

Alongside its general social meaning, Leutha's story contains evident references to concealed and overt homosexuality: The female Leutha hides within Satan's brain and stimulates his "feminine" perceptions to love Palamabron, and she also emerges overtly twice, with ruinous results. These sections have usually been viewed either in psychobiographic terms (in speculative reference to Blake and Hayley) or in a psychodynamic framework; their possible historical reference has been overlooked.[15] In part these portions of the story are specifically topical. Within the historical focus already discussed, they seize on a notorious aspect of William III's reign, his relations with several male favorites.

These include his adviser and diplomatic legate Hans Willem Bentinck, later Duke of Portland, with whom he had a decades-long constant friendship and political association, and the much younger Arnold Joost van Keppel, a nobly born page, secretary, representative, and close companion on whom William lavished gifts and properties, and whom he created Earl of Albemarle. William's relations with Keppel, particularly, became a minor scandal in 1697, when they led Portland to break temporarily with William, and again in 1699. In Jacobite circles William's court was said to have become the "chateau de derrière," and William "to have been in love with Albemarle as with a woman, and they say he used to kiss his hands before all the court" (Duchess of Orléans, quoted in van der Zee 423).[16] True or not, the rumors were food for widespread satire. "Why were your armies not turned towards Italy?" William is asked in "Jenny Cromwell's Complaint Against Sodomy."

> . . . here content with our own homely joys,
> We had no relish of the fair fac'd Boys.
> Till you came in and with your Reformation,
> Turn'd all things Arsy Versy in the nation. (16, 25–28; qtd. in Rubini 381)

Anti-Williamites professed shock "That your love is Italian, your Government Dutch / Ah! who could have thought that a Low-Country stallion / And a Protestant Prince should prove an Italian." Satirists lamented that "William van Nassau, with Benting Bardasha, / Are at the old game of Gomorrha," or abandoned the oaten reed for something a little higher:

> Proceed, my Muse; the Story next relate
> Of *Keppech* the Imperious Chit of State,
> Mounted to Grandeur by the usual Course
> Of Whoring, Pimping, or a Crime that's worse[.][17]

It cannot be proved that Blake knew of this tradition of satirical abuse. Among histories he might have read, Bishop Gilbert Burnet's pro-William *History of His Own Time,* which went through at least three editions in the eighteenth century, claims that the king "had no vice, but of one sort, in which he was very cautious and secret." Burnet may not in fact have homosexuality in mind, but later he calls Keppel's rise "quick and unaccountable" and in summarizing the king's character reiterates, "It is not easy to account for the reasons of the favour that he shewed" to Keppel and Bentinck (1: 690; 2: 224, 306). Smollett's continuation of Hume refers to the "king's affection for the earl of Portland . . . whose place in the king's bosom was now filled by Van Keppel, a gentleman of Guelderland, who had first served his majesty as a page, and afterward acted as private secretary" (1: 323). Though decorous enough, this emphasis on Keppel's history serves to suggest the rumors Smollett does not discuss directly. Other histories refer more obliquely to Keppel's rise "from a Groom of the Bed-chamber, to become a mighty Favourite," or omit such references and merely cite popular resentment of "the king's partiality to his own countrymen" (Harris 463; Goldsmith 4: 76). But the scandals were widely bruited; Swift remembered them a quarter-century later, riposting in his copy of Burnet that William's vice "was of two sorts—*male* and *female*—in the *former* he was neither cautious nor secret" (Swift 285).[18] An acquaintance of Burnet, the Earl of Dartmouth, commenting on the same passage, recalled Burnet's telling him, "some things, he said, were too notorious for a faithful historian to pass over in silence" (Burnet, 1823 ed., 3: 125 n). Though evidence is inconclusive, I hypothesize that some awareness of the rumors came down to Blake's time. If so, under the head of William's alleged homosexuality, we may find a lampoon of his relations with Parliament and perhaps of the often resented activities of the Dutch favorites in his inner circle.

Three aspects of this topic intertwine in Leutha's narrative. The first is William's efforts variously to dominate or bypass Parliament: Satan, as we know, attempts to drive the harrow in Palamabron's place, with disastrous results.[19] However, this aspect of William's reign is contained in the basic harrow plot, without Leutha's homosexual twist. Secondly, Leutha's story may allude to the public muttering over William's reputed homosexuality itself, as well as over Bentinck's and Keppel's prominence and his partiality to them, which led to repeated unsuccessful efforts to restrict membership in the Privy Council to Englishmen and to thwart William's award of huge Irish estates to these favorites. In Leutha's story, whenever she emerges from Satan's interior and directly displays herself—William's homosexuality or the activity of the favorites—the horses "terribly rag'd" and "the Gnomes recoil'd" (12:15, 38). Importantly, the satire here is arguably directed as much at the presumably parliamentary and popular horses' and gnomes' fury and panic over Satan's female portion as at the unveiling of this female portion itself. (The horses' and gnomes' actions are repeated from 7:17–19, where they seem simply a rejection of Satan's presumption—in historical terms, a parliamentary reaction against royal usurpation. Here, this same response appears partly based on sexual hostility.) Finally, in a third, related aspect of Leutha's narrative, her Miltonic affinities mean that her appearances reveal "Sin" as the hidden basis of Satan/William's rule, behind the mask of "mildness" already familiar to us.

Beyond their historical reference to William's reign, these events have a more general meaning that reaches back to Satan's consolidation of power at the conclusion of the Great Solemn Assembly. This larger moral-sexual meaning provides a kind of "parallel plot" to the political-social narrative; it is to some extent independent of the latter and contains some material not accounted for in it, though ultimately the meanings of these two narrative threads mesh. In their moral-sexual meaning, these events are a critique not of homosexuality but of sexual—including homosexual—denial and repression as the bases of state-religious oppression. This critique turns the surface content of Leutha's story, with its ostentatious apology for sin, upside down. The moral basis of the English state system turns out to be the sense of sin itself, together with the closely related idea of atonement, while its sexual basis is sexual guilt, including the repression of homosexuality and the construction of an exclusively heterosexual masculinity. Again, three strands in the story carry these ideas forward.

The first is the emphasis on Moral Law and its ruinous consequences. Already in the Satan-Palamabron narrative, Satan created "Seven deadly Sins" composed of "Moral laws and cruel punishments"; at its end, established in "Albions / Dread Tomb," he made "to himself Laws from his own identity," compelling others "to serve him in moral gratitude & submission" (9:21–22; 11:8–11). The Satan-Palamabron sequence centers on Satan's consolidation of material or social power; these references show how manipulation of moral accusation and guilt abet this process. Plate 10, one of the added plates interpolated amid this material, further identifies Satan's "Space" with our world or "Canaan," links its solidification with the onset of shrunken perception, and specifies that Elynittria and Ocalythron (Palamabron and Rintrah's consorts), motivated by "Jealousy," have helped consolidate it and Satan's rule (10:8–10, 14–21). Blake, then, charges that female jealousy abets the savagery of Moral Law and helps create the restricted existence this law cements. (In the next chapter I consider why he may have included these points.) In a parallel way, in her later narrative, Leutha recounts how, after she has been driven from Satan's brain, his Spectre lies on her "Sick Couch" and "calls the Individual Law, Holy . . . / Glorying to involve Albions Body in fires of eternal War" (13:1–6).[20] Satan is situated and acts similarly in both accounts, though the first emphasizes abstract morality and the second individualism and war. The allegory of Leutha's expulsion makes clear that these evils spring from the idea of sin itself—the illusion of driving out sin to live in perfect virtue. Further, Leutha's offering herself as "a Ransom for Satan, taking on her, his Sin" (11:30) evokes the idea of discharging sin by proxy that Blake associates with the doctrine of atonement, in contrast to the voluntary solidarity he identifies with Jesus.[21] The negative consequences of the doctrine are clear in Leutha's false reconciliation with Elynittria that leads to the ensuing century of war and tyranny.

Alongside its general moral meaning, Leutha's story is one of sexual, specifically homosexual, guilt: Leutha takes the blame both for exciting Satan's "feminine" perceptions and for the baneful results. The question is whether we are meant to endorse or criticize her guilt. Leutha calls herself "wretched Leutha," the "Author of this Sin"; bursts out, "All is my fault"; and exclaims that all is "lost! lost! lost! for ever" (12:3; 11:35; 13:8, 11). While these emotions seem straightforward, a detail of Leutha's description, her "moth-like elegance" (11:33), encourages us to view them critically; the moth, in Blake, usually suggests showy, superficial beauty. The passage parallels other Blake portrayals of female acceptance of sexual guilt, including Ona's in "A Little Girl Lost" (25–29), Oothoon's in *Visions* (2:15–16), and Vala's in *Jerusalem* (22:1–15; see chapter 6). Though the interpretation of such episodes has been disputed among recent readers, there is at least some basis for seeing them as pinpointing the wrongness of sexual guilt; in some instances, such as in "A Little Girl Lost," Blake seems clearly to counterpose a general approval of sexual desire to such self-blame. Such parallels make it as likely that we are meant to question Leutha's self-assessment as that we should take it at face value. A more specific parallel suggests this conclusion as well: Leutha's "I loved Palamabron" echoes Oothoon's "I loved Theotormon" (*VDA* iii:1), but, in comparison with Oothoon's lack of shame (iii:2), Blake now emphasizes shame and guilt concerning homosexual impulses. Though this shift in emphasis might imply a condemnation of homosexuality, the contrast with Oothoon may instead imply the wrongness of self-accusation. This idea is consistent with what occurs when Leutha appears openly, stepping out of Satan's bosom or brain; the most important point here is not that these appearances provoke the horses' and gnomes' panic and opposition but that through this reaction, homosexual desire is driven into hiding and ultimately cast out by the masculine entity that has harbored it, with evil consequences. Blake, in other words, is exploring the impulses of moral condemnation, reactive self-concealment, and, ultimately, internalized shame and repressive denial. Remarkably, Blake extends the rejection of guilt over sin and sexual desire that occurs elsewhere in his work to a new area, male homosexuality, as marked by Leutha's appearance as a female principle within Satan.

Finally, the third strand in Leutha's story, its renarration of Satan's consolidation, accords with the others and shows that Blake cannot be condemning homosexuality as such. Given the homosexual significance of Leutha's presence in Satan, his expelling her "from his inmost Brain" (12:48) is an expulsion of his homosexual portion and an effort to reconstitute himself as exclusively masculine. Yet this is the action by which Satan's Spectre comes to lie on Leutha's "Sick Couch" where "he furious refuses to repose in sleep" (13:1–2) and it is parallel to the earlier embrace of moral condemnation, or "Seven deadly Sins," that left him "Dead . . . repos'd on his Couch" while he nonetheless "vibrated in the immensity of the Space!" and "triumphant divided the Nations" (9:21, 49; 10:8, 21). Imposing "Seven deadly Sins" on humanity and driving homosexuality from Satan's brain are linked or parallel actions. As often, Blake's treatment goes so close to orthodoxy that it misleads commentators into mistaking it for orthodoxy. What initially appears as a story of the negative consequences of homosexuality is seen to be a story first of hysteria over homosexuality—on Leutha's own part and on the part of the horses and gnomes—and second of the repression of homosexuality and the creation of a rigid, exclusively heterosexual masculinity. (We recall that in *The Four Zoas,* Night 5, Luvah's affinities with Ganymede, in Urizen's pained recollection, suggested the same idea.) Not the homosexual Satan in whom Leutha moved and acted but the antihomosexual Satan who has expelled her and "the doors clos'd with thunders sound" is "the Sick-one" who glories "to involve Albions body in fires of eternal War" (12:48, 13:4–6).[22]

Homosexuality in the Bard's Song, then, is part of a parodic historical myth, a large-scale retelling of civil war, Restoration, and settlement history that refers to the founding of Satan's present rule—the rule of the English state and church. Some of the identifications in my account are certainly tentative. Some may appear arbitrary. For example, only in a general symbolic sense can Elynittria lead Leutha to Palamabron, since the Act of Settlement dealt with the succession after Anne, who was already first in line after William. But in an overall way, Parliament and crown agreeing on the line of succession does match up with Leutha's dalliance with Palamabron and the resulting horrific births. Other ways of reading the characters' affiliations may appear contradictory. Can Leutha appear *both* as Anne in her relations with Parliament (13:36–44) and as a homosexual principle in an examination of masculinity's foundations (11:35–13:6)? The answer would appear to be that in general, Blake's symbolic vocabulary often piles meaning on meaning in just this way. More specifically, Blake's conception of what thwarts Satan's rule is itself multiform and, in this instance, refers to distinct situations occurring over a historical period stretching from Milton's time to his own. We will find in the next chapter that Elynittria represents not only a female principle associated with parliamentary resistance to the crown but also female jealousy in overall, negative senses, and, for good measure, the positive female sexuality of a male entity. Her arrows (5:43, 11:38) are multiform as well: they are those that caused Satan/James to "faint" in 1688 (and, laid aside, allowed Leutha into Palamabron's tent in 1701); those that enforce Moral Law; but also those that, in a parallel to James's rout, check the Satan of Moral Law in 1810–11. Blake's use of mythic rather than allegoric characters allows this flexibility—once Elynittria has taken form as a type of female sexuality, she can express all of the contradictory aspects of female sexuality in a divided society.

While only a portion of the Bard's Song, the homosexual sequence carries major importance. Historically, it focuses satirically on a much-vilified aspect of William's reign, recalling polemical attacks on William but also suggesting their antisexual basis, so far as it is cast in Leutha's guilt-ridden voice. As sexual allegory, while Blake's initial presentation allows an antihomosexual meaning, its ultimate focus is on the ruinous effects of sexual guilt and repression, and of forced heterosexual masculinity. In both aspects, Blake presents homosexuality and the response to it as parts of the complex solidification of England's moral-political imperium after the country's last revolutionary upheaval.

Homosexual Innuendo in Blake's Milton Illustrations

Blake also explores homosexuality in a less specifically historical way in some of his illustrations to Milton's works. Unlike some of the *Four Zoas* drawings, none of these directly depicts a homosexual act, yet they allude to homosexuality through visual suggestion or innuendo. Interpreters have noted some of these suggestions but assume that Blake must have meant them negatively. In this assumption, the interpreters sometimes work at odds with their overall hypotheses about Blake's relation to Milton. Arguing in general that Blake wished to correct Milton's distrust of unfettered sexuality, respect for classicism, and ascetic conception of Jesus, they read in some of these designs *(Comus, Il Penseroso)* a negative view of homosexuality not unlike Milton's and miss implications of homosexuality in others *(Paradise Regained).*[23]

Blake's Milton designs have their own history, one of increasingly subtle and daring exploration of sexuality. In a slightly earlier set of literary illustrations that can serve as a benchmark, those for Gray's "Ode on a Distant Prospect of Eton College" (ca. 1797–98), Blake includes several images gently evoking schoolboy homoeroticism—boys gazing fondly on one another, or arm in arm. Such images seem to provide an understanding though critical account of the limited world of "innocence."[24] These depictions are consistent with Blake's handling of similar topics in *Visions* (see chapter 2). Blake already moves beyond this stance in the first of his Milton sets, for *Comus*, suggesting that adolescent homoeroticism can continue validly in the world of adult contention; and by the last Milton designs, fifteen years later, he has transcended it altogether.

Blake executed two sets of illustrations (1801, ca. 1815) for *Comus*, that "allegory of the human passage from adolescence into maturity" (Tayler, "Blake" 239) that problematically exalts the virtue of virginity. Most interpreters concur that Blake criticizes Milton's support for virginity through visual devices suggesting that the lady whom Comus holds captive is in reality immobilized by her own "idea of sexual love as bestial and corrupting" (Tayler, "Blake" 248).[25] Scholars disagree whether Blake works by showing the lady incapable of action or response (Behrendt 44–46) or, on the contrary, by depicting her gradual sexual awakening (Tayler, "Blake" 248–49; Davies, *Designs* 26), and whether the 1815 illustrations reinforce or alter the emphases of the first. All agree, however, that a crucial role is played by the lady's two brothers, who in the sixth design "rush in with Swords drawn" to rout the enchanter (*Comus* 813 s.d.) and, further, that the brothers reach this point by overcoming weakness and passivity, shown in the third design. The key issues regarding homosexuality arise from the latter, "The Brothers Seen by Comus Plucking Grapes," and its relation to the later action.

Blake's illustration apparently picks up on Comus's words about the pair, "Their port was more than human . . . / . . . / . . . I was awe-strook, / And as I past, I worshipt" (297, 301–302), and builds on this tiny hint of homosexuality, basically an undeveloped inflection in Milton's portrait of Comus's lewdness. Blake shows the brothers with their attention bent on each other (figs. 4.1, 4.2). In the earlier illustration (Huntington Library) they gaze at each other fondly as they gather the grapes individually; in the later design (Boston Museum of Fine Arts) they appear older and their glances are more contemplative as the higher of the two hands the grapes down to his sibling. Their swords in the Huntington design, side by side with their straps entwined, and the handing-down of the grapes in the Boston image—reminiscent of similar emblems of initiation to sexuality and "experience" in other works—suggest a sexual meaning to their gazes. Comus, appearing as a grave old man, regards them darkly (first version) or somewhat more benignly (later version). In the earlier design he could be looking either at the swords on the ground or at the brothers' forms, while in the later he is clearly gazing on the brothers, perhaps at the lower brother's face or conceivably the higher one's groin. In sum, the designs suggest both that

Figure 4.1 William Blake. Illustrations for Milton's *Comus*. No. 3, "The Brothers Seen by Comus Plucking Grapes." Courtesy of the Huntington Library, Art Collections, and Botanical Gardens, San Marino, California.

the brothers are sexually drawn to each other and that Comus is attracted to and/or voyeuristically fascinated by them.[26]

Whether or not they think the brothers are into anything homosexual, most interpreters think they are up to something very bad. Pamela Dunbar, apparently the first to associate homosexuality with this design, describes the brothers as "gazing adoringly into each other's eyes," adding the grapes as corroboration of sexual meaning but noting that in "The Echoing Green" they "suggest healthy, nascent sexuality but, significantly,

98

Figure 4.2 William Blake. Illustrations for Milton's *Comus*. No. 3, "The Brothers Seen by Comus Plucking Grapes." Courtesy, Museum of Fine Arts, Boston. Reproduced with permission. ©2000 Museum of Fine Arts, Boston. All Rights Reserved, no. 90.121.

it is there a girl who is the recipient of the youth's gift of the fruits" (19). Dunbar believes that for Blake, the brothers are "deeply in error" because of their espousal of virginity (in Milton's text) and their "desertion" of the lady, and she apparently feels that Blake uses the brothers' mutual attraction to express these errors; Dunbar is not sure whether the brothers represent "a pair of lovers [or] a narcissistically self-regarding single being," but believes they manifest "sterile self-regard," "lack of sexual energy," and "general submissiveness" (19–20). J. M. Q. Davies, finding the "homosexual overtones" of the brothers' glances "equally apparent in the admiring Comus," likewise believes the brothers "sexually and spiritually disarmed" and sees their attraction as "a logical consequence of the Lady's acceptance of Milton's Puritan insistence upon premarital chastity" (*Designs* 36–37). On the other hand, while not suggesting homosexual attraction, Bette Charlene Werner sees the brothers "involved in a mirrored, twining ballet of self-preoccupation" in the Huntington design, an effect she feels is softened by the grapes' "suggestion of initiation" in the Boston image (28, 39). Irene Tayler, also not suggesting a homosexual meaning, feels the brothers in the Huntington design show "fluttery femininity" and are "feminized, dreamy, indolently self-admiring . . . very dainty creatures indeed . . . sexually unthreatening men . . . [showing] wistful impotence" ("Blake" 236, 242, 245). Davies even adds, "These are 'The self-enjoyings of self-denial'" (*Designs* 36; *VDA* 7:9)—the boys are masturbators.

Some of these points are astute: The brothers in the Huntington design do show "feminine" characteristics, and the entwined sword straps may indicate genital involvement and lack of readiness for combat, though the long, straight swords cannot show lack of sexual energy. If Blake wished to suggest homosexual attraction, he may have conceived the poses as showing a "feminized" version of male sexuality. But the negative characterizations, we should realize, all rest on mere assumption: Whether "dainty" or homosexual, the brothers are *assumed* to be sexually disarmed and incapable of action or initiation into "experience." When, we might ask, does handing down grapes cease to "suggest healthy, nascent sexuality" and instead show "sterile self-regard"? Seemingly when the recipient is of the same sex and the gesture does not signify "ideal, procreative sexuality" (Dunbar 19–20).

Because so much depends on assumed meaning given to details, suggestions about Blake's meaning based on this design alone are likely to be arbitrary. We will be on firmer ground if we connect its hints at homosexuality to the continuation of the brothers' iconography in the other designs in which they appear. Those who call *Comus* 3 a negative image all feel that the brothers overcome their "self-preoccupation" and/or homoeroticism in the fourth design, in which the attendant spirit offers them the flower haemony, an emblem of sexual emergence: They "have resumed their phallic swords . . . where in the third design they were emasculated they are now armed for love and 'Mental Fight'" (Davies, *Designs* 38). The assumption, certainly, is that they are armed for heterosexual love. However, nothing about haemony in this design suggests that it can be an initiator of heterosexual experience only. On the contrary, Blake has earlier associated flowers with the advent of female sexuality, for example in *Visions* (see chapter 2). Hence the flower—with the grapes in the third design's later version—may indicate initiation into a "feminized" male sexuality instead of, or in addition to, a heterosexual maturation. Nor does the way the brothers are shown in the later designs indicate emergence from their mutual absorption into a presumed heterosexual maturity. On the contrary, in the fourth, sixth, seventh, and eighth designs they maintain the twinning relation implied by the parallel swords in the first version of *Comus* 3. They hold the swords aligned (4), rush in unison at Comus (6), bow together (7), and stand as a pair in both versions of the final design (8), ignoring the lady's reunion with their parents to focus on the departing attendant spirit but aware of each other. In the later version of this design the brother with his back to us holds his hand next to his brother's thigh. At the same time, both plot and design suggest that they *have* emerged from a protective "innocence." Indeed, in the final design, the fact that the brothers do not join the reunified family at right but observe the attending spirit, himself an emblem of public mission, suggests that they may continue as conjoined warriors in the larger world. Unlike the lads in "Eton College," the brothers remain bonded while passing from the "innocent" play of the third design into "experience."

Of the remaining designs, the sixth, "The Brothers Driving Out Comus" (figs. 4.3, 4.4) is the most significant in its own iconography and its relation to the third design. For the brothers' twinned postures and parallel swords here the significant antecedents would seem to be the Theban Band, Nisus and Euryalus, Harmodius and Aristogiton, and other lover-warriors of antiquity. Within this tradition, the brothers' coordinated actions would not be opposite to their apparent flirtatiousness in the third design but its continuation. In addition, the 1815 (Boston) version of the sixth design differs significantly from its earlier version and has further parallels with the third design in the 1815 set. Together, these interrelationships seem to pinpoint the dynamics both of unacted and of unrealized but expressed desire.

In the early (Huntington) version of the sixth design, Comus runs from the brothers with a look of alarm, and his cup seems to be wrested from him; in the later (Boston), he is almost dancing, appears in no dan-

Figure 4.3   William Blake. Illustrations for Milton's *Comus*. No. 6, "The Brothers Driving Out Comus." Courtesy of the Huntington Library, Art Collections, and Botanical Gardens, San Marino, California.

ger, and has perhaps handed off the cup to the brother who grasps it. While several commentators have made these points, none has noted Comus's mild expression as he gazes back at the brothers in the Boston design. Though Comus's face is now that of a young man, the tilt of his head and the direction of his glance are comparable to those in the Boston version of the third design, and his expression recognizably similar.

Figure 4.4   William Blake. Illustrations for Milton's *Comus*. No. 6, "The Brothers Driving Out Comus." Courtesy, Museum of Fine Arts, Boston. Reproduced with permission. ©2000 Museum of Fine Arts, Boston. All Rights Reserved, no. 90.124.

Comus in the later version of the sixth design is activated, even in defeat, by emotions similar to those that played on his features in the third. Moreover, both versions of the third design, in distinct ways, resemble Blake's *Paradise Lost* designs "Satan Watching the Endearments of Adam and Eve" (1806–1808).[27] Like Satan in *Paradise Lost,* Comus watches those who enjoy a pleasure he cannot experience; though his expression in the Huntington design seems marked by malice or envy rather than Satan's sexual anguish (1806 design) or melancholy self-absorption (1807 and 1808 designs), in the Boston image he appears wistful, contemplative, or admiring. In either version of *Comus* 3, however, he has not acted on his implied desire. These designs, like the *Paradise Lost* images, make a central Blakean point about evil and aggression: They result from the self-inhibition of sexual energy.

Thus understood, the designs resolve a contradiction in commentaries on Blake's *Comus*. Most interpreters assume that Blake criticizes Milton's belief in restraining desire; yet on the surface, at least, Comus's sexual aggression, which embodies the lady's danger, flows from active lust, not chastity or repressed desire. How can Blake be criticizing inhibition by confronting it with a figure of active aggression? Comus may, of course, be viewed as a mental projection, his aggression a fantasy construct of the lady's denied desire, but real-world male aggression remains to be accounted for. Elsewhere, Blake has made the point that this kind of aggression results from a distortion of male sexual impulse, but in the *Comus* images he seems not to show any inhibition of male heterosexual desire. *Comus* 3 does, however, focus on unrealized homosexual desire. So Comus's heterosexual aggression and tyrannical power may result from denied homosexual impulses. This point would dovetail with the Bard's Song's account of Satan's driving Leutha from his brain and with Urizen's futile regret for Luvah the cupbearer in *The Four Zoas* (chapter 3): In all these cases, repression of homosexual potentiality is shown as a component of male tyranny.

The third design, in conjunction with the sixth, also suggests the opposite side of unacted desire—the power of latent though unacknowledged desire. In the third design, Comus's aggression is in abeyance: He does not flaunt his wand of phallic danger but lets it fall as he gazes at the brothers, suggesting the power of their attraction. The earlier versions of the third and sixth design pick up on one side of this situation, that of repression: As Comus looks on the brothers with envy or malice in the third design, so the same emotions appear, inverted, as fear in the sixth. But in the Boston versions, Comus's gaze is fond or wistful in the third scene, while in the sixth, his balletic posture and almost flirtatious glance suggest that he is as much charmed by the brothers as frightened of them. These designs suggest the power of desire to influence action positively, even when unacted and unacknowledged.

These points, in turn, suggest a wider significance in Blake's reshaping of the sixth design. The 1801 version presents Milton's scenario more or less literally. But Blake is not likely to have viewed Milton's reliance on arms, or the classical warrior-lover tradition, uncritically—not in 1801 and certainly not in 1815, at the end of the war he hated and imagined as prompting Milton's return to worldly struggle. In the revision, in contrast, the brothers' victory results not from their swords but from their beauty. In this version as in the first, the continuity of the brothers' twinning and the way their poses recall the warrior-lover ideal suggest that Blake does not find homosexuality emasculating or a bar to entering "experience." But in addition, Comus's action here suggests a corrective to Milton's use of a martial ideal. Through the brothers and Comus, Blake shifts the illustrations' focus from chastity to prophetic vocation; links the latter to the classical ideal of homoerotic comradeship, further displacing any emphasis on chastity; and gives both an antimilitarist cast typical of his later work.

Besides the *Comus* images, some commentaries have fastened on one of Blake's designs for *Il Penseroso*—the third, known as "The Spirit of Plato"—as viewing homosexuality negatively. In this design (figure 4.5) Plato's spirit, appearing to Milton, is accompanied by what Blake's captions call "the Circles of Platos Heavens . . . these Heavens are Venus Jupiter & Mars" (*E*685). In Venus's circle, the goddess is flanked by a male-female couple and another whose sex is uncertain. In the first, the male, partly hidden by Plato, pushes away the female, who hides her face in a gesture like that of Eve judged in *Paradise Lost* (Butlin 529.10, 536.10). The second pair are bound back to back by entwined snakes. Damon believes the first pair indicate Blake's criticism of homosexuality: "Blake's sympathy is obviously with the woman," he argues, apparently assuming that the man's rejection of the woman is meant to represent Plato's approval of homosexuality; Damon does not mention the other pair (*Dictionary* 377, "Sodom"). Davies asserts that the first tableau depicts "[c]lassical contempt for women," while the bound pair, about equal in height, are male and "may represent an indictment of Plato's praise of homosexual love" (*Designs* 141). Though Davies does not say so, the phallic associations of snakes might support his point, and the back-to-back configuration recalls Aristophanes' fable of the origins of the sexes in the *Symposium*.

But neither grouping can present an "indictment" of homosexuality, and probably neither depicts it at all. The similarity of the rejected woman's pose to Eve's makes it clear that the male-female pair show not a peculiarity of Plato's system but a rejection of women's sexuality characteristic of "fallen" heterosexual relations in general; we recall that the judgment in *Paradise Lost* implicitly comprehends both the "sin" of eating the fruit and the sensualized intercourse that followed. Yet if this

Figure 4.5   William Blake. Illustrations for Milton's *Il Penseroso*. No. 3, "The Spirit of Plato," detail. The Pierpont Morgan Library, New York. 1949.4:9.

grouping shows "fallen" sexuality, the other, too, must depict sexuality in "fallen" form, not in general. The bound pair, even if male, cannot "indict" homosexuality any more than their biblical counterparts indict heterosexuality, but can only show what sexuality is in the present world: The lovers are tied together but also fettered by their entwining "snakes." But in fact this pair is probably not homosexual. On close inspection, the right figure shows a pronounced cleavage and fairly clearly contoured breasts, and what may be a bun of tied-back hair; her companion has short hair.[28] Probably, then, they are man and woman, like the other pair. Indeed, Aristophanes' tale is not about the origin of homosexuality but about that of divided sexuality in general. As Blake, also, is much concerned with the divisions of an assumedly pansexual primordial human, the two pairs seem to show two aspects of "fallen" sexuality— sexual rejection and chastity, and mutually binding sexual relations— without regard to their homosexual or heterosexual specifications. Balancing a visual reference to the *Symposium* with one to *Paradise Lost*—which might seem to have no place in a view of Plato's system— would suggest such a comprehensive view. And it would further suggest that the reign of "Venus," for Blake, comprises the *whole* range of sexuality in the present world.

Further, the *Symposium* is not really a tale of sexual license but of sexual restraint and the implicit superiority of mind over body, traits Socrates personifies in its narrative and in Alcibiades' reminiscence of his failed seduction of Socrates. By presenting images from Plato and from Genesis and *Paradise Lost* in tandem within the "Heaven" of Venus, then, Blake may criticize the mind-body dualism and antisexuality of both systems. The design shows that Plato's system is wrong, in other words, not by showing how bad homosexual love is, but by showing how limited all love is, and how false all division of mind and body, in what Blake sees as a debased belief system shared in essentials by classical philosophy and present Christianity.

Blake's final Milton designs, the twelve for *Paradise Regained,* contain an evolved treatment of sexuality, and homosexuality in particular. Usually seen as an artistic culmination, the set was executed in or after 1816, around the time of Blake's revisions to *Milton* and late work on *Jerusalem.* Issues of sexuality are most directly posed in the sixth design, Blake's version of Milton's banquet temptation (figure 4.6). The image shows Jesus turning from a trio of women evidently representing worldly and sexual pleasures; their poses suggest that these pleasures may in part be homosexual. Yet both Jesus' own posture and the design's overall symbolism and composition imply that his rejection may not be an admirable turn toward spiritual life but a problematic rejection of the body, the product of a mistaken opposition (Milton's) between body and mind.

Largely ignoring the issues of wealth and consumption that Milton highlights, Blake selects sexual puritanism and temptation, secondary in Milton, as his focus. What we see most clearly at the banquet table, in the space behind Jesus and the women, is the naked male-female couple seated there. However, heterosexual attraction is not Blake's main topic. By placing the three women in the foreground, Blake implies a possibly lesbian component of sexual pleasure. The two unclothed women clasp each other's wrists above their heads, and the one on the left also embraces her companion's waist. The trio has been identified with the three graces and the foremost figure with the Great Whore and other negative

Figure 4.6   William Blake. Illustrations for Milton's *Paradise Regained*. No. 6, "Christ Refusing the Banquet Offered by Satan." Fitzwilliam Museum, Cambridge.

female figures (Dunbar 177; Davies, *Designs* 168). Though these identifications are not necessarily wrong, the two entwined figures recall Blake's similar treatments of other embracing female groups such as those in *America* 15 and *The Four Zoas* 118, and they bring to mind the suggestions of homosexuality in Milton's text. Milton's "stripling youths" (*PR* 2:352–53; see chapter 1) are not present; instead, Blake has brought

Milton's female attendants at the banquet, "Nymphs of *Diana's* train, and *Naiades* / . . . / And Ladies of th' *Hesperides*" (2:355–57), into the foreground and placed them in a pose whose lesbian overtones correspond to the male homoerotic suggestiveness of the stripling youths. (The substitution, if conscious, may reflect Blake's caution about directly depicting male homoerotic poses in this period, discussed in the next chapter.)

It may seem obvious that this tableau presents lesbian relations negatively: Jesus turns from the group in emphatic rejection. Yet both Jesus' pose and the scene's symbolism and composition suggest that his rejection of the group is itself being criticized. Jesus has turned from the three women with a troubled expression unlike the assured demeanor he shows in the other temptation scenes (designs 2, 7, and 10). His hands make a shunning gesture as he "recoils, open-mouthed—as though both tempted and repelled in horror" (Hagstrum, "Christ's Body" 133). Further, the figures' positions and gestures imply that Jesus may be reacting as much to the women's open sexuality as to any specific enticement. While it is very difficult to be categorical about the meanings of figural groupings and gestures, the women do not seem directly to beckon Jesus to approach, though the one in front does make an open-handed gesture that may convey an invitation to come or to look.[29] It is uncertain that they are looking directly at him—the glances of the two women nearest him will meet Jesus' figure only if he is placed well in front of them in the picture plane. In any case, the two naked women seem as much preoccupied with each other as with Jesus. In sum, the trio seems as much a tableau exemplifying worldly pleasures as a group specifically enticing Jesus to take part. One way to look at the trio, perhaps, is in terms of conventional brothel sequences in eighteenth-century works such as *Moll Flanders* or *Memoirs of a Woman of Pleasure.* These often featured an older, worldly-wise procuress and experienced prostitutes, along with less experienced girls drawn into prostitution for economic reasons; they sometimes included a lesbian involvement among the prostitutes. With such scenes in mind, Blake's group seems not only to reinterpret Milton's scene through a familiar contemporary genre but also to show the real relations, economic and emotional, behind moralistic name-calling. Jesus' gesture and look, in turn, express disturbance at what the women are up to—his own moral condemnation—as much as a response to any invitation they might make. Blake, in sum, has spotlighted the rejection of sexuality—female sexuality in particular—that underlies Milton's conception of Jesus' self-contained masculinity.

Symbolically and compositionally as well, the design suggests that Jesus' rejection is being critically examined rather than celebrated. Sym-

bolically, the female figures must in some sense stand for the body in opposition to the spirit, or reason, as represented by Jesus—a polarity given
both by the biblical-Miltonic subject and by the female-male symbolic
gendering Blake conventionally used for these qualities. The image's
composition, then, shows a mind-body opposition that Blake opposes
philosophically and morally elsewhere—for example, in *Marriage,* plate
4, and "The Everlasting Gospel": "Thou Angel of the Presence Divine /
That didst create this Body of Mine / Wherefore has[t] thou writ these
Laws / And Created Hells dark jaws" (section f, lines 29–32; *E* 521).
Satan's figure, almost swooping between the figures, accentuates the division and may indicate, in a quite literal way, that it is Satan's work.
(Certainly Satan is not trying to bring the groups together, as he might
if indeed the women are evil temptresses.) Blake uses similarly divided
compositions, with fully interposed central figures, elsewhere: In the first
Il Penseroso design, Melancholy separates a pair of women on the left
from a pair of men on the right, and in *Jerusalem* 4, a hooded female figure divides a male figure on the left, who turns toward a group of soaring "spirit" figures, from a male on the right who probably represents the
physical body. In each case, arguably, the key idea is that the spirit-body
or mind-body split is itself wrong.[30] Compositionally as well, the banquet tableau is related to a series of earlier designs in the series, in which
the curved postures of some of the figures create an ovoid or conventionally heart-shaped composition for the whole design (see Davies, *Designs* 161–66). This motif (which recurs in the penultimate design,
considered below) is present but distorted in the banquet scene. The
configurations of the female figures at the left follow the "heart" form,
but its other side is skewed by the rigid, nearly straight form of Jesus,
suggesting in a rather direct way the "deforming" effects of antisexuality.

The idea that the banquet tableau criticizes the asceticism of Milton's
Jesus is consistent with the view that the *Paradise Regained* designs as a
group imply a sexually positive Jesus. Several interpreters take this view,
arguing, for example, that Blake wishes "to call Milton's idea of a celibate
Christ into question," since "the rationalism and the celibacy of Christ
in *Paradise Regained* exemplify the Puritan principle of liberty through
repression and restraint which is at the heart of Milton's personality and
thought," an ideal "inimical to [Blake's] own most deeply held beliefs"
(Davies, *Designs* 156). Yet these commentators view the banquet scene itself conventionally, as a representation of "love perverted in a fallen
world" (Davies, *Designs* 168) that Jesus properly shuns. If, instead, we at-
tend to the scene's content, symbolism, and composition, it will suggest
a complex victory and defeat: Jesus is right to reject Satan's sexual entrapment, as well as the temptation of wealth and ease it is part of, and

yet his rejection is deformed by hostility to the body and sexuality. This view accords with Blake's insistence on forgiveness of prostitution and adultery elsewhere in late work, with the treatment of homosexuality I have been tracing, and with the emergence of a sexually positive figuration of Jesus in the penultimate (tenth and eleventh) designs, which Davies explores in readings that I adopt here.

These images, which follow Jesus' troubled sleep in the eighth and ninth illustrations, show his third temptation on the pinnacle and his succoring by angels after it. Both designs display a radiant, transcendently spiritual Jesus who has emerged triumphant from trials. Yet his is not a triumph over the flesh. The aureole surrounding Jesus in the pinnacle design, Davies suggests, has the shape of a giant erect penis, thus inverting Milton's idea "of the Fall as an abandonment of rational self-control and an unlawful increase in sensual enjoyment" (*Designs* 175). Further, Davies proposes that the following design (figure 4.7) shows both "the moment of [male] desire . . . [and] the contrary feminine response" (176). Jesus is again surrounded by an aureole, similar in form, while the curved bodies and haloes of the lower angels supply the place of testicles (as Davies suggests) and the enclosing shape formed by the two angels at Jesus' sides adumbrates labia or perhaps the interior of the vagina.[31] Davies believes the ensemble figurally represents intercourse, but the composite figure may also represent Jesus' sexual nature, incorporating both male and female. If so, the sexual doubleness of this visionary-symbolic image—or what Blake would call its sexual unity—draws together the banquet design's division between puritan Jesus and sexualized, lesbian female figures. Compositionally as well, the design continues the motif of ovoid forms, fashioning the suggested and distorted ovoid figures of earlier images into a closed, harmonious whole. In symbolic content and formal composition, this penultimate *Paradise Regained* design suggests that the rejection of sexuality and homosexuality in the banquet scene is not merely wrong but violates Jesus' nature, which for Blake is humanity's nature as well.

Opening Satan's Doors

This chapter has isolated certain threads both in *Milton*'s narrative and in Blake's Milton designs that, though often ambiguous or hard to pick out, are central to his purposes because of what they suggest about the formation of the entities Blake calls Satan. Blake's Satan, we recall, signifies not only a principle of human consciousness, but collective entities, "multitudes of tyrant Men in union blasphemous / Against the divine image" (*FZ* 104:29–30; *E* 378). For the consolidation of these en-

Figure 4.7   William Blake. Illustrations for Milton's *Paradise Regained*. No. 11, "Christ Ministered to by Angels." Fitzwilliam Museum, Cambridge.

tities, the processes Blake explores in the Bard's Song and the images examined here provide psychic underpinning. In spite of their disparate qualities as parts of Blake's own mythic account of Milton's return on one side, and his illustration and interpretation of Milton's texts on the other, these processes have much in common.

In the Leutha portion of the Bard's Song, Satan's expulsion of Leutha from his brain helps create him as the paradoxically petrific yet expansive principle whose "Druid sons / Offer the Human Victims throughout all the Earth" (11:7–8). The attempt to cast out one's homosexual portion in creating a rigidified masculine identity, then, is part of Satan's formation, and this psychic distortion is itself a form of Satan. Similarly, in the *Comus* designs, Comus's denial of his attraction to the boys helps form the overbearing, potentially violent masculinity that seeks sexual mastery over the lady. *Il Penseroso*'s "Spirit of Plato" design stakes out philosophic ground in suggesting that the deformations of both Christian and classical views of sexuality result from what Blake sees simultaneously as the Fall and the reign of Venus—of which one aspect is the mind-body split found equally in Platonism and in Miltonic religion. The *Paradise Regained* designs then suggest that this split and the resulting denial of sex in general, and homosexuality in particular, are directly against Jesus' nature. At the same time, the brothers' development in *Comus*—especially in the later versions of the third and sixth designs, and there including Comus's response to them—suggests an alternative to Satanic masculinity; the brothers' homoeroticism, drawing on classical conceptions and yet redirecting their militarism in the direction of the power of desire, implies a potential way to open Satan's doors.

These conceptions develop over time, becoming much more visionary, daring, and heretical in the latest Milton designs. Midway in this development—after the first *Comus* set and the creation of the Satan-Palamabron and Satan-Leutha plots in the Bard's Song, but probably before the later designs—occur the revisions of *Milton,* explored in the next chapter. With these revisions, and with the designs discussed above, Blake moves toward his late synthesis of sexual liberty and human mutuality—that is, toward the world of *Jerusalem.*

Chapter Five ❊

The Cruelties of Moral Law: Homosexuality and the Revision of *Milton*

Displaying Naked Beauty! with Flute & Harp & Song

—*Milton* 4:28, copies C and D

By late 1810–early 1811, *Milton* existed as a 45–plate poem. Blake printed three copies, usually called A, B, and C, around this time; most likely he sold A first and B relatively soon thereafter. Copies B and C differ in limited but significant ways from A in their artwork— C more than B. In copy C, Blake made further extensive changes over the next several years, adding six text plates (one later removed), dropping the preface, and moving a key visual plate. Blake printed and sold copy D, incorporating all the new plates and changes in art, around 1818. Blake's major changes to the poem, then, belong approximately to 1811–18, though he seems to have continued adjusting C even after this.[1]

Most treatments of *Milton* approach the poem without considering these revisions, or regard them only as steps in the evolution of a final text. But when we consider that Blake printed, colored, and sold the poem in 1810 or early 1811, and then expanded it by more than an eighth, we should be open to the idea that the revised copies are a second, editorially distinct version of the poem.[2] This point is particularly true because the text revisions consist of significant added sections, not just line revisions, and because these text changes, with accompanying changes in artwork, shift some of the poem's thematic emphases. Among other changes, the revisions increase and refocus *Milton*'s treatment of the ravages of Moral Law, making this a more prominent theme than in copies A and B; incorporate a scene of sexualized ritual sacrifice, apparently thwarted; and, simultaneously, obscure sexual details in the artwork while shifting some of the art to underscore the increased thematic emphasis on Moral Law. Other emphases, of course, are also present in *Milton*'s added plates; moreover, rage at sexual hypocrisy has been a constant in all Blake's work since the *Songs*. But his stress now, we will see, is not just on sexual denial but on "cruelty," ritualized sacrifice, and (visually) execution. This chapter argues that these changes respond to contemporary events in London's streets.

A Contemporary Calvary:
The Vere-Street Persecutions, 1810–11[3]

On July 10, 1810, various London newspapers reported a police raid at the White Swan, a public-house in Vere-street, Clare-market, "said to be the rendez-vous of a society of miscreants of a *detestable* description" (*Times,* July 10, 1810: 3). As *Bell's Weekly Messenger* elaborated under the expressive head "Charges of a Most Odious Nature," the previous Sunday night, July 8, plainclothesmen and constables had arrested at least twenty-one men at the Swan (July 15, 1810: 223). Clare-market was a run-down area close by Lincoln's Inn Fields, and those arrested were mainly working class—as the *Times* put it, "The house was a place of call for coffee-house and tavern waiters, and most of the persons taken were of that description . . . flashy dressed fellows, in coloured clothes, with nankeen trowsers, silk stockings, &c. all hale robust fellows, the oldest not above 33" (July 10, 1810: 3). Those whose occupations were listed included a shopkeeper, a traveler in goods, a tailor, a bricklayer, ten servants and waiters (most unemployed), a corporal and three common soldiers, as well as the landlord of the house (*Morning Chronicle,* July 10, 1810: 3). Held overnight in a guardhouse, the prisoners were arraigned Monday at the Bow-street magistrate's office, amid "the fury of the crowd assembled in consequence of the cause of their apprehension becoming known" (*Bell's,* July 15, 1810: 223). Two undercover officers testified to "conversations and actions" observed on two occasions in a back parlor; the details, *Bell's* reported, were "of too gross a nature to meet the public eye" (July 15, 1810: 223). Seven persons who had been in the back room (one the previous week), plus the landlord and a waiter, were sent to prison to await trial. Twelve who had been in another room were freed for lack of evidence, but, the *Times* reported,

> their liberation was instantaneously productive of the most dangerous consequences. The multitude, men and women, fell upon them as they came out.

They were knocked down, kicked, and covered with mud through every street in their endeavours to escape. The women, particularly those of Russel-street and Covent-garden market, were most ferocious in their application of this discipline; but the lower order of male spectators were by no means lax in their exertions to mark their detestation of these wretches. (July 10, 1810: 3)[4]

Seven of the arraigned prisoners were tried at the Middlesex quarter-sessions ten weeks later; all were convicted and sentenced to prison terms, with six to be pilloried as well.[5] On September 27, the six were brought from Newgate along Fleet-street and the Strand to the Hay-market, a distance of about a mile and a half; crowds estimated at 30,000 to 50,000 (Crompton, *Byron* 164) clogged the streets, forcing the shops to close, and hurled mud, offal, dead animals, and bricks at the prisoners. "A number of fishwomen," several newspapers reported, "attended with stinking flounders and the entrails of other fish which had been in preparation for several days," which they refused to sell to the crowds, "as their proprietors, hearty in the cause, declared they wanted them 'for their own use'" (*Bell's,* Sept. 30, 1810: 311). Exposed for an hour each in two shifts (the platform was large enough only for four), the prisoners were bombarded the whole time and again when being returned to prison. The authorities connived at the violence, doing little to restrain the crowds and even letting a group of fifty women inside the pillory area to pelt the prisoners.

Probably because of the extreme brutality of the public response, the pillorying—with an unrelated pillorying, also on sodomy charges, two days earlier—excited detailed coverage. *Bell's,* for example, gave more than a full column, about seventeen inches, to the two events, an un-usual amount even in an eight-page paper. The *Morning Chronicle* traced this "crime so horrible to the nature of Englishmen" to "the unnecessary war in which we have been so long involved," as well as to "the *innovations* that have been attempted in our theatres and our *select* places of amusement." Noting that "it is horrible to accustom the people to take the vengeance of justice into their own hands," the *Morning Chronicle* called for an unspecified change in the law to stem "a torrent of corrup-tion that threatens to involve us in the gulph of infamy as well as ruin" (Sept. 28, 1810: 3). Illiberal as this position was, it was less repressive than some other accounts, which called for "making every attempt of this abominable offence punishable with instant death, without benefit of Clergy" (*Sodomy Trials,* n.d. [Sept. 30, 1810]).[6]

The raid on the White Swan was only one incident in a stepped-up antihomosexual campaign that lasted for months. Whether because po-lice activity and citizen complaints actually increased in the wake of

Vere-street, or because newspapers took greater interest in sodomy cases, or both, the months after the July raid saw a spate of reports of attempted or actual sodomy. Newspaper and other accounts show at least forty-eight persons arrested on sodomy-related charges in the last half of 1810, in twenty-three separate cases.[7] Press accounts describe the arrests in chillingly formulaic language:

> *John Carey Cole* was tried [at the Buckinghamshire Assizes] on three several indictments for an abominable crime. The prisoner was 60 years old, and was an usher in an academy, and the victims of his brutal passion were three of the boys of the school, who, awed by the situation the prisoner held there, could not resist him. On the first indictment he was acquitted, in consequence of the boy being too young to understand the necessary questions put to him to substantiate the crime; but on the two last he was found guilty, received sentence of death, and was left for execution. (*Sodomy Trials*, Aug. 12, 1810)

> A man of the name of *Carter* was brought to this [Marlborough-street] office on Monday, from St. James's watch-house, where he had been confined since Saturday night, on a charge of having assaulted a young man in the Park, with an intent to commit an unnatural crime. . . . He was handcuffed to a man charged with felony; and before they had got out of the street where the watch-house is, the features of both were covered with mud. . . . It was ascertained . . . that one of the men was charged with theft, and the unnatural miscreant having been discovered, he was assailed with double fury, and a subscription was set on foot as a remuneration for pelting the alleged thief. (*Bell's*, Oct. 14, 1810: 327)[8]

> A man of genteel appearance, of the name of *Richard Cambridge*, was on Wednesday charged at this [Marlborough-street] Office, by Thomas Mills, with a criminal assault in Hyde Park, and the disgusting evidence was so strong, that the prisoner was ordered to be committed. The prisoner . . . was conveyed with difficulty from St. James's Watch house, amidst an enraged mob, who assailed him with dirt, sticks, fists, and other offensive weapons, until his features were not discernible. (*Bell's*, Oct. 21, 1810: 334)

In December, two soldiers charged in a separate incident at the Swan in Vere-street, Ensign John Newball Hepburn, aged forty-two, and Thomas White, sixteen, a drummer-boy, were tried for "having committed an unnatural offence on the 27th of May last," a capital charge. Testimony showed that Hepburn had approached another drummer "on the Parade" in St. James's Park and asked him to arrange a meeting with White; the three met twice, the second time at the White Swan. Hepburn would seem to have been unfamiliar with the homosexual demimonde; White, described variously as a "practised *cinaed*" (passive partner) and an habitué of the Swan who was "an universal favorite," suggested the meeting place. There, according to the usual journalistic formula, "conduct the most vile and disgusting passed between the two prisoners, the particulars of which it is impossible to detail without a gross violation of decency." In July, "on the detection of the monsters in Vere-street," their go-between turned them in. The charge "was most clearly and indisputably proved, and the prisoners were both found *Guilty—Death*" (*Morning Chronicle,* Dec. 6, 1810: 3).[9] On sentencing, Hepburn struggled for life, denying the charge and denouncing the crime; White stood silent (*Times,* Dec. 13, 1810: 3). On March 8, 1811, the *Times* reported:

> EXECUTION.—Yesterday morning, *Hepburn* (late an Ensign), and *White,* the drummer, for an abominable offence, were executed before the Debtor's Door, Newgate. *White* came out first; he seemed perfectly indifferent to his awful fate, and continued adjusting the frill of his shirt while he was viewing the surrounding populace. About two minutes after, *Hepburn* made his appearance, but was immediately surrounded by the clergyman, the executioner, his man, and others, in attendance. The executioner, at the same time, put the cap over Hepburn's face, which of course prevented the people from having a view of him. White seemed to fix his eyes repeatedly on Hepburn. After a few minutes prayer, the miserable wretches were launched into eternity. A vast concourse of spectators attended. The Duke of CUMBERLAND, Lord SEFTON, Lord YARMOUTH, and several other noblemen, were in the Press-yard. (Mar. 8, 1811: 2)[10]

The persecutions continued, though with less intensity. Two days after the executions Richard Cambridge, arrested in October (see above) was pilloried, surrounded by "an immense concourse of spectators" who bombarded him "till he was completely disfigured, and appeared almost lifeless" (*Bell's,* March 10, 1811: 73).[11] And the following week another casualty was reported:

> EXCESSIVE GRIEF.—The mother of White, the Drummer, who was executed on Thursday, with Hepburn, the Ensign, died of a broken heart on the day subsequent to her son's untimely end. She never left her bed after having taken farewell of the culprit on the evening previous to his execution. (*Morning Chronicle,* Mar. 13, 1811: 3)

In the first six months of 1811, four new sodomy cases were reported in the London press. One man, Thomas Cox, was sentenced to die, two were pilloried, and one—in an indication that the mob actions of September were producing a mitigating reaction—was sentenced (for assault) to two years in prison and a fine, but without pillorying, on the grounds that "[t]he Court . . . would willingly put the prisoner in the pillory, but the indignation of the public might deprive him of life" (*Bell's,* Apr. 7, 1811: 111).[12]

This level of repression was lower than during the Vere-street months, though well above the level of earlier decades. In context, the Vere-street persecutions and the associated cases appear as an exceptional peak within a period of generally intensified repression: While prosecutions and executions for sodomitic offenses were rising between 1800 and 1818 and executions continued through 1835, the eight months from July 1810 to March 1811 seem unique in the number of incidents reported and the popular fury attending them.[13] Though conceivably the "wave" of repression is an illusion resulting from greater press attention, it seems likely that actual prosecutions rose above their already elevated base level in this period because of greater zeal by police and casual witnesses. It is also true that a countertrend can be discerned in retrospect: In the aftermath of the Vere-street mobs' violence, one judge already declined to order the pillory for sodomy-related assault (see above), and within five years reformers in Parliament introduced a bill to abolish the pillory altogether (Crompton 230–31, 251–52). But the glacial shift in opinion was not clear at the time; indeed, the law making sodomy a capital crime was reenacted in 1829 and stood until 1861 (Harvey 941). When they occurred, the Vere-street events seem likely to have had several lessons for anyone with qualms about regnant sexual morality. First, homosexuality remained an unspeakable and indefensible matter: Despite disquiet over the crowds' violence, no writer in the press then urged leniency toward any of those arrested or punished. Second, the events vividly demonstrated the degree to which working and poor people, abetted by the authorities, could be organized around hatred and repression of other poor and working people. Finally, the episode showed how stark was the gap between an ethic of mutuality and forgiveness and one of vengeance and intolerance. All these were issues close to Blake's central concerns.

"Calvarys foot": Vere-Street and Blake's revision of Milton

Blake's revisions of *Milton* increase the overall prominence of the poem's denunciation of Moral Law. This effect may be seen rather easily by comparing the work's earlier sections as they appear in the 45–plate *Milton* (copies AB) with the equivalent sections in copy D (the effect is less clear-cut in C, which lacks plate 5).[14] The reader may do this by first reading plates 2, 6–9, and 11–14 of the standard Erdman text (*E*) in sequence (skipping over added plates 3–5 and 10), and then rereading the full Erdman text.[15]

In the earlier version, Blake's narrative begins with the invocation and the opening of the Bard's Song (2), continues with a vision of Los's forge and Enitharmon's looms in present-day England (6) that merges into the Los-Satan-Palamabron story and Great Solemn Assembly (7–9, 11), and passes on to Leutha's story, the end of the Bard's Song, and Milton's descent (11–14). Key threads include the roles of the Elect, Redeemed, and Reprobate; the functions of wrath, pity, and forgiveness; and the establishment of Satan's sway over our world. Moral Law is implied as a topic in Leutha's story (11–13) and specifically mentioned when Satan creates "Seven deadly Sins . . . / Of Moral laws and cruel punishments" during the assembly, and later as Satan, "making to himself Laws from his own identity. / Compell'd others to serve him in moral gratitude & submission" (9:21–22; 11:10–11). But this idea is not singled out for special emphasis.

In the later version (*E*, based on copy D), the opening of the Bard's Song continues with an account of the formation of the body and sexes and Satan's refusal of his proper role (3); a contemporary scene of eroticized ritual sacrifice (4); and an extended discussion of the classes, their relation to Moral Law and atonement, the roles of the sexes, the narrowing of perception, and atonement again (5), before returning to the forge and looms and resuming the Los-Satan-Palamabron story (6–9, 11). Later, interpolated plate 10 again brings up restricted perception, together with women's jealousy. In this version the scourges of Moral Law become a major concern: The Elect, Blake's unreformable moral-social elite, is "Created continually / By Offering & Atonement in the crue[l]ties of Moral Law"; limited perception "brings forth Moral Virtue the cruel Virgin Babylon"—an emblem of antisexual natural religion and empire, and specifically a way of naming Rahab-Vala; and these events are related in some way to the roles of the sexes (5:5–27; quotations at lines 5:11–12, 27). Moreover, the comments on "Moral Virtue" are part of a lament by males laboring at furnaces and anvils while "the Females prepare the Victims" (5:15), linking Moral Virtue and Moral Law to the ritual preparations of "Victims" on the previous page (4:22).[16]

Visually, the first large illustration in copies AB is the view of a huge "Druid" trilith, with a figure on horseback below, on the second narrative page (plate 4; 6 in *E*). Druidism and triliths regularly signify human sacrifice in Blake, often in war or capital punishment, so the image would seem to relate to the text's evocation of "Tyburns Brook" (line 11), which usually signifies similar ideas. In copies CD, this plate comes later, and Blake has made the second new plate (plate 4 in *E*) a visual-verbal display in which as many as eight smaller triliths give form to the text's reference to "Calvarys foot" (4:21)—another reference to sacrifice and execution. (There are three or four miniature triliths separating two text segments and four at the bottom in a large design including women with spindles and distaff evidently "spinning" our world.) In the revised *Milton,* then, ritual sacrifice on plate 4 is emphasized visually and, in copy D, linked through verbal repetition to the attack on Moral Law on plate 5.

There are certainly many reasons, besides emphasizing Moral Law and its effects, for Blake to have revised *Milton* after 1810–11. I have already mentioned the sense of a succession crisis begun by renewed oppositional activity after 1807 and heightened by the king's incapacity—the Prince Regent assumed office on February 6, 1811, after a month-long parliamentary debate over the regency (*Times,* Feb. 7, 1811: 3). The first quasi-insurrectionary outbreaks among Midland weavers also occurred early in 1811 (*Morning Chronicle,* Mar. 15, 1811: 3). These events may have left their mark on the references to seventeenth-century revolution on plate 5 (see chapter 4) and on Orc's confrontation with Vala and her garment of famine, pestilence, and war on newly introduced plate 18. Other changes may be related to coverage and duplication in Blake's works. Blake's introduction of a creation narrative, for example, may be a belated response to his decision sometime during *Milton*'s gestation to leave *The Four Zoas,* with its own version of these events, unfinished. Dropping the preface may relate to its emphasis on war—by 1811–18 Blake may have felt a broader social reference was needed—or to Blake's repetition of motifs from its "Jerusalem" lyric in the prefatory poem to *Jerusalem* chapter 2, or to both factors. And so on. But among these other shifts in emphasis, the greater weight given the oppressions of Moral Law in *Milton* C and D stands out as one effect of the poem's revision.

This shift may be related to the wave of moral persecution described above. Here we must turn to one of the more obscure passages in the revised *Milton* and trace its possible reference to the Vere-street events as well as its interrelation with other elements in Blake's poem. The passage, a compressed reference to contemporary London, creates an abrupt shift from the mythic material involving Los and Satan that has begun plate 4:

> Mark well my words, they are of your eternal Salvation
>
> Between South Molton Street & Stratford Place: Calvarys foot
> Where the Victims were preparing for Sacrifice their Cherubim
> Around their loins pourd forth their arrows & their bosoms beam

> With all colours of precious stones, & their inmost palaces
> Resounded with preparation of animals wild & tame
> (Mark well my words! Corporeal Friends are Spiritual Enemies)
> Mocking Druidical Mathematical Proportion of Length Bredth
>   Highth
> Displaying Naked Beauty! with Flute & Harp & Song (4:20–28,
>   copies C, D)

Clearly a scene of ritual cruelty is occurring or about to occur in present-day London, but why has Blake set it between South Molton Street (where the Blakes lived from 1804 to 1821) and Stratford Place, the facing street on the opposite side of Oxford Street? "Calvary" in this passage has universally been explained as a reference to Tyburn's "tree," London's gallows from 1196 to 1783, at the northeast corner of Hyde Park. According to S. Foster Damon's discussion (slightly inaccurate, as we shall see), Tyburn Brook, from which Tyburn took its name, once flowed in the vicinity, descending underground near South Molton Street; Oxford Street, which divides the streets Blake names, ran west to Tyburn and Hyde Park, and so the locale Blake mentions could be "Calvarys foot" (*Dictionary* 413). (These streets' positions are the same today.) Relying instead on Oxford Street's mid-eighteenth-century name, Tyburn (or Tiburn) Road, Erdman also explains "Calvarys foot" as referring to the proximity of "Tyburn tree," though he sees "Tyburns Brook" as the Serpentine in Hyde Park (*Prophet* 397, 465). Erdman associates the "Cherubim" with England's young soldiers, "mustered before [their] sovereign in Hyde Park" in a loyalty celebration and royal review in October 1803, shortly after the Blakes moved to South Molton Street following their return to London from Felpham; for Erdman, "the first Victims were the youths' parents who brought them forth" and prepared them for sacrifice or to sacrifice others in England's imperialist wars (*Prophet* 397, 465). Extending Erdman's idea, Harold Bloom says that the soldiers display a "human beauty" in the face of their drillmasters' discipline (commentary, *E*911).[17]

Erdman's conception has much power and is likely to supply one meaning for the Cherubim. Yet there is no need for Blake to use periphrasis to name Tyburn Tree or Tyburn Brook (themselves metonymic terms for capital punishment that he frequently employs directly). One wonders whether the location has some other, more specific reference that might incorporate Erdman's view with other elements. Moreover, these glosses do not account for the soldiers' nakedness. Erdman sees naked soldiers in *The Song of Los* as those who have thrown down their arms (*Prophet* 262), but there was no rebellion among the troops in 1803 or later, though Blake may have hoped for one. Indeed, the passage has a strong erotic thread that none of the commentaries accounts for. Cherubim are conventionally male, beautiful, and fiery.[18] Here their arrows, phallic in form and associated with desire elsewhere in Blake, are "pourd forth" around the cherubs' "loins"; the "animals wild & tame," emblems of impulse and desire in other Blake passages, are found in their "inmost palaces," the recesses of their bodies or brains; and the final phrase, if in part a defense of Blake's artistic practice, identifies inferably male nakedness as beautiful.[19]

This erotic tenor is clear even though the passage's syntax and references are ambiguous. The Cherubim may be those being sacrificed (i.e., the object of "preparing"), as the passage's general drift seems to require; theirs, then, are the arrows of sexual desire, pouring around their loins, theirs are the bosoms beaming, and the animals resound in their bodies or inner palaces. Alternatively, the Victims may be preparing themselves for sacrifice; the Cherubim now become the agents of sacrifice, the arrows are those of denied desire manifested as sexual repression directed against the victims' loins, and the animals are present in the tormenters' brains. While the ambiguities alter details of the passage, and while such ambiguity is central to Blake's understanding of the dynamics of oppression, the passage's references to sexuality, desire, arousal, and male beauty are evident whether the lines denote the defiant expression of desire, its suppression and punishment, or both.

Despite Blake's presumed sympathy with soldiers caught up in an interimperialist war, there is nothing in their military situation to account for this passage's eroticism, which is absent in other passages on military victimization (e.g., *Eu* 12:5–20 or *J* 65:33–36). But the arrows of sexuality and repression, the preparation and execution of ritual sexual sacrifice, and the defiant bravery of Blake's "Naked Beauty!" are all present in the contemporary moral calvary involving soldiers, among others, that unfolded in 1810–11.

Though we have no definite knowledge, Blake is likely to have been aware of the Vere-street events. From July to December 1810 the major London newspapers reported not just the Vere-street raid and the cases of Hepburn and White, but at least twenty-one other separate police cases.[20] The quasi-official mob action at the pillorying, on September 27, 1810, covered by as many as eight London papers (Crompton, *Byron* 167), was one of the largest mass disorders in years. Hepburn and White's executions, on March 7, 1811, reported in at least three papers, were likewise an "event," if we can judge by the numbers attending, including members of the nobility. Blake—with his existing interest in repressive morality and in homosexuality—is likely to have read about these events or known of them by word of mouth. About the original arrests, arraignment, and mob hostility (July 8–9, 1810), the trials of the arrestees and, later, of Hepburn and White, and the other cases we can be less sure; these caused less stir and we know little of Blake's newspaper reading. He is known, however, to have read one paper that covered these events thoroughly, *Bell's Weekly Messenger,* though we know this specifically only for other periods. In May or June 1806, Blake wrote to a different journal, the *Monthly Magazine,* protesting a criticism of Fuseli in *Bell's* (*E* 768–69); and he copied an item from *Bell's* for August 4, 1811 into his notebook (*E* 694–95). *Bell's* was generally pro-reform in its coverage, a feature that would have appealed to Blake. We do not know whether Blake read the paper consistently. If he was a regular reader in 1806, he might have seen the paper's reports of the convictions of five members of a homosexual circle in Warrington and the executions of three (*Bell's,* Aug. 31, 1806: 276; Sept. 21, 1806: 300; see chapter 1); if he was reading *Bell's* in 1810–11, even semi-regularly, he would have seen some of its coverage of the Vere-street events, which he could also have followed in the *Times,* the *Morning Chronicle,* or other papers.[21]

In addition, the name Vere-street, repeatedly linked with the sodomy cases in all contemporary accounts, would have caught Blake's interest from the start. Blake is likely to have known Vere-street in his youth, since it was only a few blocks from James Basire's house at 31 Great Queen Street, where he lived as an apprentice from 1772 to 1779, between the ages of fourteen and twenty-one. From Basire's, Vere-street was reached by walking about fifty yards down Great Queen Street and 250 yards along Great Wild Street to Duke Street, where Vere-street began. It is quite likely that Blake's casual explorations of the area during this seven-year period would have acquainted him with these neighboring streets.[22] By a further coincidence, moreover, in 1810 there was a *second* Vere-street, almost at the Blakes' current doorstep. This one-block street, still present today, opens off Oxford Street less than two hundred paces from South Molton Street and Stratford Place, and less than three hundred steps from the Blakes' home—virtually at the site Blake names as "Calvarys foot."

Given Blake's probable awareness of the events, and his concerns with sexual hypocrisy, Moral Law, and homosexuality, plates 3–5, added to *Milton* some time after the persecutions, may contain a coded reference to them, among other details. Several aspects of the "Calvarys foot" narration fit this hypothesis.

"Calvarys foot" itself may be a fused image, referring both to executions in general and to the Vere-street events specifically. The links usually drawn between South Molton Street–Stratford Place and Tyburn are

not wrong, but they are complex and probably do not involve the closeness of "Tyburns brook" to the Blakes' home. The river Tyburn—called
"brook" in some contemporary sources (Lysons 3: 242)—rose in Hampstead, flowed south through Marylebone and along Marylebone Lane,
crossed Oxford Street probably at or just west of Stratford Place, and
wound south across Piccadilly, east and south through St. James's Park,
and into the Thames near modern Great College Street. Tyburn Brook,
a separate stream, was tributary to the Westbourne, dammed in Hyde
Park in 1730 to form the Serpentine—hence Erdman's references. Blake
does not connect Tyburn's river or brook (terms he uses indiscriminately)
to South Molton Street. When he indicates a location, Blake usually
places the river/brook in Hyde Park or Kensington Gardens (or where
the sun sets, an equivalent reference), though once in "Marybone." He
also refers to "Tyburn" alone, apparently as the place of execution, and
does sometimes link it with his own neighborhood (*J* 34/38:55–59). In
Jerusalem Blake does associate the stream with "Victims" (62:34, 90:48),
consistently with the appearance of "Victims" in *Milton* 4. And Albion
sits "by Tyburns brook" as the "deadly Tree" of "Moral Virtue" roots beneath his foot (*J* 28:14–15; see chapter 6); here the brook is linked with
execution, Moral Law, and, we shall see, homosexuality. But on balance,
"Calvarys foot" in *Milton* is probably not at South Molton Street because
of the proximity of Tyburn's brook or river.[23]

"Calvarys foot," however, has a closer connection with South Molton
Street–Stratford Place, though it is mythic in both its references. Hepburn
and White, the Vere-street victims, were executed at Newgate, but victims
in Blake die mythically on Tyburn's Tree; and a Vere-street, though not
the one in Clare-market, abutted Oxford Street close upon South Molton
Street–Stratford Place. In mythic geography, then, Vere-street would lie at
South Molton Street and Stratford Place both because a second Vere-
street was located there and because figuratively these Vere-street prisoners were hanged at Tyburn. Further, the distance along Oxford Street
from South Molton Street or Vere-street to Tyburn figuratively replicates
the actual distance from Newgate along Fleet-street and the Strand to the
Haymarket that the prisoners to be pilloried were made to traverse under
the crowds' execrations, like Jesus walking the stations of the cross. All
these associations—Tyburn, the two Vere-streets, and Oxford Street and
the Strand/Fleet-street as the *via dolorosa*—combine in the fused image of
South Molton Street–Stratford Place as "Calvarys foot."

Other aspects of the bard's London description fit the Vere-street
events as well. The term "monsters," repeatedly used for the Vere-street
and other homosexual prisoners, echoes in the "preparation of animals
wild & tame" (4:25)—with irony if the animals are in the persecutors'

breasts, and with answering defiance if they are in the sufferers'. In the "Victims . . . preparing for Sacrifice their Cherubim" we may tentatively see the enraged mobs, themselves mainly oppressed people—the *Times's* account of the initial arraignment mentions Russel-street and Covent-garden market, locales of street women, and refers to "the lower order of male spectators" (July 10, 1810: 3). The screaming rage of crowds in the plebeian areas around Bow-street and Newgate recurs again and again in the news accounts—too often to be a figment of the writers' class prejudices, and notwithstanding the noble attendance at Hepburn and White's execution. Blake's understanding of the way oppressed people can persecute their fellows is consistent with either Erdman's interpretation or mine, but the passage's emphasis on sexualized cruelty particularly fits the Vere-street events. In turn, Erdman's reading of the Cherubim as soldiers about to die becomes more powerful if extended to refer to soldiers actually sacrificed to moral virtue. One historian, referring to Hepburn and White, writes, "The involvement of the Guards, which was afterwards one of the most characteristic features of the London homosexual underworld, was already well established" (Harvey 943). But their involvement went beyond these two—we have already noted a soldier's prosecution on sodomy charges as early as 1798 (chapter 1), and four of those arrested in the July raid on the Swan—as well as White and Hepburn, accused later—were soldiers. Soldiers' participation in the homosexual world is an aspect of their double life as oppressors and oppressed that Erdman does not suspect, but that fits well with his emphasis on their victimization.

The "Druidical" proportions of "Length Bredth Highth," too, fit the context I am hypothesizing. Their "Mathematical Proportion" (4:27, 5:44) is that of rationalistic abstraction, for Blake the basis of Urizen's universe and all law, including Moral Law. That Moral Law leads to the victimization of human sacrifice in such rites as war and capital punishment is implicit in the trilith forms and the adjective "Druidical." The druidic proportions are seen literally in the triliths shown at the bottom of Blake's page—emblems of human sacrifice in Blake's work and the general discourse of his time. These references gain added force from being associated with an actual execution, since the triliths have the same form as the gallows—Tyburn's gallows specifically, originally a tripod, was later given the form Blake shows (Besant 344).

The accompanying emotions in Blake's passage are also consistent with a context of sexual repression. The arrows pouring around the loins, the gems in the Cherubim's bosoms, and the emblematic animals in their "inmost palaces" consort with the sexual nature of the Vere-street offenses, as well as with the virulent sexual hatred of their victimizers. Finally, in the sixteen-year-old White, "perfectly indifferent to his awful fate," and his nonchalant care for the set of his frill, we may see what Blake might regard as "Naked Beauty!"—naked in both Blake's usual senses: innocent and intensely sexual—in the face of a latter-day crucifixion.

In addition to explaining several aspects of the "Calvarys foot" passage itself, its possible reference to contemporary antihomosexual persecution helps make sense of its narrative and doctrinal contexts. The incident is part of Satan's attempt to gain supreme power, an occurrence both explained by and helping to bring about the rise of Blake's three classes—Elect, Redeemed, and Reprobate. In the inverted senses Blake gives these terms, Satan is very much of the Elect (7:4); Hepburn and especially White, if Blake had them in mind, certainly of the Reprobate. The passage occurs after Los's initial rebuff to Satan's ambitions, when Satan "trembling obeyd weeping along the way" (4:19). The context suggests that he is treacherously planning a comeback as he walks through London's streets, and that the present scene could provide its occasion; the description of preparation for sacrifice suggests its mode. The roles of the Elect, we know from the Bard's Song's overall content (chapter 4), include those of the British monarchy and state, especially in its imperialist mission, and of the guardians of antisexual morality. Both roles, but especially the latter, had considerable popular support, as the events of 1810–11 attest. And yet to Blake such sexually repressive rage almost certainly must have seemed the antithesis of true liberty. This point, and Satan's apparent aim of using the sacrificial scene to maneuver into power, help explain the bard's warning to his hearers against hypocritical rulers, "Corporeal Friends are Spiritual Enemies" (line 26).

However, Satan is thwarted, apparently by the display of "Naked Beauty! with Flute & Harp & Song." The upshot is that "Satan fainted beneath the artillery" (5:2). Besides the historical meanings already discussed (chapter 4), this event has a sexual meaning as well. At first glance the faint seems to be caused by Palamabron's return "with the fiery Harrow . . . / From breathing fields" (5:1–2), and several interpreters have so written (e.g., Fox, *Poetic Form* 30–31). But Blake is interweaving distinct, nonsequential narrative and thematic threads in the opening of plate 5. Satan's fate, Palamabron's return, and the discussion of sin and atonement introduced at 5:3 are all distinct lines in this narrative; the last of these is picked up again at 5:39 and the second not until plate 7. The "artillery" must be related to the remaining thread, the mocking of "Mathematical Proportion" by "Naked Beauty!" This occurrence must cause Satan's faint. Indeed, the whole sequence is repeated in reverse order at the end of plate 5, with the "artillery" now specified as Elynittria's arrows:

> . . . Satan fainted beneath the arrows of Elynittria
> And Mathematical Proportion was subdued by Living Proportion
> (5:43–44)

The end of plate 4 and the start of 5, then, form a sequence in which Satan is made to faint by "Naked Beauty!," and that they do so becomes evident when this sequence is repeated in reverse order at the end of plate 5.[24]

Blake often uses repetition as a framing device to allow thematic elaboration. Here, between the two narrations of the same events, Blake continues his account of the rise of the three classes, spelling out the link between their law and moral sacrifice:

> For the Elect cannot be Redeemd, but Created continually
> By Offering & Atonement in the crue[l]ties of Moral Law
> Hence the three Classes of Men take their fix'd destinations
> (5:11–13)

In the compressed syntax of Blake's later style, the three classes—not only moral and psychic but also political and social—are constituted through the continual creation of the Elect, and hence through the intended act Satan has witnessed "Between South Molton Street & Stratford Place," by which he has hoped to constitute himself as the Elect and as master of the Harrow of the Almighty (4:1–18). The ritualized preparation of the cherubim for sexualized sacrifice, by those who are themselves victims, strongly suggests the "Offering & Atonement" of plate 5, while the outcome, the defiant mocking of the gallows' "Mathematical Proportion," has temporarily halted these plans. Reading these narrative events as a reference to a contemporary sexual calvary deepens and enriches the discussion of the cruelty of Moral Law and its role in creating the Elect, and ties that discussion to the preceding narrative of the victims' sacrifice more fully than either Erdman's exclusively political allegory or the standard references to Blake's vocational dilemmas.

That Satan, as sexual hypocrisy and Moral Law, is checked by the bravery of those facing sacrifice allows one possible explanation for the "arrows of Elynittria." We have already noted several of Elynittria's roles, revolving in sometimes contradictory ways around her function as Palamabron's consort; we will see yet another below. Here, her identity as the female aspect of a male entity creates a variant of these roles: Her arrows would signify the phallic eroticism of this female aspect, that is, homosexual male eroticism. This is an appropriate meaning if the events at "Calvarys foot" do refer to the Vere-street persecutions. Indeed, since they have the same effect—both make Satan faint—the arrows and the

"Naked Beauty!" of 4:28 must be the same: Both signify phallic homosexual desire. Further, the cherubim's "Naked Beauty!" is manifested by their arrows "Around their loins pourd forth"—another parallel with Elynittria. In this case, the implied meaning of Satan's quest—that constructing Moral Law through sexual cruelty shared by the populace creates oppressive power—is balanced by a suggestion that defiant male homosexual desire can be a counterforce against this power. (To be sure, in 1810–11 this suggestion could only be wishful.) Analogues to the Orc-Guatimozin passage in *The Four Zoas* should be palpable.

A final aspect of plate 5, continued on the fourth of *Milton's* added plates, 10, is its treatment of male-female divisions and what Blake seems to feel is women's embrace of sexual repression. On plate 5, at the start of the interpolated discussion already mentioned, we are introduced to the "Daughters of Albion in their beauty" (5:5), here probably a figure for British women in general rather than the twelve named daughters prominent in *Jerusalem*.[25] Among other qualities, they take "whom they please / . . . into their Heavens in intoxicating delight" (5:10–11), and these choices seem to play a role in the creation of the Elect and Moral Law, detailed in the next lines (12–13). Logically enough, then, "the Females prepare the Victims" and, as they do, "the Males at Furnaces / And Anvils dance the dance of tears and pain" (5:15–16). The males in turn sing of how the senses are narrowed in the formation of the material body, ultimately creating "Moral Virtue the cruel Virgin Babylon" (5:28). The creation of the body, division of the sexes, and diminution of perception are here bound up with the foundations of morality and sexual cruelty. Though males as well as females create the three classes (5:38), females seem to bear the brunt of the bard's criticism. On plate 10, in turn, following Satan's fall into his "Space," Los affirms his religious, political, and cultural dissidence—"their God / I will not worship in their Churches, nor King in their Theatres" (10:12–13)—a fairly direct reference to continuing Dissenting traditions under the restored monarchy (see chapter 4). But in naming aspects of Satan's rule, Los also singles out Elynittria—here personifying female "Jealousy"—and "British women," as a group, for binding the "Internal light" to "a deadly fading Moon" (10:14–18). In other words, Los holds British women's jealousy specifically responsible for helping create a world of restricted sense experience under Satan's power; and the restriction itself is gendered, a shackling of inferably male inner light, or inspiration, to a classically female entity, the moon.

Sexual division in general is a major theme in *Milton;* but Blake is also concerned here with the specific relation between class and political tyranny and sexual jealousy and victimization—as manifested by women in particular. If we interpret Blake as primarily making a general statement on women's psychology, plates 5 and 10 can only seem thoroughly misogynist. However, they appear in a different light if we relate them narratively to plate 4—also an account of victims and sacrifice—and historically to the events of 1810–11. In the newspaper accounts, we repeatedly read of "the enraged multitude, the majority of whom were females"; the "fishwomen [who] attended with stinking flounders" that they insisted on hurling themselves; and the group of "[u]pwards of 50 women" whom the authorities let inside their cordon, who "assailed [the pilloried prisoners] incessantly with mud, dead cats, rotten eggs, potatoes, and buckets filled with blood, offal, and dung, which were brought by a number of butchers' men from St. James's Market" (*Bell's*, July 15, 1810: 223; Sept. 30, 1810: 312; *Sodomy Trials*, Sept. 30, 1810). If these reports are accurate at all, in a direct and literal sense London's women did "prepare the Victims," and so far as the bard's comments follow the narration of the scene of sacrifice on plate 4, he is recognizing this fact. More broadly, plates 5 and 10 are not concerned with the nature of women in some abstract sense, but with gender relations under a system of "Satanic" rule in which women's sexuality is distorted into victimization (5) and jealousy (10), and in this form helps prop up that rule. But Blake's development of this point is incomplete in *Milton;* much of his intermittent complaint against women for restricting men's sexual enjoyment and imaginative faculties is still present, alongside his exposure of the workings of Moral Law.

The focus of plate 5 on Moral Law, its cruelties, and their connection with social inequality helps confirm the interpretation of the calvary of plate 4 as one of sexual persecution and helps explain its introduction into the poem; put another way, introducing the plate 4 scene reinforces, and helps explain, the focus of later material in the poem on the effects of Moral Law. At the same time, plates 4–5 add a second, sexual level of meaning to the historical allegory noted in an earlier chapter. What we saw as events of Milton's century that checked resurgent absolutism we now also see as events of Blake's time that challenge Moral Law. If "Satan fainted beneath the artillery" (5:2) has not only a historical meaning keyed by the events of 1688 but also a sexual meaning based on continuity with plate 4, then not only are sexual and political liberty equivalent (as Blake's readers already know) but sexual and political resistance are linked as well. In Blake's universe, where Satan has complex political, religious, and moral-sexual meanings, these events are parallel and related: As sexual cruelty and repression underpin Satan's political power, so moral-sexual defiance may undermine it. But for this to happen effectively—I believe Blake would argue—requires more than simple defiance.

It requires a general toleration, in fact a reconstruction of consciousness, to which *Milton* itself, by reshaping how we see Moral Law and homosexuality, is to contribute.

The Homosexual Plates and Blake's Revision of Milton

The homosexual subtexts in the text of *Milton* 3–5 have a counterpart in several visual plates that evoke qualities of fraternity, mutual support, and moral heroism. These include the paired figures of "William" and "Robert," that of Milton supporting a swooning male or female figure, and that of Blake turning to meet Los in a sunburst (plates 32, 37, 45, and 47; figs. 5.1 to 5.5).[26] These plates have their own relation to *Milton*'s revision. All were present in the poem's initial version, copy A, and there they give strongly homoerotic overtones to the heroic qualities they depict. Differences in design in copies B, C, and D mute their visual homoeroticism, but at least in plate 47, other changes thematically heighten the poem's emphasis on positive male homoeroticism.

The mirror images of William and Robert show Milton's spirit entering as a falling star into William Blake and his long-dead, beloved younger brother, not otherwise mentioned in the poem. Both figures fall backward with arched backs and outflung arms in postures that suggest both crucifixion and sexual ecstasy (Essick and Viscomi 27; Storch, *Sons* 144). In copy A's "Robert" (figure 5.1), a tubular form against the right thigh suggests an erect penis; it is white-gray with a dark outline and a central ventral line, with a suggestion of an opening at the end, but no testicles. A heavily inked black shape in the appropriate position in copy A's "William" (figure 5.2) has been viewed similarly (*IB* 248). Close inspection shows that the inked form, a relatively distinct penis, has been partly obscured by coloring. Dark gray wash begins along the left thigh and continues partway up the shape; at its top, two tangent ovoids of light-gray wash partly cover its tip, which can be discerned beneath the wash; the effect is to slightly shorten the shape.[27] Evidently, the moment of Milton's spiritual accession is also a moment of sexual exaltation, and the implication is that it is experienced simultaneously by the living William and the dead brother whom he saw as a spiritual guide. In effect, the images' subject-matter—William's accession through Milton's spirit to spiritual exaltation, brotherly love, and prophetic vocation—becomes a triple spiritual and sexual union among the two brothers and Milton, manifested in the brothers' simultaneous orgasmic body spasms.[28]

The two remaining images, especially plate 47, have been frequently seen as implying oral-genital contact or sexuality; Robert N. Essick and

Figure 5.1   William Blake. *Milton a Poem.* Copy A, plate 33 [*IB* plate 37]. © Copyright The British Museum.

132

Figure 5.2   William Blake. *Milton a Poem*. Copy A, plate 29 [*IB* plate 32]. © Copyright The British Museum.

Joseph Viscomi comment that "[i]f this is a valid perspective, then Blake [in plate 47] has extended his central theme of brotherhood . . . into an erotic dimension as a powerfully physical embodiment of the union between the artist and the imagination" (33–34).[29] More is involved than simply union. Plate 47, Essick and Viscomi add, records "an influx of imaginative strength" (34). In both images the possible source for this influx—in a general way rather than as a specific illustration of oral sex— is the male genitals. This function is more clear-cut in plate 47, showing Blake's union with Los, than in 45. The latter (figure 5.3) has sometimes been seen as showing fellatio, but the primary visual effect is that the swooning figure has collapsed upon Milton. In fact, the kneeling figure is positioned so as to be unable to keep its balance during a sexual act; nor is Milton supporting him or her. (However, Blake's use of posture is often inexact.) Though the figure could receive a vivifying impulse from Milton's genitals, the image does not suggest that this is occurring, and there is no defined textual analogue for the image that conveys this idea. If the figure is Urizen, as most who view it as male believe, the clearest textual reference is not to Milton's hostile "baptism" by Urizen, as W. J. T. Mitchell feels ("Style" 56, citing text events at 19 [21]:7–9), but rather the moment when "Urizen faints in terror striving among the Brooks of Arnon / With Miltons Spirit" (39 [44]:53–54). But in this case the image cannot show a reviving homosexual contact, or even fellatio as a "hierarchical relationship" reinforcing a "position of dominance" (Kaplan 169). Rather, the scene must present a visual analogue for Urizen's terror in the text, much as images in *The Four Zoas* explore implications not present in their verbal texts. Visually, Urizen's faint appears to be brought on by Milton's nakedness itself, perhaps even by the proximity of oral-genital contact. In other words, Urizen faints at the sight of the naked male body and—inescapably in the figures' positioning—the possibility of homosexual contact.[30]

Plate 47 (full view, copy B: figure 5.4; detail, copy A: figure 5.5), as all commentators have noted, refers to the earlier textual description of Los's advent to Blake, on the plate following the image's original position as plate 21. The image records the moment when Los appears as "a terrible flaming Sun: just close / Behind my back; I turned round in terror, and behold. / Los stood in that fierce glowing fire"; and it anticipates the moment when Blake stands "with fear & terror . . . / . . . but he kissed me and wishd me health. / And I became One Man with him arising in my strength" (22 [24]:6–8, 10–12). The image's head-to-genital proximity—very close, as Los's left foot is almost on a plane with Blake's buttock—replaces the two acts of love that Los performs in the text, binding on Blake's sandals and kissing him, and instead suggests a genital kiss.

134

Figure 5.3   William Blake. *Milton a Poem.* Copy B, plate 41 [*IB* plate 45]. This item
is reproduced by permission of The Huntington Library, San Marino, California. RB
54041, plate 41.

The implication of sexual arousal is clearest in copy A. Here the Los figure has a visible erection, clearly discernible though a little obscure amid
dark rose-gray shading for the whole pubic area. Two round shapes are
below it, where testicles should be and just over Blake's cheek; the one
on the right is indistinguishable from Blake's nostril but the one on the
left is quite distinct, and definitely not a cheekbone. Blake's genital area
has been blocked out with a bar of black wash—not necessarily by
Blake—but on close inspection one can see what lies beneath the wash.
Surprisingly, it is not a penis but a black triangle, in the space formed by
Blake's left heel and squatting thighs. These shapes form a concave-sided
triangle with its apex at the top, colored black in a darker pigment than
the covering wash. We are not seeing the cleavage of the buttocks, which
would not be visible from this angle on either a male or a female figure.
Blake, in sum, despite his figure's defined overall male bone structure
and musculature, has portrayed himself either with no genitals or with
female genitals, as some faint lines in the position of labia suggest.[31]

Plate 47 is inescapably ambiguous. If Los is a figure of resplendent nobility, there would seem to be no getting round the fact that in copy A
this nobility centers (literally) on his aroused genitals, which are directly
before Blake's head and also occupy the focal point of the composition.
Even when the viewer fails to note this consciously, the image must visually suggest that Los's glory and the inspiration he imparts are manifested in his genitals; in the same way the image must suggest that Blake
will receive both through his mouth or face. But the image also denies
the implication of literal sexual contact. Aside from the mythic dimension that Los is stepping out of the sun and is therefore more a visionary
apparition than a physical figure, Blake's posture of twisting to face
someone behind him is an unlikely configuration for an actual sexual act
or kiss. For this reason—but also, no doubt, because of powerful inhibi-
tions against recognizing the image's implied sexuality—many observers
have read this plate in nonsexual terms. But, at least in recent years, as
many have done the opposite.[32]

The sexual implications of the "William," "Robert," and Los-Blake
tableaux are driven home when we realize that the figures in them are
variations on those in *The Four Zoas* 78. The figures of the brothers—
particularly Robert, whom we see from the left side, like Orc—replicate
Orc's arched back and cast-back head, as well as Blake's alternative sketch
of a flexed leg, although the figures are rotated upward to represent a
backward fall and their arms are flung outward. The erect penises in the
first versions of both images repeat what we have noted in Orc. In the
Los-Blake tableau, Los's figure echoes, in less extreme form, the same
arched-back, bent-leg posture, but with head bent down and arms raised;

136

Figure 5.4   William Blake. *Milton a Poem.* Copy B, plate 21 [*IB* plate 47]. This item is reproduced by permission of The Huntington Library, San Marino, California. RB 54041, plate 21.

Figure 5.5   William Blake. *Milton a Poem*. Copy A, plate 21 [*IB* plate 47], detail. © Copyright The British Museum.

in a general way, the plate shows a rotation of *The Four Zoas* 78 upward into a vertical plane, maintaining the overall relationship of the two figures although their specific placement and postures, as well as the viewer's perspective, differ. These comparisons show that the sexual implications in these *Milton* designs are not some artifact of the positioning of figures with different, nonsexual meanings, but result from distinct reworkings of a preceding design to retain its essential elements while removing the overt depiction of a specific homosexual act. In effect, "Robert" and "William" retain the posture suggesting sexual climax without the two male bodies directly joining, while the Los-Blake image retains oral-genital proximity without implying sexual climax.

One further imaginative rotation is suggestive. Rather than viewing Los and Blake along a horizontal axis with the characters upright, the viewer may rotate the scene into a horizontal plane viewed vertically from above. In this case Los appears to be lying on a bed of flames with Blake, also supine, between his legs, twisting over to kiss him. The grass and the positions of the characters' feet make this an impossible literal reading, but the exercise helps us to see that Los is positioned almost exactly like a man lying down to receive fellatio.

While these images do not directly show sexual contact, in copy A all three show or suggest male sexual arousal. In later copies, differences in line, color, and shading, the addition of clothing, or both, obscure the signs of arousal. Generally, the changes are less extreme in copy B, in which Los and Blake remain naked and "William" and "Robert" have only a suggestion of covering shorts, than in C and D, which clothe all the figures. In copy B, William has been given just the waistband and cuffs of otherwise invisible shorts. Yet William has no distinct genitals; copy A's inked shape can be picked out with care but is obscured by coloring and shadow effects. Robert is also given waistband and cuffs, and added pen lines suggest folds in the garment. Wash and ink lines almost conceal the shape prominent in copy A, while an equivalent shape along the figure's left thigh, *not* noticeable in A, also appears as part of the drapery. These differences from A suggest by comparison that the effect of a male organ in A was achieved through careful use of color to outline some parts of the printed impression and cover others.[33] In copy C, in which the shorts are more definite, "William's" inked shape is visible, but has printed differently and is rather indistinct. "Robert's" penis-form is fairly clear in outline despite the vivid green-gray shorts Blake has added; though visually the shape appears to be under the shorts, it is actually separately colored in a lighter yellow-green. Since a tiny sliver of the shorts' green-gray comes over part of the shape's ventral edge, it would appear that Blake added the shorts after coloring the body, and went around the shape's outline to preserve its distinctness.

Los and Blake, too (plate 47), are treated more chastely in copies B-D than in A, though the characters' overall relations still emerge from their postures. In B, though the figures are still unclothed, dark pink-gray shading in Los's pelvic area above Blake's face obscures the anatomic detail; only an indistinct rising form is visible, not a defined penis, and the arc-shape above Blake's cheek, though visible, is not clearly related to the form. Altogether, one must look carefully to see even a suggestion of sexual organs. In Blake's thigh and pelvic area, rough handling of ink and wash achieves an effect of indistinct shadow. The outlines of the left foot and both thighs are thickly inked and not clear in detail; black shadow forms an irregular rising shape where genitals would be. In C and D, both figures wear shorts, with color and shadow effects completing the makeovers.[34]

These changes could stem from any motivation, including the desire to make the works acceptable to buyers. But it is also possible that the revisions reflect increased nervousness about displaying all-male sexual images at the time when Blake was coloring the later copies.

Despite retouching, these plates retain their thematic importance. This emerges both from their visual form and from their relation to *Milton*'s other material on homosexuality and Moral Law. For "William" and "Robert," the relationships are general and were present in the poem's earlier state (copies AB), before plates 3–5, 10 [11], and others were added. These images show Milton's descent to our world to correct the insistence of the "Elect" on sin, punishment, and submission. This insistence is detailed in several passages already examined, such as those describing Satan's consolidation of his position through creating "Seven deadly Sins" (9:21). In the face of Satan's efforts, Milton's descent sparks in "William" and "Robert" a prophetic exaltation that is also vividly "reprobate": Their erections, in the initial versions of these plates, confront and defy the "Elect's" sexual denial, as do their postures once we tease out the images' relations to each other and to others suggesting sexual ecstasy.

The Milton-Urizen plate (45), which shows the outcome of the two characters' struggle, can also be related to the inception of that struggle, in plates 15 [17]–20 [22]. There, as Milton plunges into our world and into Blake's body (15 [17]:45–50, also the referent for "William"), the narrator describes Milton's three wives and daughters, who, in a typically dense Blakean fusion, are identified with Rahab, Tirzah, and others and with mountain regions of Palestine (17 [19]:10–16). In turn, the sons and daughters of Rahab and Tirzah offer Milton domination over Orc and over the world of labor, war, sexuality, and natural religion (19 [21]:36–20 [22]:6). They tempt Milton, that is, not to struggle for the full liberation of human potentiality but to become ruler and limiter of humanity. Urizen, who in the AB text appears for the first time as Milton reaches our world (17 [19]:36), wrestles with Milton to enforce this choice. Milton's victory over Urizen, then, is the victory of a struggle for human transformation over compromise with social oppression. Part of the sons' and daughters' temptation, however, has been psychic and sexual. One of Tirzah's powers, which they offer to Milton, is that she "ties the knot of milky seed into two lovely Heavens" (19 [21]:60), i.e., the testicles; his rule is to be based partly on the limited expression of sexuality, implicitly linked to the overall sway of Moral Law. With this material as backdrop, the Milton-Urizen plate (45), generally a depiction of Milton's triumph over these temptations as represented in Milton's wrestling, can be seen to accentuate their sexual aspect: Urizen faints before a Milton who is a figure of prophetic dedication *and* of untrammeled male nakedness, and the postures of the characters imply that part of this nakedness is the possibility of homosexual expression, an appropriate opposite to the fettered sexuality included in Tirzah's world. Further, Urizen's collapse implies that it is exactly the liberation of sexual potential, including that of homosexual expression, that he cannot bear and denies in his body and mind—he faints before Milton's sexuality almost literally because he cannot face it.

These three designs, then, form part of the poem's overall opposition to restraint, including sexual restraint and the Moral Law. So does the Los-Blake design (47), but this image takes on added significance when it shifts position in copies CD. It is the only full-page plate whose relative position changes in different copies of *Milton*. In copies A and B, where it is plate 21, this image directly follows the verbal depiction of Los's appearance in the sun (plate 20 in these copies; 21 in C; 22 [24] in *E*). In C and D, it moves to become the fourth plate from the poem's end (43 and 47 in the two copies). Thematically, its meaning has usually been related only to the Los-Blake narrative where it was first placed (e.g., *IB* 263–64), though W. J. T. Mitchell suggests that its new position is meant to contrast with a negative portrayal of homosexual contact in plate 45 ("Style" 67). Its displacement has also been explained in nonthematic ways, for example as an expedient to avoid renumbering subsequent plates (Essick and Viscomi 37, 40 n. 17).

Surely the basic reason for moving the plate was pictorial and thematic in a general way: to introduce, near the end of the poem, an overwhelmingly magnificent image of prophetic vocation. But in addition, the repositioning in C and D coincides with the introduction of new verbal material earlier in these copies, including the "Calvarys foot" narration, and juxtaposes the Los-Blake image with a passage thematically related to this material. On plate 40 [46] (42 in C), the plate preceding this image, Milton's female counterpart Ololon describes Milton contending with the zoas in the Brooks of Arnon; when Ololon ceases, the narrator tells us that

> Rahab Babylon appeard
> Eastward upon the Paved work across Europe & Asia
> Glorious as the midday Sun in Satans bosom glowing:
> A Female hidden in a Male, Religion hidden in War
> Namd Moral Virtue; cruel two-fold Monster shining bright (40
>   [46]:17–21)

Rahab here is Blake's familiar figure for the fusion of war and false religion under the aegis of sexual denial, and the text refers to the geographic arenas of war and imperialism in Blake's time. But besides these overall religious and political references, the passage recalls the ritual cruelties on plates 4–5; and it directly echoes the "crue[l]ties of Moral Law" and "Moral Virtue the cruel Virgin Babylon" on plate 5 (5:12, 27; present only in copy D), as well as similar references elsewhere (e.g., 9:22, 22 [24]:44). Rahab Babylon and the "Virgin Babylon" of 5 are of course the same; the names build on a conflation of Rahab with Babylon the mother of harlots (Rev. 17:5) that Blake has used in *The Four Zoas* (Night 8, 115 [111]:1–21, *E* 385–86).

While echoing the references to ritual victimization and moral cruelty on plates 4–5, the passage also serves as a textual opposite to the visual plate that follows it: In the text Rahab Babylon appears on the pavement like a glowing sun within Satan's bosom, while in the visual image Los steps onto the green grass *out* of the fiery sun. The text presents a verbal image of moral orthodoxy and punishment, while the Los-Blake plate is a visual image of moral transgression. These oppositions can hardly be coincidental; they seem pointedly to juxtapose text and opposed image in a way that adds meaning to both. Repositioning the Los-Blake image, then, relates it directly to a restatement of the cruelties of orthodox morality and their connection to war and imperialism. In addition, we see here Blake's inversion of conventional categories: The image of hermaphrodism is used to convey Rahab's horror, yet the term does not refer to moral-sexual transgression but to its opposite, orthodoxy—Babylon in plate 5, unlike in *The Four Zoas*, is virgin, and here is Moral Virtue. Not transgression but sexual orthodoxy, Blake suggests, is hermaphroditic, because in suppressing the inferably dual impulses present in everyone, it forces female to hide within male, and male within female.[35] Sexual transgression, in contrast, becomes a source of highest moral heroism.

The fullest recent discussion of this image views it in a way diametrically opposite to mine, with assumptions and implications that are worth noting. Starting from the thesis that Blake's "mythic cosmos is not only gendered, but hierarchical and masculinist," Marc Kaplan argues that the homosexual implications in this and other plates are "conscious and intentional" (151, 168). Yet they do not disturb male-dominated sexual hierarchies, because "males of [Blake's] time . . . viewed sexual acts between males as much less disturbing (assuming always that one identified with the dominant/penetrator) than a perceived femininity 'invading' the male personality" (168). Plate 47 seems, however, to depict exactly such an "invasion," since Blake presents himself as the receptor and, in copy A's underlying image, lacks male genitals. Kaplan is unaware of the latter point, and he argues, consistently with his overall thesis, that the plate shows an acquisition of "masculine power" through fellatio that complements the poem's deprecation of women. The threatening idea of male submission, Kaplan believes, is avoided because, "[t]hough Blake is nominally the submissive partner . . . he and Los in fact become equals" (169). Kaplan appears to argue that the ordinary male of Blake's time viewed homosexual acts by "dominant" males with equanimity. This idea is almost certainly untrue; judges, juries, satires, polemics, and mobs showed no tolerance toward homosexual penetrators (such as we assume Cole and Hepburn to have been) or interest in distinguishing between the roles. But Kaplan is forced to minimize the culture's antihomosexualism because he wishes to see Blake's apotheosis of oral-genital contact as completely supportive of male hierarchy.

Kaplan's assumption that Blake's prohomosexualism is entirely congruent with misogyny deserves serious consideration nonetheless. Briefly, I believe, first, that for anyone in Blake's time to suggest, in however veiled a way, that males could "become equals" through fellatio was a considerable departure from conventional ideas of masculine identity; second, that casting both male comradeship and male homosexuality in a heroic light need not imply denigration of women. Indeed, the assumption that it does is close to the classical Freudian idea that male homosexuality is based on unreadiness for mature sexual relations and involves symbolic humiliation of women; traces of this idea turn up not only in Kaplan's account but in Webster's and Storch's as well. Homosexuals have had to learn to reject this charge. In fact, rather than reinforcing masculinist assumptions, such a presentation as Blake's can become part of an undermining of male-female hierarchies, as we shall see when discussing *Jerusalem.*[36]

The Los-Blake image, then, in its new location, graphically and explicitly answers Rahab Babylon's cruelties of moral virtue by showing moral transgression as heroic triumph. It gains added resonance from its relation to plate 4. Both allude to violation of moral laws, but plate 47 gives this violation an aura of visual splendor and moral heroism; it is an *image* of "Naked Beauty!," the quality that—with its homosexual tonalities drawn from the Vere-street persecutions—momentarily halted Satan on plates 4–5, as he will be definitively thwarted in the poem's plot outcome on plates 40 [46]–43 [50]. Just as the text material about Rahab Babylon presents an equivalent to the moral and sexual repression on plates 4–5, the Los-Blake image presents a visual equivalent to the verbal tonalities of defiant male beauty on those plates.

In offering this equivalent, the image, together with the text material on plates 4–5, reshapes and particularizes *Milton*'s meaning. One of *Milton*'s purposes, we know, is to show an awakening of the British people through the infusion of Milton's spirit. But, Blake suggests, that cannot happen unless "Milton"—the prophetic spirit in the British people—recognizes and changes false ideals. Broadly, there must be a shift from sectarianism and imperialism to fraternity (plates 22 [24]–23 [25], 25 [27]); specifically, from sexual persecution to toleration (plates 4–5). *Milton* itself contributes to this latter shift both by denouncing Moral Law directly and by pictorially implying one of the most despised acts in hierarchic male culture, sucking the penis, as the source of moral fraternity and prophetic inspiration. The revised *Milton*'s images and text suggest that male homosexual acts may further an accession of prophetic power and mission, contrary to the teachings of antisexual religion; heroize the limited acts of defiance of moral law that occur in everyday life; and imply that such acts may be steps toward the larger social and cultural resistance that can end Satan's rule and that it is *Milton*'s aim to promote.

Chapter Six ✺

Blake's Synthesis: *Jerusalem*

they shall arise from Self,
By Self Annihilation into Jerusalems Courts & into Shiloh
Shiloh the Masculine Emanation among the Flowers of Beulah

—*Jerusalem* 49:45–47

Jerusalem is Blake's synthesis of his ideas concerning homosexuality
with those concerning economic and political justice, religious and
sexual freedom, gender, and the means of change and renewal. In
Jerusalem these multiple concerns of earlier works reappear, merged,
compressed, and at white heat, in a drama of division and reunification
through conscious solidarity—a remaking of human consciousness not
as an end in itself but as the means to confront intellectual error and political, sexual, social, and religious tyranny as manifested throughout history. Acceptance of homosexuality, in *Jerusalem*, is both a component
part and an emblem of these changes.

Blake's concern with homosexuality broadens in *Jerusalem* to include
and even emphasize lesbian relations. This focus counterbalances the emphasis on male relations that many observers have noted in *Milton*. In
Jerusalem, homosexuality in general appears among the supposed vices
condemned by Moral Virtue; in addition, Blake introduces a specifically
lesbian narrative that highlights the evils of moral condemnation and embodies an alternative to possessive sexuality. As the latter, in turn, is one
of several kinds of possessiveness opposed by the principle of brotherhood
embodied in Blake's Jesus, the lesbian narrative has a larger, synecdochic
significance in *Jerusalem* as a whole. Homosexuality becomes both an embodiment and an emblem of mutualistic and equalitarian sexual and social relations. In addition, in a more immediate, less utopian perspective,
attitudes to homosexuality among other transgressions become a sign of

the "Universal Toleration" (*E* 635) that for Blake is required if Albion, the British people, are to awake to liberty. Finally, in a reconsideration of the role of the sexes, Blake broaches the parity of homosexual and heterosexual relations, as well as of women and men.

Community, Private Property, and Moral Law

Jerusalem's concerns with moral condemnation, social possessiveness, and private property—and, by implication, with alternative, mutualistic social and sexual relations—are announced in the poem's opening sequence, when Albion, spurning Jesus' plea for brotherhood and mutuality, declares that Jesus is

> Seeking to keep my soul a victim to thy Love! which binds
> Man the enemy of man into deceitful friendships:
> Jerusalem is not! her daughters are indefinite:
> By demonstration, man alone can live, and not by faith.
> My mountains are my own, and I will keep them to myself!
> The Malvern and the Cheviot, the Wolds Plinlimmon & Snowdon
> Are mine. here will I build my Laws of Moral Virtue!
> Humanity shall be no more: but war & princedom & victory!
> (4:25–32)

Recalling evocations of "Moral Law" and "Moral Virtue" in *Milton,* Albion's reference to moral virtue counterposes it to loving human relations (what he sees as "deceitful friendships"), much as, in *Milton,* the narrator opposed moral abstraction to "Naked Beauty!" and "Living Proportion" (4:28, 5:44). Moral Virtue as such—its cruelty and oppression—becomes a major focus of the poem. Episodes such as that of Jerusalem's condemnation as harlot, with the contrasting story of Mary's pardon (61:1–62:34), exemplify moral strictures and the opposed ethics of forgiveness. In symbolic geography, the Blakes' own neighborhood becomes the site of moral punishments that are also the sufferings of England's youth in the European war: The Daughters of Albion, "with Moral Virtue the fair deciever," "divide" Reuben and the other sons of Jacob and "sen[d] / Him over Europe in streams of gore . . . / . . . / The Wound I see in South Molton S[t]reet & Stratford Place" (74:33–55).

Moral judgment here is general, but in other cases coded references implicitly connect it with the condemnation of homosexuality, as in an early sequence in which Los refers to the foremost of Albion's renegade sons, Hand:

Hand sits before his furnace: scorn of others & furious pride:
Freeze round him to bars of steel & to iron rocks beneath
His feet: indignant self-righteousness like the whirlwinds of the
   north:
Rose up against me thundering from the Brook of Albions River
From Ranelagh & Strumbolo, from Cromwells gardens & Chelsea
The place of wounded Soldiers. (7:71–8:03)

Hand's scorn and pride, then, condense to prison bars, while his self-righteousness, that brother of moral virtue, rises against Los. A second level of diction establishes Hand's denied sexual excitement: His rocks, or stones—testicles—have become iron, while his self-righteousness rises in erectile form. Of particular concern here are the place names, which, as often in Blake, encode part of the passage's specific meaning. Though the difficult diction first seems to say Ranelagh and other places are indignant against Los, their character makes it more likely that they prompt or reflect Hand's self-righteousness, which rises against Los. The brook, of course, is Tyburn's, seen as flowing into the Thames, while the Chelsea Hospital was an old soldiers' home (Damon, *Dictionary* 79). So Blake names by metonymy two results of "indignant self-righteousness," capital punishment and war. The other place names probably identify targets of this same self-righteousness: Ranelagh, Strumbolo (or Strumbolo House), and Cromwell's Gardens were pleasure gardens, the first located in Chelsea itself (Damon, *Dictionary* 95, 341, 389). Blake refers to Ranelagh, with Vauxhall, as a fashionable venue in "An Island in the Moon" (*E* 457), and so was probably familiar with its reputation.

"Pleasure gardens," however, does not convey the full character of these places. Ranelagh, in particular, was famed as a site of that characteristic eighteenth-century night entertainment, the masquerade. While some masquerades were genteel entertainments, others were scenes of sexual, class, and gender rule-bending, offering opportunities for assignations, prostitution, cross-dressing, and sexual license. As Terry Castle, historian of the masquerade, notes, "At the classic eighteenth-century masquerade . . . the roiling, disreputable public assembly—a distinctly ungenteel liberty was the goal: liberty from every social, erotic, and psychological constraint" (*Masquerade* 53). There "[a]ll state and ceremony are laid aside; since the *Peer* and the *Apprentice,* the *Punk* [prostitute] and the *Duchess* are, for so long a time, upon an equal Foot," according to the London *Weekly Journal* in 1724 (qtd. in Castle, *Masquerade* 30).

Besides this general freedom, masquerades provided "a locale for homosexual seduction. . . . [J]ust as heterosexual men and women used the masked ball to make illicit sexual connections, so homosexuals made similar if more discreet use of the occasion" (*Masquerade* 50). The masquerade not only offered such opportunities, both male homosexual and lesbian, but—importantly in assessing Blake's allusions—was famed for doing so. Literature and polemic alike made the homosexual connection; as the author of *Short Remarks Upon the Original and Pernicious Consequences of Masquerades* (1721) put it, "These Sallies of Gallantry, I fear, will soon metamorphose the Kingdom into a *Sodom* for Lewdness" (qtd. in Castle, *Masquerade* 46).[1] Though the masquerade declined in the 1780s and 1790s, and died out in the new century, it was a live institution in Blake's younger years and, as Castle sums up elsewhere, "remained a subject of fascination throughout the century"; "[w]hether or not they attended, the majority of English people knew about the masquerades" ("Culture" 172). If we associate Hand with contemporary moralism, his "indignant self-righteousness" at Ranelagh and the other sites would have been provoked by their encouragement of homosexuality as well as general sexual looseness and crossing of class boundaries.

These sites of moral trespass, and Hand's "iron rocks," are recalled a page later when Hand "Condens'd . . . / . . . his infant thoughts & desires, into cold, dark, cliffs of death" and his "condens'd thoughts . . . / Into the sword of war" (9:1–5). The channeling of repressed intellect and sexuality into war is a general Blakean theme. Here it is inflected by specific connections with infant sexuality: Hand as moralist channels his own past and present fantasies into "cliffs of death." But these fantasies, in adults, have their own locus in social life, sites of license such as the masquerade, whose play-acting and use of visual and vocal disguises, including communication in peeps and squeaks, suggested "collective reversion . . . into an earlier stage" (Castle, *Masquerade* 36). So Hand's sublimating sexuality into death here and his self-righteousness against Ranelagh and Strumbolo a page earlier are connected; Blake is including moralistic hatred of perverse sexuality among the causes of war and oppression and so upending a rhetorical strategy of liberal moralists, who blamed moral laxness on foreign influences and war (chapter 5).[2]

Besides having intrinsic importance, moral constraint in *Jerusalem* is linked with broader social oppression, which it both epitomizes and helps prop up. Like its focus on Moral Virtue, *Jerusalem*'s concern with possession, private property, and their opposite, mutualism, traces back to the opening sequence, when Albion, branding the Jesus who is "mutual in love divine" (4:7) as a "Phantom of the over heated brain," rejects the love "which binds / Man the enemy of man into deceitful friendships" (4:24–26). Affirming the Hobbesian-Lockean idea of a natural-rational "man alone"—isolated from a social community—who knows "by demonstration" (line 28), Albion lays claim to Britain's mountains, hills, and uplands as personal, familial, or national property. The Malvern Hills of the Cotswold region, the Wolds of north-central England, the Cheviot Hills straddling the Scots-English border region, and Welsh Plinlimmon and Snowdon he appropriates as "mine," in a simultaneous evocation of the formation of private property from community ownership and of English conquest of Britain's other peoples. On the twin foundations of this claim and the governance of "Moral Virtue" (line 31), Albion erects the social world of historical oppression and eighteenth- and nineteenth-century British imperialism: "war & princedom & victory!" (line 32). Blake thus links moral-sexual restriction to social issues of private property and imperialism.

Appropriately, then, positive sexual relations also appear both as exempla of a larger social mutuality and as a focus of *Jerusalem* in their own right. Alternatives to Albion's "man alone," posed by implication in his own speech and directly in the Saviour's plea to him that "Thy brethren call thee, and thy fathers, and thy sons, / Thy nurses and thy mothers, thy sisters and thy daughters, / Weep at thy souls disease" (4:11–13), emerge in numerous episodes of mutual assistance throughout the poem. Some are political and social, such as those in which Erin aids Los and his sons and in which the "Friends of Albion," England's cathedral cities, attempt to aid Albion (plates 11, 36/40–39/44). In others, the pleasures of sexuality appear alongside other forms of mutuality, as in a passage in which they are cursed by Hand and his brothers: "No more the sinful delights / Of age and youth and boy and girl and animal and herb, / And river and mountain, and city & village, and house & family. / Beneath the Oak & Palm, beneath the Vine and Fig-tree. / In self-denial!—But War and deadly contention" (18:16–20). ("Self-denial" apparently refers not to restraint but literally to mutuality, the refusal of selfishness.) Finally, positive mutual sexuality is also stressed in its own right. The sustaining value of bodily love, along with the values of community and family, is affirmed specifically and lyrically, as the "Grain of Sand in Lambeth that Satan cannot find / Nor can his Watch Fiends find it . . . / But he who finds it will find Oothoons palace, for within / Opening into Beulah every angle is a lovely heaven / But should the Watch Fiends find it, they would call it Sin" (37/41:15–19).[3]

This issue is important not only intrinsically but because of the common impression that the older Blake rejected material life, sexuality, and the body for things of the soul. This impression, certainly, is supported by some of Blake's own emphatic statements, for example in *A Vision of the Last Judgment:* "I assert for My self that I do not behold the Outward Creation & that to me it is hindrance & not Action it is as the Dirt upon my feet No part of Me" (*E* 565). Yet however important such statements are, in *Jerusalem* Blake's attitude to material nature and its concomitant, sexual life, is more nuanced. Desire to be done with things of the body is balanced by a knowledge of their value in our present existence. For example, Los, in a statement consonant with others on the value of everyday life, argues that "the Religion of Generation which was meant for the destruction / Of Jerusalem, [must] become her covering, till the time of the End" (7:63–64). Here the body and sexuality, or "Generation," serve to protect Jerusalem as apocalypse matures, and the idea of a "covering" or veil of flesh (often negative in Blake) has positive significance. Clearly, the poem encompasses the redemptive possibilities of ordinary sexual love, and Los indeed continues his discussion of the "covering" by calling generation the "Birthplace of the Lamb of God" (line 67)—meaning not simply that the female genitals are Jesus' birthplace but that sexual love as a whole is the birthplace of the human form, Blake's lamb of God. One aspect of sexual love in *Jerusalem*—one room of Oothoon's palace—is women's homosexuality.

Lesbianism, Repression of
Homosexuality, and Vala's Veil

While the implications and consequences of Albion's choice of social and sexual isolation stretch through *Jerusalem* until his recognition of brotherhood in its final pages, alternative possibilities centering on women's love are sketched late in its first chapter, in an episode involving Jerusalem, Vala, Albion, and Albion's sons. The fallout from this episode helps consolidate both Albion's regressive identity and the character structure and symbolic identity of the poem's major negative female entity, Vala.

In this part of the narrative, Albion's sons, "join'd in dark Assembly" (18:5), intone a chant of sexual guilt, atonement, social injustice, and "War and deadly contention" (18:20) that seems both to mirror and to harden Albion's "self-righteousness," helping to close his "Circumference" (19:31, 36). Then:

> . . . Albion fled inward among the currents of his rivers.
>
> He found Jerusalem upon the River of his City soft repos'd
> In the arms of Vala, assimilating in one with Vala
> The Lilly of Havilah: and they sang soft thro' Lambeths vales,
> In a sweet moony night & silence that they had created
> With a blue sky spread over with wings and a mild moon,
> Dividing & uniting into many female forms: Jerusalem
> Trembling! then in one comingling in eternal tears,

Sighing to melt his Giant beauty, on the moony river.

But when they saw Albion fall'n upon mild Lambeths vale:
Astonish'd! Terrified! they hover'd over his Giant limbs. (19:39–20:2)

The events leading up to this scene, and its consequences, make it pivotal. Just before it, following a major text segment focused on Los (pages 6–17), the narrator has turned to a direct account of oppressed existence. Each of the "Four Regions of Human Majesty," we are told, has "an Outside spread Without, & an Outside spread Within / Beyond the Outline of Identity both ways, which meet in One: / An orbed Void of doubt, despair, hunger, & thirst & sorrow" (18:1–4). These "outsides"— separated areas of existence, where "Man [is] the enemy of man" (4:26)—are, then, both social and psychic ("Without" and "Within"). In subsequent lines, still leading toward our scene, Hand and Albion's other sons condemn sexual delight (as already examined above) and invoke Vala as their presiding spirit (18:28–30), and we see Albion-England's landscape blighted as "flocks die beneath his [Albion's] branches / . . . his trumpets, and the sweet sound of his harp / Are silent on his clouded hills, that belch forth storms & fire" (19:2–4).[4] We recognize here the hills of *Milton*'s preface (copies AB) and the fire of its "mills," variously of war industry or the industrial revolution (Erdman, *Prophet* 396; Bronowski 176–77). So the general context for the riverbank scene is social and psychic repression and division.

But the scene on the riverfront is not simply a component part of a divided world. It may also contain part of an explanation of how and why Albion falls. While Albion has *already* fallen, "his Giant beauty and perfection fallen into dust" (19:8), in the lead-up to this passage, the scene also seems to *cause* his swoon (20:1)—the fallen Albion has turned "inward" into his thoughts, where he sees Vala and Jerusalem, but what he sees threatens to "melt his Giant beauty," so that his swoon also appears as a reaction to unbearable sights. Finally, the scene leads to the burgeoning of the world of suffering we inhabit. Its aftermath includes a complex later sequence involving Vala's veil (20–23). That episode, discussed more fully below, generates social misery and moral victimization, meanings the veil retains in several later references. The veil episode, in turn, leads on to Albion's death-throes, which end chapter 1 and chapter 3 and create the prostration and crisis that are shattered only in the poem's final pages. The Vala-Jerusalem scene generates much of *Jerusalem*'s later action.

The scene is remarkable first for its frank depiction of lesbian relations. That they are indeed lesbian is clear both from the description itself and because Albion, in a later reference that seems to include this scene, condemns the delights of Eden as "labours / Of loves: of unnatural consanguinities and friendships / Horrid to think of when enquired deeply into" (28:6–8).[5] Though the scene has sometimes been viewed as "pre-sexual" (Paley, *City* 168), perhaps a majority of interpreters have taken it as actively lesbian, as perhaps also a majority have taken the figures seated on a water lily, in the illustration that begins chapter 2, as female and as referring to this scene.[6]

The scene echoes others, in contemporary literature and in life. Lesbian scenes occurred in several novels, including Richardson's *Pamela,* Fielding's *Shamela,* and Cleland's *Memoirs of a Woman of Pleasure,* which narrates Fanny's initiation in and subsequent withdrawal from "foolery from woman to woman" (34; 10–34 passim; see chapter 2). Real-life instances of women living together were fairly common, and Blake is likely to have had some knowledge of them. He may have had contact with one such couple. Keri Davies notes that Blake's first known collector, Rebekah Bliss, shared a household with a companion, Ann Whitaker, for thirty-five years and was buried with her. There is evidence, though it is not conclusive, that Bliss acquired her Blake works directly from him (220–21, 224, 226). If so, Blake might have known of Bliss's living situation. In any case, other such couples were widely known. Eleanor Butler and Sarah Ponsonby, for example, daughters of Irish gentry, eloped in 1778 to Llangollen in Wales, where they lived as socially prominent if often impoverished landowners for the next fifty years and became celebrated as the "Ladies of Llangollen." Though they slept in the same bed through life and addressed each other in journals as "Beloved," their lives were outwardly proper; in later years they were patronized by everyone from the Prince Regent and Wordsworth (who composed a squib in their honor) to Hester Thrale Piozzi, a coveted friend who privately called them "damned sapphists" with whom women feared staying over unless accompanied by men (Donoghue 150). But in the beginning Butler and Ponsonby had to struggle for acceptance. The issue of their possible lesbianism surfaced in a suggestive newspaper article in 1790 but lapsed when their friend Edmund Burke advised them not to sue. Anna Seward, another friend, struck a blow against the still-current threat of vilification and for women's autonomy, and simultaneously established the Ladies' public image, in "Llangollen Vale, Inscribed to the Right Honorable Lady Eleanor Butler, and Miss Ponsonby," the lead work in her *Llangollen Vale, With Other Poems* (1796). Seward makes the Vale a symbol both of Welsh freedom and of a "friendship" that is superior to masculine traditions of war and romantic love, and impervious to "Bigotry" (86, 102, 132, 158). Seward never specifies the precise nature of the bigotry; Blake's treatment of Vala and Jerusalem, however, makes the directly sexual nature of their encounter all but explicit, and in any case leaves no doubt of Albion's suspicions.[7]

Though fleetingly, Blake presents in the riverfront scene a positive conception of cooperation—and therefore also a positive view, even an idealization, of lesbian relations as mutualistic and embodying possibilities of female autonomy. These points are suggested both by the narration itself and by Jerusalem's later recollections. The narrative presents Jerusalem and Vala's encounter as both adult and mutually responsive. While the participants themselves retrospectively view it as a "virgin" dalliance (20:6), and while both Jerusalem and Vala are apparently virgins, there is no sign in the scene itself that they are immature or that they see the episode as preparation for an initiation into heterosexual love. Indeed, their self-sufficiency and, in particular, Vala's love for Jerusalem provoke Albion's jealous seizure of Vala (20:34–36). There is also no sign in the narration itself of coercion or hierarchy, beyond the fact that Vala appears as the initiator: Jerusalem is "soft repos'd" in Vala's arms, and the expressions describing their actions are plural: "they sang . . . / . . . / Dividing & uniting . . . / . . . in one comingling," etc. (19:42–46). Jerusalem's subsequent recollection implies the same mutuality. She recalls, "[T]hou [Vala] hadst caught me in the bands / Of love; thou refusedst to let me go" (20:31–32). Though several of the poem's characters see this action as an entrapment—including Los's sons, who anticipate the scene by regretting that Jerusalem gives substance "to her [Vala] . . . whose life is but a Shade" (12:1)—Jerusalem herself expresses no regret. Indeed, Jerusalem's language of entrapment here is no more than the ordinary language of love, and in this we mark the depth of Blake's shift from his early use of this language in a poem like "How sweet I roam'd." When that poem's speaker laments that the "prince of love" has "shut me in his golden cage" and "mocks my loss of liberty" (3, 12, 16; *E* 413), we hear genuine regret and the narcissistic desire to enjoy love's fruits without entangling obligation. Here, Jerusalem refers to mutual delights.

Noteworthy in themselves, these aspects of Blake's scene revise its contemporary literary analogues and Blake's own previous treatment of lesbianism in *Visions*. Of note, for example, in Cleland's lesbian episode are the implicit superiority of heterosexuality and the firm but relatively guiltless way in which Fanny, recognizing that superiority, withdraws from the relationship (see Donoghue 202–206; Kopelson 177). Blake changes both elements. In *Jerusalem,* the heterosexual factor in the riverbank encounter is Albion's seizure of Vala, whose consequences, we shall see, are negative; and Jerusalem regrets the relationship with Vala when it has

ended. In *Visions,* we recall, Oothoon experiences a quasi-lesbian encounter with Leutha that strengthens her in preparation for her advance
to an implicitly mature heterosexual union; the sojourn with Leutha, sexual only by implication, is preadult and easily seen as confined to "innocence." *Jerusalem's* scene replicates this encounter in an Edenic tonality,
but with clearly indicated physical expression and as a self-sufficient relation among grown women, supplying the awareness of women's autonomy that some commentators have found lacking in *Visions.*

Aside from its overt lesbianism, for experienced readers of Blake this
scene's positive treatment of Vala is its most striking aspect. Rather
than the vaunting, deceptive, destructive figure of *The Four Zoas, Milton,* and some other passages in *Jerusalem,* she appears benign, even innocent. The knowledgeable reader will immediately find an
explanation, firmly based in interpretive tradition: Vala's seemingly
sympathetic qualities are part of her deceptiveness, signaled in such
phrases as "soft repos'd," "assimilating," and "moony"—Blakean short-
hand for the limited paradise of Beulah, or human sexuality. To Harold
Bloom, for example, the scene has a "sinister beauty"; Bloom believes
Jerusalem's love for Vala, a siren of material nature, is "a disaster, a mistaken mingling of man's freedom [symbolically, Jerusalem] with his
bondage" (*Apocalypse* 429–30). Nevertheless, we shall see, the seemingly naïve response is right. Blake's treatment of Vala—complex, far-
reaching, and deeply radical—suggests a potentially and initially
benign role for nature and the flesh, and thus sexuality and lesbianism
in particular. Further, far from treating Jerusalem and Vala's love as a
source of bondage, Blake inverts the republican tradition's link between homosexuality and social corruption by making *guilt* over homosexuality a wellspring of war and oppression.

These issues are best approached via Vala's "veil" imagery. Consistently with Vala's generally benign initial role, her veil also initially appears in a positive light, and again this appearance is not deceptive.[8] We
first see the veil through Jerusalem's eyes as she looks back on the love af-
fair, in a statement partly quoted above: It is a "beautiful net of gold and
silver twine; / Thou [Vala] hadst woven it with art, thou hadst caught me
in the bands / Of love; thou refusedst to let me go" (20:30–32). The veil
here is closely similar to the "covering" that the religion of generation
provides for Jerusalem, even though the latter is, by implication, heterosexual. Jerusalem recalls the veil as protective and as a sign of shared love:
"The Veil shone with thy brightness in the eyes of Albion, / Because it
inclosd pity & love; because we lov'd one-another!" (20:34–35). This
meaning of the veil is consistent with Blake's positive revaluation of the
body, discussed earlier. If, indeed, the human covering of flesh may have

positive significance in *Jerusalem,* so also, specifically, may Vala, or nature, have an originally positive meaning. This meaning is seen directly in the leadup to the riverbank scene, when the narrator specifies that in the process of generation "Vala produc'd the Bodies. Jerusalem gave the Souls" (18:7). From the dualistic standpoint (often assumed to be Blake's own) that strictly counterposes body and soul, or Vala and Jerusalem, providing the bodies must seem a negative activity. But if indeed body and sexuality are necessary "till the time of the End" (7:64), then Vala's and Jerusalem's must also be a necessary collaboration.[9] The implication, in turn, is that Albion should accept, even welcome, this collaboration, as specifically manifested in the riverfront scene. Hence, the guilt, condemnation, and regret of nearly all participants after this scene are a triumph of repressive moralism, exclusive possession, and hierarchy in sexual and social relations—the evils repeatedly associated with Albion's errors—over the mutuality and equality that Albion's joining Vala and Jerusalem's idyll might have embodied.

For the riverbank idyll does not last; it is disrupted by Jerusalem and Vala's sight of "Albion fall'n upon mild Lambeths vale: / Astonish'd! Terrified! they hover'd over his Giant limbs" (20:1–2). Both women internalize responsibility for Albion's faint; they treat his horror at their lesbian relation as signifying their own guilt, though only Vala fully accepts this guilt. In doing so, they make Albion's needs primary over their own. This response leads on to a short segment in which Jerusalem recalls, as a prior event, Albion's violation of Vala:

> Albion rent thy beautiful net of gold and silver twine;
> Thou hadst woven it with art, thou hadst caught me in the bands
> Of love; thou refusedst to let me go: Albion beheld thy beauty
> Beautiful thro' our Love's comeliness, beautiful thro' pity.
> The Veil shone with thy brightness in the eyes of Albion,
> Because it inclosd pity & love; because we lov'd one-another!
> Albion lov'd thee! he rent thy Veil! (20:30–36)

It is possible that this seizure indeed occurred in the past, and therefore that the Vala-Jerusalem relation too occurred in the past; Vala and Jerusalem, prompted by Albion's swoon, feel retrospective guilt. Alternatively, Albion's rending the veil may be a version of his swoon; Albion in one aspect loses consciousness on seeing the lesbian tryst, and in another becomes a sexual aggressor interrupting it. In either case, Jerusalem and Vala's responses merge into a third stage of internalizing Albion's own reactions, as Jerusalem transfers to the situation following the seizure the love she previously seemed to feel with Vala:

> thou forgavest his furious love:
> I redounded from Albions bosom in my virgin loveliness.
> The Lamb of God reciev'd me in his arms he smil'd upon us:
> He made me his Bride & Wife: he gave thee to Albion.
> Then was a time of love: O why is it passed away! (20:37–41)[10]

Despite their common assumption of responsibility for Albion's swoon, Jerusalem and Vala respond quite differently at the moment it occurs, as well as after. Vala's responses are expressed through a change in the veil imagery, and, perhaps, in the veil's own nature. Jerusalem, we shall see, rejects guilt, yet she feels its impact—emanating from Vala—as she speaks "weeping in pleadings of Love, in the web of despair," which Vala is simultaneously creating as a "veil of tears," a pun on the traditional term for our mortal life (20:3–4). Vala, then, is reconstituting the veil as one of tears and despair.[11] She shuns Jerusalem, shutting her "into the winter of human life," which appears a few lines later as a winter of economic exploitation (20:5, 12–20). Central to Vala's action is her conviction of her own guilt, as well as Jerusalem's: "Thou art my sister and my daughter! thy shame is mine also!" (20:19). Later, she finds her guilt mirrored—or replicated—in Albion's reproaches: "Where shall I hide from thy dread countenance & searching eyes / I have looked into the secret Soul of him I loved / And in the dark recesses found Sin & can never return" (22:13–15).[12] Blake centers this guilt not in Jerusalem but in Vala.

As with the homosexual encounter itself, Vala's response to Albion's violation varies a similar episode in *Visions*. There, Oothoon begins by accepting that Bromion's rape has "defiled" her bosom (2:15) but ends by moving from a sense of rejection to her own rejection of the Urizenic universe. This outcome belongs to *Visions'* relatively optimistic world, shaped by the voices of Wollstonecraft, Helen Maria Williams, and other radical women writers of the 1790s. However, it is also possible that oppression, even violation, may produce positive identification with the oppressor and his values. This conception, perhaps, helps explain why Oothoon appears in negative as well as positive roles in *Milton,* notably as Leutha's "charming guard" in the consolidation of English political and sexual repression (13:44; chapter 4). In *Jerusalem,* Albion's seizure of Vala—which may be seen as rape or, more radically, simply as male-dominated marriage—leads to a similar result, a deformation of the victim's personality in which she internalizes Albion's values and redirects his sexual aggression outward. Simultaneously, Blake varies the popular brothel-scene genre I have referred to before, in which the harlot is an amiable, if hardened, sapphist. Understanding the profound self-abhorrence that a realization of homosexuality may cause in members of a sex-denying society, Blake has Vala incorporate this disgust into her emerging role as deceiver and harlot.

The veil embodies these complex responses to the lesbian scene, to Albion's swoon, and to his rape-embrace. In part, Vala responds through self-concealment: "Vala replied . . . hiding in her veil" (20:11). Simultaneously, she displaces her guilt, making Jerusalem's imputed shame the source of her own and implying that the sin she sees in Albion's eyes may be his own. These reactions belong to a psychic complex that Blake understands profoundly: Guilt is internalized only to be denied and projected externally as oppression and war. Logically, then, the veil also appears as one of social oppression:

> When winter rends the hungry family and the snow falls:
> Upon the ways of men hiding the paths of man and beast,
> Then mourns the wanderer: then he repents his wanderings & eyes
> The distant forest; then the slave groans in the dungeon of stone.
> The captive in the mill of the stranger, sold for scanty hire.
> (20:12–16)

The verbs in this social vision—"rends," "hiding," "mourns," "repents," and "groans"—replicate the terms that describe Albion's violation, Vala's response, and the veil itself: "rent," "tears," "shame," "hiding," "despair" (20:36, 3, 19, 11, 4). This social world *is* the world of Vala's internalized but displaced sexual guilt. Vala's role as a religious-psychic "veil" for these evils is well established in other Blake works; *Jerusalem* probes the origins of this psychic function in sexual guilt and denial, and especially denial of homosexuality. The disruption of the primal scene of lesbian harmony is a direct source of these evils, so far as Vala's guilt actuates them; through metonymy, it stands for the loss of other harmonies of brotherhood—social, sexual, psychic, and religious—whose fracture also leads to these social evils.

The veil's nature and meaning now consolidate in the form Vala has given them. In a subsequent episode, Albion mourns, "All is Eternal Death unless you [Vala and Jerusalem] can weave a chaste / Body over an unchaste mind!" and sew up "the deep wound of Sin," the vagina (21:11–13). That is, he tries to recreate the maidenhead as a woven and sewn covering or veil. This, of course, cannot be done, except in psychic denial, and so the resulting veil is one of deception and outward projection of the sense of sin. Albion further accuses Vala of *not* weaving the veil of "Natural Virtue" needed to protect his daughters from Luvah (21:11–16; quotation at 15). Luvah, here, has many meanings, including

the emotions in general (Damon, *Dictionary* 255) and his specific political identity as France (see 66:15 and elsewhere)—i.e., the lure of revolutionary ideas, seen as destructive of male-female hierarchies among others.
Finally, Albion himself tears away the intact veil, now become the "Veil of
Moral Virtue, woven for Cruel Laws," and casts it "into the Atlantic
Deep, to catch the Souls of the Dead" (23:22–23). The dead, as elaborated elsewhere in the poem, include oppressors in Britain and imperialist armies rampaging across Europe (e.g., 47:9–10, 63:30–34, 73:46–48),
but also those who suffer under the "Polypus" (a developed form of the
veil) with its "Laws of Sacrifice for Sin" (49:24–25). Albion's act brings his
fall, and chapter 1, to a climax. As he sinks in living death and the world
of guilt, tyranny, and war coheres, "Thundering the Veil rushes from his
hand Vegetating Knot by / Knot, Day by Day, Night by Night; loud roll
the indignant Atlantic / Waves . . . turning up the bottoms of the Deeps"
(24:61–63). What seems to be a narrative contradiction—the veil is rent
at one point (20:36), stripped off whole at another—actually makes deep
sense. Albion's rending the original veil, a female curtain, emblematic of
the maidenhead, which was the sign of Vala and Jerusalem's love, *creates*
the veil of moral virtue. The latter is a veil of denial of mutual sexuality
generally, and lesbianism specifically, which then serves to "catch the
Souls of the Dead," as the net of religion and war.

The implications of the veil's transmutation are profound. If its sinister development is a direct manifestation of Vala's sexual guilt over the
riverfront scene, a guilt that makes her accept her seizure by Albion
(20:32–37), then she *becomes* the Vala familiar to us elsewhere in
Blake—a deeply deceptive sexual mystifier of war and delusive religion—by acceptance of coercive male love, Albion's "furious love"
(20:37), and by denial of her own homosexual aspect. Here, as in *Milton's* Leutha episode, Blake implies that repression of homosexuality is
one of the psychic constituents of social repression and war. This would
be a remarkable conception in any time and place, and is particularly remarkable amid the deep hatred of homosexuality in Blake's England.

Jerusalem's response to Vala, in contrast, rejects sexual guilt, implies
an acceptance of lesbian relations, and speaks for a politics of general toleration. Jerusalem is treated as a complex character, not just a doctrinal
mouthpiece for Blake. Her words convey her struggle with her own guilt
and her longing for the past, and they betray considerable retrospective
confusion. Jerusalem recalls her love of Vala as virginal and nonsexual,
partly displaces its happiness onto the period when Albion has already
seized Vala and offered Jerusalem as the Lamb's bride (20:39–40), and
idealizes both as "a time of love: O why is it passed away!" (20:41). Overall, however, she speaks against imputing unforgivable guilt to lesbian

acts. She recalls her and Vala's love as mutual (20:35, quoted above), comely (20:33), and experienced in "sweet regions of youth and virgin innocence / . . . / Where we delight in innocence before the face of the Lamb" (20:6–9). Though intellectually Jerusalem accepts Vala's new-found ideal of antisexual purity, she cannot attain it: She "cannot put off the human form" (20:29). And she rejects the self-righteousness of moral judgment and its connections to war and injustice:

> O Vala what is Sin? that thou shudderest and weepest
> At sight of thy once lov'd Jerusalem! What is Sin but a little
> Error & fault that is soon forgiven; but mercy is not a Sin
> Nor pity nor love nor kind forgiveness! O! if I have Sinned
> Forgive & pity me! O! unfold thy veil in mercy & love!
> Slay not my little ones, beloved Virgin daughter of Babylon
> Slay not my infant loves & graces, beautiful daughter of Moab
> I cannot put off the human form I strive but strive in vain
>   (20:22–29)

> Why should Punishment Weave the Veil with Iron Wheels of War
> When Forgiveness might it Weave with Wings of Cherubim
>   (22:34–35)

These words are consonant with a larger concept of forgiveness and mutual love stated elsewhere by the poem's authorial voice and by other characters, such as Erin.

Jerusalem does not challenge the idea of sin directly, but terms it a minor "fault" and calls for forgiveness. This aspect of Blake's treatment merits discussion in my conclusion, but can be specifically related to the dramatic situation in these episodes. Both speeches cited here are aimed at winning over other characters—in the first Jerusalem addresses Vala, in the second Albion, with reference to Vala's veil. Jerusalem is not stating abstract doctrine but appealing for a change in public and private actions: for reconstituting the veil in its remembered original form as a covering of kindness. She makes her appeal in terms recognizable to her audience, that is, as a plea for a crucial first step in toleration rather than a total change in ideas and behavior. Moreover, Jerusalem's speech to Albion occurs when he has called on Vala to slay him for *his* sins (22:29–30); Jerusalem is calling on the British people to forgive *their own* errors and live. Most immediately, the sin in question is Albion's murder of Luvah—France, in one aspect of Blake's symbolism—and the page leading up to this episode includes Albion's self-condemnation for England's war policy: "I hear my Childrens voices / I see their piteous faces gleam out upon the cruel winds / . . . / I see them die beneath the whips of the Captains!" (21:37–42). Less directly, Albion has rural poverty, Hand's condemnation of the delights of sexuality, and much else to answer for—the whole landscape of suffering and struggle that opened out in the decade 1810–20. Both Albion and Jerusalem, then, are speaking of social ethics, not personal morality alone. So Jerusalem is calling for a shift in social life toward broad tolerance, a change whose importance should be clear in the context of the events sketched in my previous chapter, and one that must occur for Albion/Britain to liberate himself.

Albion's condemnations of homosexuality, finally, reverberate through his own self-accusations and his dedication to self-punishment and the torture of others. These condemnations take Jerusalem as the embodiment of female sexuality in general, and woman-woman love in particular: Albion looks "into thy [Jerusalem's] bosom: / I discover thy secret places," and blasts her for an "unlawful pleasure" that is also his own "phantasy" (21:18–19; 23:2). And as the last comment suggests, Albion also dimly recollects his own pleasure in male-male nakedness. He remembers a time when he and others, implicitly male (they have "Giant limbs"), raised "mighty Stones" and "danced naked around them: / Thinking to bring Love into light of day, to Jerusalems shame: / Displaying our Giant limbs to all the winds of heaven!" until "Sudden shame siezd us, we could not look on one-another for abhorrence" (24:4–7). The dance is one of male sexual display and comradeship. Though Albion recalls its eroticism as a rejection (shaming) of woman, Jerusalem's imagined shaming may be a projection of Albion's and his cohorts' own recoil at their actions. Both female and male homosexuality, then, are among the imputed sins for which Albion feels he must turn from love and mercy.

Amid these evocations of sexual and homosexual guilt, Albion's retrospective attack on "unnatural consanguinities and friendships," at the start of the poem's second chapter (28:7), ties the specifically homosexual content of the scene to *Jerusalem's* largest concern, the opposition of dominance and property to mutualism in all fields of life. As S. Foster Damon notes, the condemnation comes from the power-mad Albion who has set himself up as "punisher & judge" (line 4; see *Dictionary* 376). Indeed, Albion speaks as he sits "by Tyburns brook," and, when he finishes, "underneath his heel, shot up! / A deadly Tree, he nam'd it Moral Virtue, and the Law / Of God" (28:14–16). The speech's content, setting, and outcome emphasize the connections among antihomosexuality, the entirety of moral law, and the ritual sacrifice of moral victims.[13]

In its sexual reference, the speech harks back to Albion's swoon on beholding Vala and Jerusalem in one another's arms. That faint reflected

Albion's own perception of the scene, which we saw from his perspective. In Albion's perception, Vala and Jerusalem's love was directed against him, and its potential to create a multitude of "female forms" (19:45) independent of men also threatened to "melt his Giant beauty" (19:47), that is, to undermine his own form and definition—in one meaning, to soften his erection. But in fact, Albion's own faint was equivalent to his beauty melting; his sight of the tryst weakened his own psychic solidity. In this latter aspect—in yet another backward glance at *Visions*—Albion's faint contrasts with Oothoon's imagined delight in watching Theotormon copulate (*VDA* 7:25–26; chapter 2); unlike Oothoon, Albion is unable to take pleasure in another's love. The parallel, and Blake's general presentation of Albion's "self-righteousness" (19:31), imply that males, as well as females, should be free of sexual possessiveness, able to take unselfish vicarious pleasure in the sexual bliss of others, and that males—so far as Albion is meant as an archetypal male psyche—are wrong to be incapable of doing so. That Blake has previously presented similar points as a criticism of women's jealousy makes his application of the idea to male sexual possessiveness in the context of tolerating lesbianism noteworthy.

But while "unnatural . . . friendships" must refer back to the lesbian scene, Albion's speech has a far broader application. In effect, it returns to and adds to the opening scene of the entire poem, as Albion pronounces judgment on Eden's "ornament[s] of perfection" and "labour[s] of love" (28:1):

> And Albion spoke from his secret seat and said
>
> All these ornaments are crimes, they are made by the labours
> Of loves: of unnatural consanguinities and friendships
> Horrid to think of when enquired deeply into; and all
> These hills & valleys are accursed witnesses of Sin
> I therefore condense them into solid rocks, stedfast!
> A foundation and certainty and demonstrative truth:
> That Man be separate from Man, & here I plant my seat. (28:5–12)

Albion's speech—from a stance of condemnation that recalls Hand's and echoes contemporary moralism—identifies the lesbian relations of the riverbank scene with Eden's "ornament[s] of perfection" (line 1), places them among the "crimes" of mutuality, or "labours / Of loves" (lines 6–7), and returns to the poem's opening in affirming "Man's" separation from "Man." With Albion's swoon (20:1), his seizure of Vala (20:36–37), and now his moral condemnation of all the works of Eden, the intermeshing pattern that joins lesbianism to Eden's loves and the horror of homosexuality to the destruction of brotherhood and the creation of private property and war is complete.

Blake's mythic setting has obscured the multiform, partly contemporary reference of the riverbank scene. Several interpreters have seen the scene as a "primordial" sexual encounter occurring "in illo tempore" and leading to the creation of our "fallen" world (Paley, *City* 167–72). But though it may partly refer to them, there are several reasons not to restrict the scene's scope to an account of mythic beginnings. First, as I have argued elsewhere, Blake's evocations of Eden and the "fall" generally do not refer to objectively "real" past time within his narratives, but are explanations of current reality that also project unrealized possibilities of mutuality backwards onto a mythic past.[14] More specifically and, in this case, more importantly, the riverfront tableau refers to contemporary scenes as well. The narrator's statement that Albion "fled inward among the currents of his rivers. / He found Jerusalem upon the River of his City" (19:39–40) must mean that he fled into his own brain and body, so that in one aspect the scene is an enactment of the homosexual potentialities—and horror at them, as the swoon makes clear—existing in Albion's (every person's) inner being. In addition, Albion's city is London, and its river the Thames, so that Albion is also observing in imagination real scenes of lesbian activity in Blake's contemporary London. Hence, the shock, guilt, and appeals to forgiveness that follow are parts simultaneously of (1) a remembered or imagined primal "fall"; (2) a psychic reaction to homosexuality "inward," in everyone's brain generally; and (3) the present-day life of England. So also the implied loves of Eden must exist on these three planes.

Reconsidering Gender: Shiloh, Hermaphrodism, and "Emanations"

So radical a reconception of eighteenth-century ideas about homosexuality must imply some shift in conceptions of sexuality in general. In *Jerusalem*, this revision takes place partly through introducing a masculine "emanation," Shiloh, and partly through a meditation on the idea of "emanations" in general, late in the poem; to understand the latter fully, we will have to look briefly at Blake's conception of hermaphrodism as well.

"Emanations" first appear in Blake's work in *The Four Zoas*, as a way of conceptualizing portions of Blake's "giant forms" that appear separately from his male primary characters when the sexes emerge. They are generally female, correspond to female characters already sheared off or extruded by male entities in Blake's earlier work, such as Enitharmon

and Ahania, and come to represent human attributes and aspects of reality that Blake treats as primarily female, such as emotivity, material nature, etc. Elynittria, for example, in my discussions of the "arrows of
Elynittria" in earlier chapters, could be considered Palamabron's emanation, though I have avoided the term because Blake does not use it of her.

The idea of "emanations" evolves gradually. In *Europe,* for example,
Blake presents Enitharmon simply as Los's consort; her daughters,
Leutha, Elynittria, Oothoon, and others, are likewise paired with male
characters without any implication that they emerged from or separated
from them. Most, even when they return in later works, are never called
emanations. Nevertheless, Damon applies the term to almost all of them,
including, egregiously, Oothoon, who possesses her own autonomous
history in *Visions* prior to meeting Theotormon; most commentators
have followed Damon's nomenclature. (See Damon's *Dictionary* articles
on the individual daughters.) The concept of female extrusion, though
not the term "emanation," appears in *Urizen* and *Ahania,* in accounts of
Enitharmon's emergence from Los and of Ahania as Urizen's "parted
soul" (*U* 18–19; *Ah* 2:32). The origins of this treatment seem rather
clear. In *Europe,* Blake essentially treats male and female as coeval (as in
Genesis 1, though he is not concerned with creation per se). In *Urizen,*
where he is inverting the biblical creation story, he seizes on the canoni-
cally favored story of woman's extraction from man in Genesis 2, seeking to show this aspect of biblical creation, like others, as an evil
stemming ultimately from Urizen's "assum'd power" (2:1).[15] Nevertheless, despite this initially polemical context, the idea of emanations—the
term itself is introduced in *The Four Zoas* 4:2—becomes an ongoing part
of Blake's conceptions, applied to a wide range of characters. In *The Four
Zoas, Milton,* and *Jerusalem,* Jerusalem is Albion's "emanation" and
Enitharmon implicitly Los's; and in *Jerusalem,* Albion's twelve daughters
are "the beautiful Emanations" of his sons (5:45).

The idea of "emanations" as used in these works, including most of
Jerusalem, has two implications germane to the present discussion. First,
as often noted, it reinforces conventional sexual hierarchies by assigning
assumedly "higher" qualities, such as spirit as opposed to nature, to the
male-gendered entities; indeed, the term "emanation" itself assumes the
priority and primacy of the non-"emanative" male forms. This notion of
hierarchic and derived "female" qualities is only partly compatible with
several aspects of *Jerusalem's* action: the initiatory, prophetic, and explanatory roles played by some female entities, such as Erin (Ireland);
Jerusalem's embodiment of the poem's most basic values, mutuality and
forgiveness, to which Los's prophetic role—here, as opposed to the presentation in *Milton*—is adjunct; the poem's criticism of possessive male

sexuality as seen in Albion's seizure of Vala, and of possession and competition in general; and, perhaps most basically, *Jerusalem*'s new emphasis on the salvific qualities of sexual and domestic life and child-nurturing, traditionally gendered as female realms. Second, the idea of male primary entities and female "emanations" implies the primacy and normative character of heterosexuality—not necessarily in the characters' imagined and possible Edens, but certainly in the present—and so is incompatible with the poem's depiction of lesbian relations as a possible alternative to possessive heterosexuality.

Blake varies his scheme in *Jerusalem* by introducing "Shiloh the Masculine Emanation among the Flowers of Beulah / [Who] dwells over France, as Jerusalem dwells over Albion" (49:47–48). Shiloh has appeared twice before, in *The Four Zoas,* where he is Albion's counterpart and, in context, seems to be France, "ruin[ed]" as Albion is oppressed (21:9–10; 21 [19]:5). His identity as an "emanation"—the only masculine emanation named specifically—and his status as Jerusalem's coequal are new in *Jerusalem.* He has been seen as "peace," as French liberty, and, by Warren Stevenson, as France's toleration of homosexuality, decriminalized in the 1791 penal code and the 1810 *Code Napoléon* (42; see Crompton, *Byron* 17, 37). Shiloh was a redemptive, messianic symbol in much biblically based literature of Blake's time, and his appearance as an embodiment of gender fluidity and homosexuality would be highly significant.[16] Stevenson's point, though not elaborated, is supported by references to sexualized torture in some passages dealing with Shiloh and by his appearance in others that focus on sexual love.

Shiloh is first mentioned in *Jerusalem* in Erin's speech at the close of chapter 2 (48:54–50:17), a speech whose length (105 lines) and position suggest its central importance in the poem. Erin focuses on the depredations of the "Giants" or "Sons" of Albion and of the "Polypus of Death." She tries to reconcile forgiveness for individuals, and even sinning nations (France), with the necessity to "Remove from Albion, far remove these terrible surfaces" (49:60; repeated, 49:76)—the sons and the Polypus, or, in general terms, oppressive rulers and institutions, and moral-sexual guilt. And she foretells that Albion's children will one day "arise . . . / . . . into Jerusalems Courts & into Shiloh" (49:45–46). The crimes Erin decries are committed against Albion's "Children" or "little-ones" (48:58, 49:11), and generally represent those of poverty, prostitution, and war. But Erin modulates into more specific references:

> Jerusalem is cast forth from Albion.
> They [the Giants] deny that they ever knew Jerusalem, or ever dwelt
>   in Shiloh

The Gigantic roots & twigs of the vegetating Sons of Albion
Filld with little-ones are consumed in the Fires of their Altars
(49:8–11)

O Polypus of Death O Spectre over Europe & Asia
Withering the Human Form by Laws of Sacrifice for Sin
By Laws of Chastity & Abhorrence
. . . .
        [striving] in Natural Selfish Chastity to banish Pity
And dear Mutual Forgiveness; & to become One Great Satan
Inslavd to the most powerful Selfhood: to murder the Divine Hu-
manity (49:24–30)

The Polypus, in the second passage, is a transformation of the "Veil of
Moral Virtue, woven for Cruel Laws," that Albion cast into the Atlantic "to catch the Souls of the Dead" (23:22–23, discussed above). As
a compound organism, the Polypus may be an imaginative version of
the netlike veil with its catch of souls, and its laws of chastity and sacrifice for sin, its repudiation of forgiveness, are the same as those of Albion's veil, constituted, we remember, from Vala's assumption of sin
after the riverbank scene. These correspondences, besides embodying
general themes, tie the Polypus to the veil, the riverbank scene, and the
repudiation of homosexuality. In this context we should notice that the
giants/sons of the first passage, burning the little-ones in root and twig
cages—a version of the wicker man of Scandinavia, referred to several
times in *Milton* and *Jerusalem*[17]—deny that they "ever dwelt in
Shiloh." Shiloh's associations with France suggest a denial of fraternity,
and the passage can easily be seen to reject the war's fratricide. But
Shiloh's identity as "Masculine Emanation among the Flowers of Beulah" suggests a further sexual meaning. Emanations, we know, are sexual counterparts of male mythic entities; here the emanation is
masculine and found among flowers (traditionally gendered feminine).
In this context, just as for the giants/sons to "know Jerusalem" would
mean to know a world of bodily desire and mutuality characterized by
love of women, so to "dwell in Shiloh" would mean to experience such
a world that includes the love of men. Roughly, then, for the
giants/sons to deny that they ever "dwelt in" such a world means they
deny ever potentially or actually knowing its pleasures. The burning of
the "little-ones" by these self-blinded beings would then suggest victimization of women or, especially, male homosexuals for sexual
crimes. The parallel between the burning of the little-ones by the giants opposed to Jerusalem and Shiloh and the murder of divine humanity by laws of chastity and sacrifice for sin supports this inference

as well, and we recall that the divine humanity, in a boy of sixteen, was figuratively burnt in a wicker cage for such a crime (see chapter 5). Shiloh as male homosexuality, furthermore, has a parallel in Jerusalem's homosexual sojourn with Vala, and the joint opprobrium visited on sexually transgressing women and homosexual men seems to match the parallel redemption by which the murdered and exiled children "shall arise from Self, / By Self Annihilation into Jerusalems Courts & into Shiloh" (49:45–46).

Later in *Jerusalem* Shiloh appears twice in contexts that can have to do only with sexuality. Los, trying to persuade Enitharmon that the world of the sexes must vanish with human regeneration, mentions him as part of that world, among the "Emanative Visions of Canaan in Jerusalem & in Shiloh" (92:21). As "Canaan" essentially refers to the world of "generation," the point of the reference seems to be that the "emanative visions" of that world include female and male aspects; Blake is emphasizing the parity of female and male "emanations," and perhaps including homosexual visions as part of the generative world. And in an earlier complementary passage on the need for the body and sexual love in preredemptive life, the narrator avows:

> Nor can any consummate bliss without being Generated
> On Earth; of those whose Emanations weave the loves
> Of Beulah for Jerusalem & Shiloh, in immortal Golgonooza
>   (86:42–44)

Here Shiloh, with Jerusalem, receives the loves of Beulah—those of sexual fulfillment—from unnamed emanations in the daily life on earth that sustains us in our own time. It is not likely that in each of these passages Blake goes out of his way to specify France as well as Britain. But in a poem concerned with sexual accusation and guilt, which turns partly on an incident of lesbian love and its fallout of self-laceration and blame, homosexual love fits very well as at least one component of Shiloh's identity. In the second passage specifically, the difficult syntax might mean that the emanations provide (weave) Beulah's loves for (toward or to be experienced by) female and male entities; in this case the speech could refer to heterosexual loves, though it would not have to be limited to them. Or, the "loves / Of Beulah for Jerusalem" could be a term for heterosexual loves in general, and those for "Shiloh" could signify homosexual loves. Shiloh then is certainly "peace" in all senses, and France in several topical passages, and the condemnation of cruelty associated with his name involves war and other ways of slaying "Divine Humanity," but his identity as "Masculine Emanation" and therefore homosexual love is central.

Though partly signifying homosexuality, Shiloh is also an expression of the greater fluidity Blake introduces into his gender scheme by revising the idea of "emanations." This revision makes use of another idea that we must briefly examine to understand it adequately, that of hermaphrodism. This might seem a key term in any discussion of Blake and homosexuality, especially given its importance in contemporary ideas of lesbianism and Blake's use of lesbian images in *The Four Zoas* that recall contemporary medical and popular discussion of "double-sexed" females (chapter 3). Blake's references to hermaphrodism, in which "Double-sexed," "Female-male," "Male-female," and similar terms are prominent (e.g., *M* 19:32–33), obviously draw on this theoretical and popular vocabulary. But in fact Blake does not use the ideas of hermaphrodism or double sexes to refer to homosexuality. Blake introduces the terms "hermaphrodite" and "hermaphroditic" in late works, starting in *The Four Zoas,* Night 8.[18] Textual references lead an independent life from the visual suggestions of "hermaphrodism" (which are not continued in *Milton* or *Jerusalem*); the terms do not appear, for example, on pages whose illustrations show possible lesbian or male homosexual activity. Nor are these terms—almost always used in a negative way—ever used textually to refer to actual homosexual relations; they are not applied, for instance, to the Satan-Palamabron plot in *Milton* or to the Vala-Jerusalem scene in *Jerusalem.* The terms do not at first signify a sexual conception (in the ordinary sense) for Blake at all, but a political and social idea. Hermaphrodism is initially the meshing of disparate entities in war, and then the link between war and religion. Each of the latter, for Blake, is based on suppressed or distorted sexuality; they become "hermaphroditic" because, gendered male and female in Blake's symbolism, they are fused in one system as Rahab Babylon. From this starting point the term expands in *Milton* and *Jerusalem* to denote cultural-historical stages while continuing to refer to the war-religion complex, and finally evolves to embrace sexuality in the narrow sense. In these last uses, Blake employs the idea in a complex inversion of its ordinary connotation to signify our usual, single sexual identities, within which the "opposite" gender or sexual characteristics remain present, but suppressed.

In Blake's first uses, Urizen's battle, waged by mingled human and bestial forms, is a "Shadowy hermaphrodite black & opake," which also harbors the yet-unformed Satan and for this reason, too, is "Hermaphroditic . . . hiding the Male / Within as in a Tabernacle Abominable Deadly." The "Hermaphroditic" war subsequently extrudes Satan, "A male without a female counterpart . . . / Yet hiding the shadowy female Vala as in an ark & Curtains" (*FZ* 101:34–37, *E* 374; 104:20, 23, 25–27, *E* 377). The battle and Satan seem to develop successively, and they are hermaphroditic in that they lack sexual partners ("without a female counterpart") yet conceal opposite-sexed entities within themselves—Satan within bestial battle, Vala within Satan. They are hermaphroditic, then, in a specialized usage of the term's ordinary sense, and yet Blake's use clearly does not refer to ordinary physical hermaphrodism or homosexuality.

Subsequently something like the development just seen is recounted in cultural-historical terms as the sequence of twenty-seven "churches" from Adam to Luther in *Milton* and *Jerusalem,* of which the first nine are "Giants mighty, Hermaphroditic," the next eleven "the Female males: / A Male within a Female hid as in an Ark & Curtains," and the last seven "Male Females: the Dragon Forms / The Female hid within a Male: thus Rahab is reveald / Mystery Babylon the Great: the Abomination of Desolation / Religion hid in War" (*J* 75:12, 14–15, 17–20; see the comparable description on *M* 37). Jean H. Hagstrum glosses the last two stages well as "sexualized religion" and "the sexualized state" ("Babylon" 114), though the last would best be understood as a fusion of idolatry and empire, as "Rahab" and "Babylon" suggest.[19] The same conception of hermaphrodism appears in a passage from *Milton* examined in the last chapter, describing Rahab Babylon as "A Female hidden in a Male, Religion hidden in War / Namd Moral Virtue; cruel two-fold Monster shining bright" (40:20–21), though the term "hermaphroditic" itself is not used there.

Hermaphrodism develops other senses related to these. Milton, for example, descends to our plane and enters "his own Shadow; / A mournful form double; hermaphroditic: male & female / In one wonderful body . . . / . . . the dread shadow, twenty-seven-fold / Reachd to the depths of direst Hell, & thence to Albions land" (*M* 14:36–40). As we trace Milton's "shadow" through the poem, we realize it is not his mortal form, as might first appear, but the form of his errors, extending through history (the twenty-seven folds) and equivalent to "the Covering Cherub & within him Satan / And Raha[b]," which itself contains the twenty-seven churches (37:8–9). The Covering Cherub's functions include both sustaining idolatrous warfare and creating and enforcing humanity's sexual division. In a later elaboration, "A Double Female . . . / Religion hid in War," appears within its stomach and, as humans "become One with the Antichrist [an aspect of the Covering Cherub] & are absorbd in him," they take form as distinct sexes, "The Feminine separat[ing] from the Masculine" (*J* 89:52–53, 89:62–90:1, discussed below). We should be cautious, then, about concluding that "for Blake the hermaphrodite symbolizes a condition of mutual oppression between the sexes," as W. J. T. Mitchell remarks with regard to Milton's hermaphroditic form ("Style" 63); Mitchell's point is correct only when "hermaphrodite" is redefined into almost the opposite of its usual meaning. Not only does Blake's hermaphrodite have nothing to do with hermaphrodism as ordinarily understood, but sexual difference is one of its creations.[20]

This last sense of hermaphrodism as a state of sexual differentiation, not amalgamation, becomes part of Blake's reconsideration of the idea of "emanations," found in a complex scene near the end of *Jerusalem* that combines a continuation of the Los-Enitharmon narrative with doctrinal statements. In it Los tries to resolve the issues of sexual difference that have been central in the poem. The scene follows Los's decision not to oppose the earthly power of Cambel and Gwendolen (Hand and Hyle's counterparts) but to labor in preparation for a future apocalyptic upheaval (83–85); it comes after Los's watch-song of praise to Jerusalem (85–86) and is part of the movement leading up to the solidification of Antichrist, Los's final confrontation with his Spectre, and the waking of Brittannia and then Albion (89, 90–91, 94–95). Hence Los speaks at a moment of major tension in the poem, during which he is incongruously enmeshed in a struggle to dominate Enitharmon:

> Los answerd sighing like the Bellows of his Furnaces
>
> I care not! the swing of my Hammer shall measure the starry
>   round[.]
> When in Eternity Man converses with Man they enter
> Into each others Bosom (which are Universes of delight)
> In mutual interchange. and first their Emanations meet
> Surrounded by their Children. if they embrace & comingle
> The Human Four-fold Forms mingle also in thunders of Intellect
> But if their Emanations mingle not; with storms & agitations
> Of earthquakes & consuming fires they roll apart in fear
> For Man cannot unite with Man but by their Emanations
> Which stand both Male & Female at the Gates of each Humanity
> How then can I ever again be united as Man with Man
> While thou my Emanation refusest my Fibres of dominion (88:1–13)

The passage's emphases on the meetings of emanations and the presence of children are consistent with *Jerusalem*'s overall recognition of daily life, the family, and domesticity. Yet Blake goes beyond earlier statements of this idea in two ways. The first is that emanations appear in "Eternity." Readers of Blake are used to a dualistic conception in which, in our extant world, people are divided and couple through their mortal bodies, while in "Eternity" humanity exists in fourfold forms, unified and without "emanations." "Emanations," Blake's "fall" narratives since *Urizen* have stressed, were unknown among the "Eternals." In this restatement, Blake sweeps away the dualism of this world and "Eternity," and of the human forms within them.[21] The human forms in Eternity (Man and Man, in Blake's gendered formulation) have not jettisoned their emanative portions, nor has sexual difference melted into an undifferentiated androgyny. The eternal forms coexist with their emanations and their children, and can enter one another's bosoms only if the emanations embrace and "comingle." As the children's presence shows, Blake is speaking of ordinary human families, and the emanations must be the forms' real human bodies. The implication, certainly, is that "Eternity" is not an immaterial realm but the present earth, cleansed and renewed; and there eternal forms mingle through the sexual love of ordinary human bodies.

The idea of "emanations" now acquires a double or overlapping meaning, likewise going beyond Blake's earlier presentations: The "emanations" are ordinary human bodies, which may be either male or female, and they are also female and male aspects of *each* human, standing "both Male & Female at the Gates of each Humanity." Hence both men and women, in their reality as fourfold forms, possess equivalent male and female aspects; and both male and female bodies are equal derivations from the forms. Nor are the emanations female portions of male characters, even of male eternal forms (more or less how the matter has been presented in Blake interpretation); eternal forms have emanations that are both female and male, so that both Enitharmon and Los, as ordinary human characters, are emanations, and every "Four-Fold Form" possesses both. Roughly, then, the idea presented in Los's speech is that fourfold forms mingle only if their emanations mingle, and these may be male and/or female. What earlier seemed to be the anomalous case of Shiloh—a "Masculine Emanation among the Flowers of Beulah"—is now presented as the norm for "emanations" in general.

Further, though these emanations are female and male bodies, they are not "sexes" in Blake's specialized sense—entities whose identities or essential characteristics are female or male. We know this because of a complex passage in which the narrator describes the consequences of Antichrist's consolidation. As the "multitudes of those who sleep in Alla" become "One with the Antichrist & are absorbd in him" (89:58, 62),

> The Feminine separates from the Masculine & both from Man
> Ceasing to be His Emanations, Life to Themselves assuming!
> And while they circumscribe his Brain, & while they circumscribe
> His Heart, & while they circumscribe his Loins! a Veil & Net

Of Veins of red Blood grows around them . . .
. . . .
          . . . that no more the Masculine mingles
With the Feminine. but the Sublime is shut out from the Pathos
In howling torment, to build stone walls of separation, compelling
The Pathos, to weave curtains of hiding secresy from the torment.
          (90:1–5, 10–13)

We notice again that whereas earlier presentations of the "emanations"
idea designated them as female, here both feminine and masculine are
seen as emanations. Besides this point, the passage criticizes the solidification of male and female identities (what we would call genders) that
"circumscribe" the human brain, heart, and especially loins, while taking
bodily form (generating blood vessels, etc.). The result is that "No more
the Masculine mingles / With the Feminine." But as the earlier passage
in which "emanations" meet "Surrounded by their Children" shows
(88:6, discussed above), the evil is not the formation of male and female
bodies as such but their "Ceasing to be . . . Emanations, Life to Themselves assuming," i.e., the solidifying of bodily forms with defined gender identities.

Both "Masculine" and "Feminine," it should be noted, limit "Man."
Though it views the separation of "Masculine" and "Feminine" from
"Man" as resulting from the Antichrist's influence, the passage still leaves
open the possibility that women are its initiators ("the Sublime is shut
out from the Pathos"). But the passage's main point is to attack rigid gender identities as Satanic, and it attributes the evils of sexual alienation to
both genders—the masculine or "Sublime" builds walls while the feminine or "Pathos" weaves curtains. The abrupt appearance of Burkean categories—gendered male and female in Burke's aesthetics—helps make
this point, since it is used to criticize (not rationalize, as in Burke) both
gender and aesthetic separation.[22] Ironically and paradoxically, but in a
way true both to Blake's general conception of sexual polymorphousness
and to his treatment of homosexuality in this poem, these specifically
male and female identities are hermaphroditic:

          . . . when the Male & Female,
     Appropriate Individuality, they become an Eternal Death.
     Hermaphroditic worshippers of a God of cruelty & law! (90:53–55)

Hermaphrodism, then, with deep logic comes to mean the differentiation of exclusive gender identities; since individuals truly contain both
masculine and feminine qualities (and all other universal characteristics),

male and female identities must be either female-within-male or male-within-female. And these gendered identities, themselves responsive to the twisted moralism we have come to recognize as Hand's "iron rocks" and Vala's reconstituted veil, become enforcers of that moralism, "worshippers of a God of cruelty & law."

Los's speech about emanations has its own constituent ironies. Los is still ruled by his power-lust to dominate Enitharmon (88:13), and the immediate winner is the Spectre, who smiles "Knowing himself the author of their divisions . . . gratified / At their contentions" (88:35–36). The three-sided confrontation unwinds ambiguously. Los smashes the Spectre (91:41–52) but works to persuade Enitharmon. The emphasis on mutual consent and the positive role of sexual and familial relations signified in this plot action is consistent with other aspects of *Jerusalem's* handling of sexual relations and political persuasion, and contrasts with the comparable moment in *Milton* when Milton commands Ololon, "Obey thou the Words of the inspired Man" (40:29). But the plot shows Enitharmon clinging to her distinct gender identity, and the issue is not resolved; the two are still "convers[ing] upon Mam-Tor" (appropriately, one of the breast-shaped twin prominences of Derby Peak, site of sexual and class suffering elsewhere in the poem) when first Brittannia and then Albion awake (93:27, 94:1–95:4). At first sight frustratingly ambiguous, this denouement possesses deep logic: Brittania's and Albion's waking, not just individual dialogue, will resolve history's sexual wars; the preceding exchanges, fraught with contradiction and self-interest, can only achieve sufficient clarity to make the awakening possible.

For the purposes of my discussion, however, the key point in Blake's reconsideration of the roles of the sexes is Los's statement that "Man [may] unite with Man" through emanations that are "both Male & Female." Though part of Los's contention with Enitharmon, his words are consistent with Erin's and the narrator's comments on Shiloh and the "emanations," and can be taken to represent a "redeemed" consciousness in the poem. Hence, each "Humanity" may unite with another through male and female, or male and male, or female and female emanations.[23] Whether the emanations are conceived as sexual bodies or as mental aspects within individuals or large populations, the male and female emanations—and, therefore, heterosexual, lesbian, and male homosexual relations—stand on the same level. Humanities may unite through male and female emanations (William and Catherine Blake), female emanations (Butler and Ponsonby), or male emanations (Hepburn and White).

Further, the unification spoken of here is not *only* that of two humans in sexual love. It is the unification of "Man . . . with Man," or of two "Humanit[ies]," and these terms resonate with their earlier uses in

Jerusalem, in Albion's "Man the enemy of man," "That Man be separate from Man," "Humanity shall be no more" (4:26, 28:12, 4:32). The echoes are not accidental. In the humanist revolutionism of *Jerusalem,* sexual love is at once a consolation and sustaining force in present oppression; a component of approaching human mutuality; and an emblem of a larger, general human unification. And in these pages, that love includes both heterosexual and homosexual manifestations.

Conclusion ✳

What is Liberty without Universal Toleration

—"Annotations to Boyd," *E*635

Though Blake made sexual freedom central to his idea of liberation from an early date, his sexual attitudes seem initially to have been conventionally male-centered. If unusual even in the *Songs* and *Visions* in his empathy for female sexual desire, Blake nonetheless imagined this desire brought to ripeness by male attention and, frequently, male aggression. And he shared his age's prejudices against "nonprolific" sexuality, including masturbation and, in part, homosexuality. Blake differed from the current of his time, however—even the radical 1790s—in the depth of his radicalism, both sexual and political. A poem like "A Little Girl Lost," for example, shares its theme of inderdicted sexuality with a dramatic narrative such as Wordsworth's Vaudracour and Julia (*Prelude,* 1805–1806, 9:555–934); it is even superficially less radical, as it does not include the element of aristocratic tyranny. What sets "Little Girl" apart is, first, its emphasis on sexual delight in and for itself and, second, its sense of the utter incompatibility of this delight with the present world, embodied in the father, whom Blake can treat sympathetically without compromising his own radicalism precisely because he knows the unashamed pleasure he has in mind can be enjoyed only in "the future Age." Allied with the awareness of ruling-class self-righteousness found (in a nonsexual context) in the sister poem, "A Little Boy Lost," this sense of sexual delight as the essence of a freedom impossible in present society sets Blake on a course of suspicion toward every kind of sexual restraint and hatred of all moral punishment, despite his initial narrowness of perspective. And these Blakean conceptions form part of a social perspective in which freedom goes beyond political representation to leveling and communitarian liberty. From the 1790s onward, sexual enjoyment is both a good in itself and an emblem of mutuality in a cooperative commonwealth.

While these links between sexuality and Blake's political ideals have been much discussed, what has been less noticed is how, in the pressured atmosphere of the *Visions,* Blake's commitment to sexual delight is forced through the interstices of his male-centered conceptions into an accommodation of sexual perversion, which then spreads to a partial reconsideration of masturbation and a continuing concern with homosexuality. In the later poems that have been my main focus, male homosexuality plays several roles. It is an emblem of resistance to political and moral tyranny in *The Four Zoas* and *Milton* respectively; its repression is part of the construction of the tyrannic personality and polity in *Milton* and some of the illustrations of Milton's works; and it affords a target for Urizen's incomprehension and Hand's ire in *The Four Zoas* and *Jerusalem.* Lesbianism, already in *The Four Zoas,* is an alternative to male-dominated sexual relations and, perhaps, a portion of the joys of apocalypse. It retains these meanings, deepened by Blake's tracing of the links between homosexual guilt and social and political oppression, in *Jerusalem.* Striking in Blake's consideration is how earlier episodes such as the rationalization of heterosexual male rape in *America* 1–2 are replaced by an exposure of the socially, as well as sexually, destructive outcome of male sexual coercion in the rape sequences of *The Four Zoas* 7b and *Jerusalem* 20. As Blake reverses or extends earlier views, homosexuality in *Jerusalem* comes to embody a persistent Blakean theme, the true worth of the outcast: the "unnatural consanguinities and friendships / Horrid to think of" are in reality the "labours / Of loves" (*J* 28:6–8). Simultaneously, homosexuality also stands for a new point, the tolerance needed to advance toward liberty, which will be my focus below.

Blake's homosexual episodes and visual displays, we have seen, are usually encoded even more than was his usual practice. Exemplary of his overall approach are the homoerotic male images in *Milton,* whose explicit sexuality Blake disguises or literally covers in most copies. This reticence is certainly understandable. Professionally, Blake had every reason to make these images less potentially offensive, as sales of his engraved books depended primarily on their visual elements. In a more general way, the atmosphere of the age, manifested in events from William Beckford's exile to the bombardment of the Vere-street "monsters" with bricks and filth, imperatively demanded concealment; we recall that neither Bentham nor Percy Shelley published his own works on homosexuality. Along with retouching or erasing sexually explicit visuals, Blake conceals verbal allusions to homosexual themes behind symbolic vocabulary, esoteric allusion, and seemingly random uses of place names, so that careful, historically informed contextualization is needed to bring them forth. Exceptionally, the lesbian episode in *Jerusalem* is quite straightforward, once one is willing to focus on lesbian implications and to realize that characters' condemnations of moral transgressions are not necessarily Blake's.

If relatively few, the homosexual elements in these poems are placed at moments of central significance. In *The Four Zoas,* one occurs during Orc's transformation, raising questions about sexual comradeship and its absence in the resistance to tyranny. In *Milton,* encoded homosexual references occur in the poem's consideration of English political and moral tyranny; others are found in contemporary and historical material added in the second version of the poem, with echoes in the visual depiction of prophetic vocation near the end, and these references heighten the defense of moral transgression and the attack on moral law. And in *Jerusalem,* homosexual elements are introduced in the narration of the central conflict among Vala, Jerusalem, and Albion, and again in the preparation for the closing apocalyptic sequences, so that they encapsulate both the refusal of human mutuality and the sexual aspects of its recovery. So these episodes emerge as parts of the poems' central meaning. In particular, they epitomize the sexual dimension of Blake's Christian sexual anarchism, which continues to affirm social upheaval as his early poems did, now on the basis of an inclusive communalism freed—among other disfigurements inherited with the English republican tradition—of glorification of male sexual violence and denigration of homosexuality.

Homosexuality and Blake's Ideological Evolution

Blake's response to homosexuality plays a part in the evolution of his radicalism toward a later, inclusively popular conception of social renovation. Blake's final long poems, *Milton* and *Jerusalem,* remain committed to achieving liberty through apocalyptic upheaval. *Milton* closes as "Los listens to the Cry of the Poor Man: his Cloud / Over London in volume terrific, low bended in anger" (42:34–35). In *Jerusalem,* Erin urges her sisters, the Daughters of Beulah, to "remove from Albion these terrible Surfaces" (49:76). Since the "Surfaces" signify institutions of law and restrictive justice as well as rulers' oppression, fraternal hatred, and sexual victimization,[1] Erin is speaking of changes both in individual behavior and in social power. And the poem's climax comes as Albion, finally moved to brotherhood, throws himself "into the Furnaces of Affliction," calling to "my Cities & Counties / Do you sleep! rouze up! rouze up.

Eternal Death is abroad" (96:35, 33–34). Blake's imagery denotes popular awakening and rebellion (though they are seen as provisionally nonviolent), based on a mobilization of the whole people rather than conspiracy or coup—hence Albion's descent and call, which echoes contemporary broadsheet agitation. Further, the polity emerging from this upheaval is seen as noncoercive, functioning through debate and exchange—"they conversed together in Visionary forms dramatic" (98:28)—and without government of any kind.[2]

This scheme, it should be clear, depends on the ability of Britain's common people, Albion's "Cities & Counties," to live together in free mutuality; if they cannot, neither collaborative insurrection nor noncoercive democratic commonwealth can be possible. With this need in mind, apparently, Blake devotes several lengthy passages to the ethical preconditions for apocalypse, such as forgiveness and recognition of the particularity of each individual (e.g., *M* 22:27–24:43; *J* 45/31:2–38, 48:54–50:17, 91:1–30). Blake's later emphasis on spiritual preparation, then, should not be seen as a turn away from social radicalism. And it is both more, and more positive, than a disillusioned response to the failures of the French and American revolutions. It is a recognition of the need to overcome the obstacles—in popular prejudice, authoritarianism, and chauvinism—to the kind of radical self-government that Blake's presentations of apocalypse imply.

Homosexuality has its own place in this conception. It offers, we now know, a prototype of mutual, non-dominant relations, and exempla of resistance to tyranny and moral law; its acceptance is related to Blake's continuing commitment to sexual freedom and his renewed affirmation of the life of the body and conjugal love. As I have covered these aspects of Blake's treatment fairly fully, I will not explore them further here. Acceptance of homosexuality serves, in addition, as both emblem and part of the broader changes in Albion—the British people—needed to build a cooperative society. Blake remarks elsewhere, in opposition to religious conformity, "What is Liberty without Universal Toleration" (annotations to Boyd, *E* 635); in his later works, female and male homosexuality serve as markers of this broad toleration.

The Vere-street experience—if I am right that Blake knew of these events and responded to them in *Milton*—seems likely to have had an impact on *Milton*'s and *Jerusalem*'s presentations of forgiveness and toleration, alongside other factors such as popular war-chauvinism. Besides any earlier examples of antihomosexual persecution that Blake may have known of, Vere-street's demonstration of virulent public hatred and support for moral victimization is likely to have been deeply disturbing to anyone as committed to sexual nonconformity as he. Further, these events would have been likely to have an impact on Blake's ideas about mass action. Most biographers and critics have agreed that these were favorable. If we accept Erdman's reconstruction, Blake was strongly and positively influenced by the mob actions in London during the Gordon Riots of 1780—taking them as a prototype of Albion's rising and discounting, or perhaps then sharing, their anti-Catholic bias. The six-day bread riots of September 1800, both Erdman and David Worrall suggest, may have had a similar impact; their demands, Worrall argues, echo in the agrarian commonwealth shown in Night 9 of *The Four Zoas* (Erdman, *Prophet* 7–11, 344–46; Worrall, *Radical Culture* 44–47). With or without these specific echoes, Night 9 includes a powerful and stirring account of the resurrection of the dead as class uprising, in which the risen victims of history "shew their wounds they accuse they sieze the opressor howlings began / On the golden palace Songs & joy on the desart" and the dead children of six thousand years "Rend limb from limb the Warrior & the tyrant" (123:5–10). But Vere-street showed mobs, very nearly, rending limb from limb the members of a sexual minority. The episode, therefore, could be seen as revealing the depth of sexual and moral repressiveness in the English commons, and thus adding to the necessity for a spiritual cleansing before and/or as part of a democratic-revolutionary awakening that would be at least in part a release of sexuality. *Milton,* we have seen, responds to this need through a heightened emphasis on the ravages of Moral Law and the defiance of the Reprobate.

At the same time, bigotry of such depth and intensity heightens the need for toleration on any basis, and thus seems related to an aspect of Blake's late poems already mentioned—his emphasis on "forgiveness" rather than an upending of conventional moral categories as in earlier works. Blake conceptualizes this point in the preface to *Jerusalem*'s first chapter: "The Spirit of Jesus is continual forgiveness of Sin: he who waits to be righteous before he enters into the Saviours kingdom, the Divine Body; will never enter there" (3, prose). This idea has multiple applications, public as well as private, and refers to the judge as well as the judged. It must represent—this aspect should need no elaboration—the older poet's awareness of the profound harm we do to one another and the deep imperfection of our nature, also emphasized in the preface to the poem's third chapter. In addition, with regard to "sins" like homosexuality, forgiveness is an attitude Blake would urge on Albion: to be forbearing in judging what is different. Jerusalem, for example, uses "mercy" and "forgiveness" in this way after the riverbank encounter (20:22–25). At the same time, the idea may seem to express acceptance of common morality: One forgives only what is wrong. Yet Blake's embrace of forgiveness need not signify his acceptance of conventional moral terms, for the idea of forgiveness is flexible and need not be urged only on the conventionally moral on behalf of the conventional sinner. On a second level, *Jerusalem's* emphasis is on *Albion's* sins—those of anticommunitarianism, war, and moral condemnation among others. On this level "forgiveness" does not validate conventional morality because it is Albion's own moral condemnation that must be forgiven. Further, Albion with his sins of intolerance is the imperfect being who will wake up to fraternity; hence, toleration rather than a full reversal of moral prejudice can be a crucial step in *his* spiritual cleansing.

Blake's point, further, applies not only to private morality, but to the focus of much of his late thought, the awakening of the British people. The social action of democratic-revolutionary rebellion must be made by imperfect people, in a particular time and in the wake of particular events. In relation to the Vere-street experience, this idea would mean that people may still affirm various kinds of restrictive morality—against women's sexuality in general, against prostitutes, adulteresses, homosexuals—on the eve of a democratic uprising. In any real way, one would expect full acceptance of unconventional morality to mature only with time and/or in shared experience of struggle, and yet, in 1811–20, the issue of a democratic uprising seemed to be posed for the immediate future. In such a situation, there is a distinction between asking people to cleanse themselves of brutal sexual hatred and asking a full shift to a new morality; the ideas of tolerance and forgiveness could perhaps bridge the gap between existing and fully reformed morality, as well as expressing a basic idea in Blake's own later ethics.

Blake had been aware of the popular capacity for sexual victimization for many years, of course; it is present in *Songs of Experience* and *Visions*. But it is likely to have been driven home with exceptional force by the eight-month display of sexual hatred following the Vere-street raids, along with the many other examples of opprobrium for sexual "sins" one could read of in the daily or weekly press.[3] Together with such similar issues as the need to forswear vengeance against France, stressed in Erdman's reading of *Jerusalem* (*Prophet* 462), and with an immediate, direct public urgency because of the rise in popular struggles from 1811 to 1820, the force of sexual bigotry may have provided much impetus for Blake's emphasis on Albion's errors, on spiritual preparation, and on the need for "forgiveness" in *Milton* and *Jerusalem*.

These aspects of the late poems dovetail with another: Blake's united front with organized religion, seen, for example, in the respectful treatment of Wesley and Whitefield in *Milton* and of "Bath" in *Jerusalem* (*M* 22:55–23:2; *J* 39/44:43–41/46:16). By "united front" I mean the readiness to make common cause around limited issues with those with whom one disagrees in general, while criticizing or opposing them on other matters and leaving open the ultimate meaning of the points on which one agrees. This approach is central to *Jerusalem*. It is implicit in the preface to chapter 1 and present at crucial points such as the full-page crucifixion scene of plate 76, strategically placed at the start of the poem's final chapter. This sublime image conveys the full religious import of wonder at Jesus' sacrifice and yet, when read in the context of *Jerusalem*'s closing apocalyptic passages, it also signifies Albion's emulation of Jesus in his own willingness to sacrifice his life for humanity.

This emphasis on limited unity that leaves final meanings open occurs also in Blake's treatment of sexual tolerance and may stem partly from the Vere-street experience. Just as Blake is ready to make a united front with "Bath" over opposition to the war (Erdman, *Prophet* 476–80), so he is ready to state his position on Moral Law in terms broad enough to be agreed to by others; such terms include "forgiveness of sins," "universal toleration," and the entry of the unrighteous into the Savior's kingdom. Simultaneously, Blake gives these ideas his own specific content: "liberty both of body & mind to exercise the Divine Arts of Imagination" (*J* 77, prose). While in the immediate context of *Jerusalem*'s address "To the Christians" this phrase refers to "the labours of Art & Science," for Blake those labors amount to the whole of civilized culture; he is not speaking narrowly of artistic freedom, though of course it is included. The mental and bodily arts of imagination have inferably broad meanings elsewhere: the bodily-spiritual acts shown on *Milton*'s plate 47, the victory of "Naked Beauty!" over "Druidical Mathematical Proportion" on *Milton* 4 (27–28). Thus Blake's formula is flexible and expansive. In a similar way, the words of the voice/Jesus, "Every Harlot was once a Virgin: every Criminal an Infant Love!" (*J* 61:52), make common cause with those who can embrace a limited toleration, in terms accessible to ordinary religious thought; but, at the same time, Vala and Jerusalem's idyll offers a more extensive, positive meaning for toleration, while the linkage of Vala's doctrine of virginity to war and oppression undercuts the superiority of virginity that Blake's apothegm seems to assume.

Finally, "What is Liberty without Universal Toleration," too, has a dual meaning. Liberty is *not* possible without toleration: People who deflect blocked sexuality outward in attacks on sexual deviants cannot forge bonds of love and sacrifice with others to "remove from Albion these Terrible Surfaces"—with which, in the Vere-street events, they were in league. At the same time, universal toleration—its opponents are well aware—erodes the assumed superiority of the conventional over the merely tolerated, and so promotes acceptance of deviance, not just toleration. This latter point might seem more sexually radical than the need for mere toleration, but in fact, the need to provide a broad public basis for toleration is equally fundamental in what I am calling Blake's "united front" with religion. In *Jerusalem,* the prefaces (especially to chapters 1 and 4) and some doctrinal pronouncements plead for unity around ideas of forgiveness and toleration, while other parts of the narrative prompt discussion of whether these mean simple toleration or fuller acceptance of sexual deviancy. The enormity of the Vere-street persecution suggests tolerance as an immediate goal in the spirit of Jesus while allowing the larger understanding implied by the *Milton* artwork, *Milton* 4–5, and *Jerusalem* 19–22 and 88 to develop. And this fusion of toleration with continued contention over its full meaning becomes part of Blake's idea of how to prepare for rebellion. Blake's continuing exploration of homosexuality, then, in the context of its savage repression in the streets of his city, provides part of the ferment leading to his late, inclusive ideas of liberty and toleration.

Blake, Gender, and Romanticism

Blake's view of homosexuality, besides casting light on his ideological evolution, also illuminates the scope of Romantic views of sexuality and Romanticism's now much-controverted status as social criticism. On both issues, opinions have reversed dramatically since the 1970s. At that time, Blake was commonly hailed for his advocacy of sexual freedom. And the Romantic movement in arts was assumed to have offered a utopian critique of society, partly focused on interior and/or archaic alternatives—the life of imagination or the integrity of "primitive" or medieval social relations—and partly offering a projected future alternative to the market-dominated societies developing in 1750–1830. When we think of Romanticism in the visual arts or literature, poetry, or drama, these are the ideas that come to mind, and when we think of Blake in particular, we have in mind variants on them: childhood innocence and its violation, the mental fetters of "experience," the freedom of untrammeled sexuality, visions of utopian communalism.

Since the 1980s, the tide has turned. A series of trenchant critiques (most mentioned earlier in this study) have charged Blake and other male Romantics with failing to free themselves from dominant ideas of gender; others have questioned more generally how much Romantic social conceptions broke with the regnant ideologies of their times. The drift of my study of Blake and homosexuality, it will be evident, runs in the opposite direction, challenging the downgrading of Blake's reputation and reaffirming some of the claims for Blake's and Romanticism's social vision. In so arguing, I am not returning to an idea of the timeless validity of Romantic preoccupations—with the transcendent powers of art, for example, the consoling role of nature, or the reconstruction of the world through internal vision. Blake's continuing concern with his own society's political and social struggles does not in any case fit these stereotyped images of Romanticism. Rather, I am arguing, with Blake as a case in point, that the Romantic critique of society raised issues and sketched utopian prospects that remain relevant to our present society. My specific focus, of course, is Blake's view of sexuality, and involves four topics: the limits of Blake's view of gender; the idea of a distinct, less bounded women's Romanticism; related issues of how ideological change occurs; and the overall assessment of utopian potentialities in Romanticism.

The criticisms referred to above share a dissatisfaction with what has become known as "the Romantic Ideology." Jerome J. McGann's 1983 book of that title offered a politicizing attack on dominant interpretations of Romanticism for incorporating and replicating some Romantics' conceptions of the transcendent power of imagination and glossing over their evasions of social reality. McGann's clarifying polemic both paralleled and furthered a growing skepticism about several aspects of Romantics' self-presentation. In Wordsworth's case, Marjorie Levinson's chapter on "Tintern Abbey" in *Wordsworth's Great Period Poems* (1986) typifies this trend; rather than endorsing Wordsworth's celebration of mind and nature, Levinson argues that the poem "represents mind . . . as a barricade to resist the violence of historical change and contradiction" (53). In a somewhat parallel way, Steven Goldsmith's *Unbuilding Jerusalem* (1993) links Blake's concern with undermining linguistic authority to Paine's agitation for democratic representation and faults both for being preoccupied with verbal opposition and evading issues of social power. Criticisms of Blake's view of women, though they began and continue independently of the broad critique of "the Romantic Ideology," dovetail with it; Anne K. Mellor and Richard E. Matlak, for example, suggest both that Blake failed to break with dominant gender categories and that this failure marks his overall radicalism as incomplete:

Although Blake radically contested the boundaries between almost all of the binary structures he inherited from his culture (he reconceptualized the relationships between good and evil, man and God, reason and imagination, freedom and slavery, etc.), he never contested the *fundamental* binary of sexual difference: the ideal human form divine is always in Blake's system male; the female is either an "emanation" from the male (and happily subservient to him), or essentially different from and lesser than the male (and therefore wrong in asserting opposition to him). (275; my emphasis).

Blake's treatment of gender, however, particularly in late work, is a good deal more fluid than statements like this suggest, and it follows that his entrapment within conventional gender categories is less rigid than they suppose. Erin, for example, fits neither of the roles sketched here— subservient "emanation" or destructive lesser being. She is not identified as an "emanation" at all, and she has no paired male entity. As Ireland, she plays an important active role at several points in *Jerusalem,* joining Los and helping to free him from the "Cliffs of Albion" in chapter 1 (11:8–15) and exercising independent doctrinal and prophetic functions in chapter 2. Nor do the comments above fully account for *Jerusalem's* direct consideration of gender and sexuality—its reformulation of the "emanations" as male and female entities, its criticism of the formation of distinct male and female sexual identities, its implied attack on Los's demands for "dominion," and, most of all, its recognition of homosexuality as a category transcending masculinity and femininity—hence the emanations that stand "both Male & Female at the Gates of each Humanity." These latter aspects of *Jerusalem* are quite directly contesting the "binary of sexual difference," whether or not we regard it, with Mellor and Matlak, as more fundamental than others.

Blake's consideration of homosexuality itself plays a role in prompting his reconsideration of gender inequities. While fully misogynist defenses of male homosexuality are well known historically, such a defense does not seem to be what Blake was about; rather, Blake's intellectual engagement with homosexuality led him to an awareness of female homosexuality and to a reformulation of doctrinal elements of his view of the sexes. The views that emerge are certainly not fully consistent or clear; *Jerusalem's* attempt to reposition emanations as both male and female and the interactions of "Men" in "Eternity" as occurring through male and female "emanations" jostles against the continuing conception of general "Humanity" as male. Similarly, *Jerusalem's* reformulation of the meaning of "emanations" coexists with more sexually hierarchical formulations of the same idea in this and the other two long poems. Nevertheless, both the dramatic treatment of homosexuality in these poems and these doctrinal reformulations move significantly toward recognizing parity between male and female, and the autonomy of female social and sexual relations.

In sum, whatever combination of specifically "Romantic" notions (such as belief in the power of imagination) and other concerns (such as biblical redemption and protest over social and moral injustice) one takes as determining Blake's outlook, these ideas were able to disrupt existing gender categories to some degree, not just claim special privileges for male satisfaction within them.

The same fluidity in gender conceptions raises some questions about the effort to define a set of concerns and a kind of poetics that are the province of women Romantic writers. While the description itself may be valid, the idea that it applies only to the group in question may involve false binaries. It is striking, in fact, how much some of Blake's later concerns overlap with those seen as specific to women's Romantic writing. Mellor has outlined several of these in her *Romanticism and Gender,* in a necessarily preliminary way. Some, though not all, are in fact present in Blake's work. Mellor argues, first, that "women Romantic writers tended to celebrate, not the achievements of the imagination nor the overflow of powerful feelings, but rather the workings of the rational mind, a mind relocated—in a gesture of revolutionary gender implications—in the female as well as the male body" (2). Blake, who never shows women as less intellectually capable than men, retains his suspicion of reason in late works, but reason is counterposed not to the overflow of feeling in a Wordsworthian sense but to faith and prophecy, qualities manifested, in Jerusalem and Erin, by women as well as men. Blake's insistence that truth resides in particulars rather than generals (e.g., *J* 55:60–61, 91:18–30) is also an approach to knowledge traditionally thought more characteristic of women than of men.

Mellor's second salient feature, a "commitment to a construction of subjectivity based on alterity" (3), is harder to find, even in late Blake. While Blake's revision of the idea of "emanations" allows for sexual difference, and while Blake always endorses intellectual contention in the abstract, he shows little true awareness of "alterity," i.e., the legitimacy of distinct *ways* of thinking, feeling, and acting, distinct *kinds* of existence. In his long poems, perhaps only Los's debate with Rintrah and Palamabron in *Milton* (22:27–24:47) shows an actual debate with contending positions; in *Jerusalem,* Los, Erin, and others present a *single* conception of redemption, presented mainly in oracular pronouncements and with little conception of alternative roads.

In the area of conduct in our present world, however, Blake's overlap with Mellor's sketch becomes palpable. Mellor notes that women Romantic writers embraced an ethic that

> insists on the primacy of the family or the community and their attendant practical responsibilities. They grounded their notion of community on a cooperative rather than possessive interaction with a Nature troped as a female friend or sister, and promoted a politics of gradual rather than violent social change, a social change that extends the values of domesticity into the public realm. (3)

Jerusalem indeed bases fundamental values on "the family or the community." Its action, we have seen, unfolds from Albion's rejection of community, expressed in the calls of his "brethren . . . thy fathers, and thy sons, / Thy nurses and thy mothers, thy sisters and thy daughters," and from his mistaken claim to possess the natural and social landscape, "The Malverns and the Cheviot, the Wolds Plinlimmon & Snowdon" (4:11–12, 30). So, too, does *Jerusalem* insist on "a cooperative rather than possessive" relationship with nature, "troped as a female friend or sister," as Vala is in the riverbank scene. Finally, continuing to believe in social revolt (Mellor's implied endorsement of gradualism is one of the more clearly ideological parts of her scheme), Blake finds domestic and social culture crucial in preparing the soil for cooperation. In a passage mentioned earlier, "those who disregard all Mortal Things" (*J* 55:1) debate and recognize the importance of daily and sexual life, apparently disavow the need for a transcendent guardian principle, and instead counsel:

> Labour well the Minute Particulars, attend to the Little-ones:
> And those who are in misery cannot remain so long
> If we do but our duty: labour well the teeming Earth. (*J* 55:51–53)[4]

Blake too, then, "extends the values of domesticity into the public realm," where they play a major part in preparing for a freed existence.

I present this comparison not to validate Blake against a "checklist" of women's Romanticism, but to point to the complex and contradictory ways in which new intellectual conceptions emerge. Ideological change frequently occurs not as a result of breaking through to fully altered conceptions, but through seeking new implications within existing ones; then, over time, either these conceptions are abandoned for the new ones, or they are in fact redefined. Mellor's and several other critiques of Blake's treatment of women have focused on Blake's use of hierarchic metaphorizations of male and female, on the hostile, negative portrayals of "Female Will" in his middle work, etc. Such criticisms have measured Blake against modern conceptualizations of sexual equity and, in part, against women's writing of his time. But such comparisons tell only half the story. In a complex way, Blake adds to his dramatic portrayal of female entities and stretches his theoretical categorizations, especially of the "emanations," to the point at which they partly negate the metaphoric system in which they originate. Thus, Blake's late works hold ideas that are in contradiction. Nor is contradiction Blake's trait alone. Wollstonecraft, for example, intent on the case for women's rationality, devalues female emotion and sexuality in *Vindication;* only in *The*

Wrongs of Woman does she reach a fuller "vindication" of these qualities. In such cases we need to ask about the direction of development, not seize on one or the other side of a contradictory mix to "prove" a thesis. If one does not tailor one's criteria specifically to validate what women writers were doing, both Blake and Wollstonecraft seem to react in distinct, complex ways to inherited ideas that they work to bend into new shapes. Blake's conception of women's intellect is comparable to that of his women contemporaries; his devaluation of the "female" realms of family and domestic life is retrograde compared to theirs, until *Jerusalem;* his recognition of women's sexual desire, though partly driven by male concerns, is fuller than that of some women writers; and his conception of homosexuality (female and male) as part of human sexuality is far in advance of most other contemporary thought. But in any case, Blake's evolution shows that ideological change occurs neither by sequential evolutionary steps nor by a total break with earlier thought, but by half-steps and sudden leaps that redefine earlier categories while still partly coexisting with them.

If, finally, Blake's uses if gender are fluid, even contradictory, featuring restrictive conceptions alongside others that dissolve fixed categories; if Blake's late poetics and social concerns significantly overlap with those posited as a humane, nonhierarchic set of values peculiar to women writers; and if Blake's and contemporary women authors' writing both show a roiled mix of older and newer modes of thinking, continuities and breaks with the past, then, too, it is wrong to discount or dispute the capability of Romantic vision to criticize oppressive relations and to project, in however contradictory a way, a utopian alternative of continuing relevance. Robert Sayre and Michael Löwy point to these capabilities in one of the fullest and most generous recent essays on Romanticism as a cultural phenomenon, written from a Marxist standpoint that nonetheless sharply criticizes standard Marxist views. Examining "Romantic anticapitalism," Sayre and Löwy reject the charge that it is merely backward-looking, and they refuse, too, to localize Romanticism as a phenomenon of late eighteenth- and early nineteenth-century society. They argue that "*romanticism is an essential component of modern culture,*" and that it originates in a "hostility toward present reality" that rejects "not the present in the abstract but a specifically capitalist present conceived in terms of its most important defining qualities," particularly "the all-powerfulness in this society of exchange value." Hence "the romantic fire *is* still burning. It is alive not only in social movements (pacifism, ecology, feminism) . . . but at the same time in new religious currents ('liberation theology')" (23, 32–33, 90).

Though Sayre and Löwy mention feminism only in passing and homosexuality not at all, there is much in their discussion that applies to mine. In *Jerusalem*'s dramatization of Albion's refusal of mutuality and his embrace of private and imperialist possession, one finds pinpointed the elements of society that Sayre and Löwy view as targets of Romantic revolt. In the historical-sexual mythic allegory of *Milton*'s Bard's Song, one finds a serious effort to anatomize the origins of Britain's imperialist polity and antisexual morality, in their intermeshed political, religious, and sexual dimensions. Most relevant to my present discussion, and going beyond Sayre and Löwy's Marxist framework, Blake's focus on sexual division as part of civilization from its inception (in *Urizen, The Book of Ahania, The Four Zoas,* and *Milton*) parallels recent feminist scholarship emphasizing the presence of male supremacy in earliest prehistory.[5]

Simultaneously with his critical account of oppression's origins—and this point is central to Sayre and Löwy's view of Romanticism's continuing relevance—Blake projects an alternative to divided and hierarchic sexuality, grounded in sexual love, aspiring to a sexualized interchange of whole persons, uncoupled from defined social gender roles, and including homosexuality and sexual perversion. In part this alternative rests on the idea of tolerance. In this respect it shows the capacity of Blake's vision to go beyond the majority thought of the time, even beyond that of Romantic social criticism. Tolerance of homosexuality was, of course, *not* part of Romanticism's common coin; yet the "spirit of the age" (any age) is not uniform any more than that of an individual. Blake's sexual radicalism leads to a formulation of liberal tolerance that was beginning to show itself faintly in the thought of the day—for example, in the first calls in parliament to abolish the pillory (chapter 5). Blake, a Romantic Christian radical; Percy Shelley, a Romantic atheist radical; and Bentham, a rationalist liberal, all shared in this nascent development. Their doing so shows that a broader social intellectual shift was in the air, in which some strands of Romanticism participated, rather than initiating.

Still within the limited framework of anticipating later intellectual trends—which really means representing one barely visible thread within current thought that would later grow in strength—Blake's conception of homosexuality as a component of everyone's sexuality, with Bentham's similar ideas, anticipates a developing intellectual trend that could not have been evident to him or other contemporaries. In this area, Blake's thought is of his time but of a future time as well; it is one very early manifestation of a contrary trend in thought that would, over the next century and a half, displace the repressive norm of Blake's time first through the ambiguous idea of homosexuality as medical condition rather than sinful choice, then through broader lesbian-gay assertiveness and partial public acceptance.

In yet a more far-reaching way, Blake's conceptions represent an element in Romantic thought that reaches even beyond the liberalized, still hierarchic and sexually restrictive social order of the next two centuries. This envisioned alternative is still today generated as an aspiration by the continuing sexual hierarchies and repression that seem inescapable in present, as in past, society. Blake's envisioned world of sexual liberty turns out to be a present utopia—not in the sense of being incapable of human achievement, but in that of representing real aspirations to transcend present society. So it should be no surprise that, in 1995, the House of William Blake, a graphic arts collective situated in the poet's house at 17 South Molton Street, London, would mount "The Genitals Are Beauty," an exhibition of works by forty-seven contemporary artists inspired by Blake's celebration of the genitals' holiness.[6] In this way, as Sayre and Löwy posit for "Romantic anticapitalism" generally, Blake's critique of sexuality begins from conditions given historically—in this case also prehistorically, but in no way extrahistorically, i.e., as part of human life in general—and fashions both a destructive criticism of a destructive system and a positive utopian vision achievable through collaborative democratic collectivity.

Paradoxically, relating Blake's view of homosexuality to events of the day and to other contemporary outlooks such as Bentham's more thoroughly historicizes Blake, yet places him within deviant but really existing intellectual threads that go beyond the dominant or even dissident thought of his time *and* ours. Just as we read "A Little Girl Lost" in the confident belief that the "future Age" is ours, only to discover that we have yet to build it, so Blake's view of homosexuality both reveals what could be conceived within the thought of his time *and* points to the cultural achievements that remain ahead of us.

Of course, no discussion focused specifically on homosexuality can resolve debates over how Blake treats gender relations overall, much less disputes over Romanticism's outlook and significance. Nevertheless, the place of homosexuality in Blake's later works and its connection with their overall themes, including those of gender, suggest that some (male) Romantic criticisms of sexual norms were capable of partly transcending hierarchic conceptions, and of projecting a positive vision that retains considerable power. Blake's remains a *partial* questioning. Nonetheless, in historical context, the degree to which Blake's treatment did move toward gender equity is impressive and noteworthy. And, regardless of these broader implications, Blake's view of homosexuality, with Bentham's, enlarges our knowledge of what was intellectually formulable within eighteenth- and early nineteenth-century modes of thought. Expanding his already catholic conceptions of sexuality, Blake found it possible to imagine homosexual "rivers of delight" upon "the River of [Albion's] City" that was his own city, in his own time, cleansed and renewed by universal human cooperation.

Notes

Preface

1. See, for example, discussions of Beckford's *Vathek*, Knight's *Priapus,* or Cleland's *Memoirs of a Woman of Pleasure,* all cited subsequently.
2. If often inaccurate; see my "The Myth of Blake's 'Orc Cycle'" and chapter 2 of my *The Chained Boy.*
3. I borrow from the overview in DiSalvo, Hobson, and Rosso, Introduction (xxix-xxx).
4. Peter Ackroyd's *Blake* (1995) reflects a newer sexual climate in referring rather casually to homosexual content in the designs but unfortunately does not discuss their meaning or their relation to Blake's verbal texts. Ackroyd's reference to the depiction of fellatio in *The Four Zoas* (281), though not specific, may refer to page 78, which I discuss later. For other references to homosexual content in designs, see references in later chapters.
5. For examples of Foucault's influence in historical studies see, e.g., Trumbach, "Sodomites" 9. For a restatement in theoretical terms, see Halperin 15–40 and 41–53; on the tentativeness of Foucault's initial formulation, see Halperin 5–7. Haggerty, discussed below, takes a Foucauldian view throughout. For an overview of recent critical approaches, see B. Smith.
6. Boswell argues for the twelfth century as the point of transition from ancient and early medieval acceptance of homosexual behavior to late medieval, Renaissance, and modern intolerance. Boswell's approach is generally "essentialist."
7. See Carolyn Dinshaw's illuminating discussion of this line and its social and linguistic contexts (156–68, 256–64 nn. 1–18). Halperin himself argues that Greek "homosexuality" was sanctioned exclusively between older men and younger boys in conjunction with male-female marriage, and he makes this point central to his argument that ancient male-male sex could not have been "homosexual" in our sense at all. But in a revealing afterword, he is compelled to recognize new artistic evidence of Greek adult-adult same-sex relations and role reversals in man-boy relations, a major breach (sorry) in his argument. (See 47, 130–31, 160–61, 225.)
8. Emma Donoghue, Robert F. Gleckner, and Jon Thomas Rowland, to cite only three authors of recent books on the period, have used "homosexual"

or "lesbian" to refer to an identity or sensibility common in the period. Rowland combines his usage with approving references to Foucault on secondary points. For critiques of the Foucauldian view, referring both to the "long eighteenth century" and to earlier periods, see Murray and Donoghue, and in part Cady and Patterson. In a variant of Foucault's approach, Trumbach argues that during the eighteenth century, northern European sexuality became organized in a system of "three genders composed of men, women, and sodomites" (*Sex and the Gender Revolution* 3). This thesis and Trumbach's related view that in earlier centuries "probably most" males enjoyed bisexual relations (5) seem overly schematic to me. (Trumbach's book focuses on heterosexual relations; a planned second volume should cover the material on homosexual relations that Trumbach has published over the years as articles, many cited below.)

9. See the anthologies edited by Gerard and Hekma, Maccubbin, Rousseau and Porter, and Summers.

10. See Trumbach, "Birth" 130, 130–33; Haggerty 6–11, 23–43.

11. See Burg; Kaplan 168, discussed in chapter 5.

Chapter 1.
Eighteenth-Century Homosexuality
and the Republican Tradition

1. For further discussion of this image, see chapter 3.

2. I present here an overview of recent historical research with incidental contributions of my own. For my use of *homosexuality* as an inclusive term of discussion, see preface.

3. For occupations and prostitution, see Trumbach, "Sodomites" 19–20, and "Sodomy Transformed" 116–17. For venues of occasional and regular homosexual contexts, cruising areas, etc., in the 1720s, see *Hell upon Earth* 43; Trumbach, "Sodomites" 15–17, 23; Norton 54–69. On mollies and molly houses, see *Hell upon Earth* 43; Bray, 81–104 passim; Norton 70–91; Trumbach, "Birth" 137–39, and, for a caution on the reliability of evidence, Patterson. *Hell upon Earth* (1729), much cited in writing on this topic, is an idiosyncratic production, targeting "Fox-Hunters, Peace-Hunters, Money-Hunters, Men-Hunters, Whore-Hunters, Death-Hunters, Levee-Hunters, News-Hunters," the printing of coffee-house "Prittle Prattle," cursing, gluttony, and more, in addition to sodomy (title page and passim).

4. On masquerades, see Castle, *Masquerade,* chapter 1 passim, and discussion in chapter 6 below. See also G. S. Rousseau, "Pursuit" 143, 155.

5. The comparison of the number of establishments in the 1720s and 1813 is Harvey's. Harvey calls the houses "brothels," but descriptions indicate a mix of homosexual activities in them. *The Phoenix of Sodom,* cited also below, is of questionable reliability. Its author, Robert Holloway, is concerned to rescue the reputation of James Cook, the landlord of the White Swan (apparently the "J. Cook" named on the title page as seller of the pamphlet), who

had been jailed for extorting money from former clients. Holloway himself was sentenced to eight months in Newgate for defaming one James Stewart in the pamphlet (*Sodomy Trials,* July 1, 1813; *Phoenix* 47, 50–51). *Phoenix* contains much evident inaccuracy, e.g., identifying "Tommies" (a term for some lesbians) as married male homosexuals' name for their wives (11). Nevertheless it supplies many plausible details not available elsewhere.

6. *The Trial of Richard Branson* 26. By comparison with Branson's £100 fine, £52.10s. paid the fees for Blake's seven-year apprenticeship starting in 1772 (Ackroyd 42). On the statutes, see Harvey 941 (the best discussion); Gilbert 63–64; Trumbach, "Sodomites" 21; Rubini 377 n. 57; and, for the Netherlands, Huussen 173. Penetration of a woman or animal also constituted sodomy, but in general the statute was applied only to acts with men. There is some disagreement among these sources on prevalent legal practices. On the 1698 trials of Captain Edward Rigby for public solicitation and blasphemy, see Bray 98; Bredbeck 6–8; Rubini 355–56. For some examples of successful and unsuccessful prosecutions, see Trumbach, "Assaults" 409–21 and *Gender Revolution* 55–62.

7. For discussion see Bray 90–97; Trumbach, "Assaults" 409, "Sodomites" 22, and "Sodomy Transformed" 115. Trumbach's further reference to raids on taverns or other establishments during 1798 ("Assaults" 409) cannot be verified from the *Times; see* below.

8. See also Harvey 940, 942; Norton 185. Harvey's reference drew my attention to this case. "Respite" often led to reprieve, and I have not found a report that the men were later executed in *Bell's* or in *Annual Register* 1806–1807. (The *Register's* ambiguously placed phrase, "one of the most affluent men in Warrington" [438], may refer to Hitchin or the man he attempted relations with, but the former is more likely.)

9. *The Women-Hater's Lamentation* is reproduced in facsimile, with engravings, in *Sodomy Trials* (unpaged); text only, Rubini 379–80. For another satire, *Love-Letters Between a certain late Nobleman And the famous Mr. Wilson* (1723), see Kimmel's edition, with commentary; for other polemics, etc., see Trumbach, "Sodomites" passim; Bray 81–104 passim; G. S. Rousseau, "Pursuit" 153–54, and "Introduction to the *Love-Letters*" passim; Kimmel, "Greedy Kisses" 2–6, and further references below. On Beckford, see Lonsdale passim; Crompton 119–26, 232–34; Haggerty 136–51. Haggerty's generally excellent account fails to mention Beckford's semi-exile (149–50). For two cases at Oxford in the 1740s, see Norton 159–68; for the ruin of the impresario Isaac Bickerstaffe, see 174–84.

10. This case was mentioned in Lillian Faderman's *Surpassing the Love of Men* (147–54) and popularized in her *Scotch Verdict* (1983), and has since been discussed by several scholars; a facsimile of the legal records was published in 1975 (*Miss Marianne Woods . . .*). The complexities of the legal documents have led to several misconceptions, all revolving around the idea that lesbianism was thought inconceivable, at least in England—as Faderman puts it, the judges thought "women did not engage in sex together . . . simply be-

cause there was nothing they could do in bed" (*Surpassing* 149). In fact, the lawyers and judges were well acquainted with the possibility of various kinds of lesbian sex; it was only direct vaginal penetration with the clitoris alternately by each of the women that the reporting judge, or Lord Ordinary, urged was "impossible in this country to commit," on grounds of general anatomy; the judge's summary, crediting this claim along with circumstantial evidence and the lack of allegations of using hands or "instruments," or of "particular conformation" (i.e., enlarged clitorises), correlates with Woods and Pirie's own position, which freely admitted the possibility of "tribadism" in general but denied it here based on anatomy, circumstance, etc., as well as the usual arguments about character. (See "State of the Process," June 14, 1815: 13–15, summarizing hearings held Dec. 1810-Feb. 1811; Woods and Pirie's "Additional Petition," Oct. 10, 1811: 24–27.) Regardless of some statements by individual judges, the implausibility of lesbian sex in general occurring in England or Scotland was never a serious issue in the trial. For the precedents cited by Gordon's lawyers, see "Authorities with Regard to the Practice of Tribadism," immediately following "State of the Process." (The documents are all separately paginated in the facsimile.) Faderman's references in *Surpassing the Love of Men,* it should be noted, sometimes misconstrue the focus of lawyers' or judges' statements, and *Scotch Verdict* is highly fictionalized (more than Faderman's prefatory note, vii-viii, indicates); compare, e.g., Faderman's version of Lord Meadowbank's speech, *Verdict* 257–62, with "Speeches of the Judges" 5–14 and 40, on which it is based.

11. Donoghue 7, 3; Trumbach, "Sapphists" 125, 131–32. On hermaphrodism and lesbianism, see chapter 3. On medical and sex education publications, which covered some of these topics but not homosexuality, see Porter and Hall.

12. Information in this paragraph is based on Donoghue and on Trumbach, "Sapphists." For Charke, see Donoghue 97–100, 164–66; for Damer, Donoghue 145–48, 262–65, and Trumbach, "Sapphists" 131–32 and 139 n. 26. Trumbach gives the name Ann Seymour Damer and the birth date 1748, relying on a 1908 biography.

13. I have not been able to locate a copy of, or bibliographic listing for, Cannon's pamphlet. For another partial exception, Anna Seward's "Llangollen Vale" (1796), see chapter 6. Rictor Norton, seeking defenses of homosexuality, turns up a self-justifying popular air, "Let the Fops of the Town Upbraid" (43), which may be a hostile satire; a few molly-house songs recorded in trial records; and a pamphlet defense of effeminacy that, as Norton notes, is actually a satiric attack. Among "serious defences" Norton counts Voltaire's, Swift's attribution of homosexual tastes to "art and reason" in *Gulliver's Travels* 4.7, and Earl Strutwell's apologia in Smollett's *Roderick Random,* chapter 51 (119–20); but both the latter are hostile gibes. Searches of relevant databases (e.g., British Library online catalogue, Eighteenth Century Short Title Catalogue) using such terms as sodomy, pederasty, Sodom, Socratic, Ganymede (and other mythological, classical and biblical tags),

"Greek" and the like, along with contemporary terms such as *pathic* and others, fail to turn up titles favorable to or even neutral toward homosexuality. Selective reading of more neutral-sounding pamphlets or books yields the same result. This is a rough and ready research method, and no doubt some positive treatments can be found, but the overall pattern seems clear.

14. For assessments of some these texts see Kimmel, "Greedy Kisses"; G. S. Rousseau, "Pursuit" 146–51 and "Introduction to the *Love-Letters*" passim; Trumbach, "Sodomy Transformed" 117–22; different accounts of the positive and negative valences of Cleland's tavern sodomy scene by Kopelson, Mengay. Cleland omitted the graphic description of sodomy (158–59) from *Fanny Hill,* his expurgated version of the novel (1750), yet was dogged with the reputation of a sodomite—illustrating some of the difficulties in depicting such material even with negative commentary like that supplied by Fanny and Mrs. Cole (159–60). The description appears in both Penguin and Oxford editions of the *Memoirs,* but not in twentieth-century texts based on *Fanny Hill.* On Hervey, see Rowland 65–87; Norton 146–58, and a brief but extremely perceptive comment by Patterson (260).

15. Gleckner, as he acknowledges, builds on Jean H. Hagstrum's groundbreaking, discerning "Gray's Sensibility" (1974).

16. Blake had no great respect for West but knew him and would have been likely to approve of any major patronage for a project based on Revelation. Nancy L. Pressly is probably right in arguing that "Blake would have had to be familiar with West's Revelation paintings, and it is clear they had some influence on his ideas" (67 n. 19). Blake may also have been aware of Beckford's quasi-radical politics (see Pressly 64–66). For West's relations with Beckford, see Pressly 57–67 and Alberts 221, 244–49, 255–57; on Blake and West see *E*573 (Blake's dismissive comment in the notes now known as the "Public Address"); *BR* 50 (West's praise of Blake); *BR* 169, 193, *BRS* 42, and Bentley, "Blake and Cromek" passim (West's promotion of Blake's designs for Blair's *The Grave*).

17. Knight's plate 2 shows three priapean figures: a flying erect phallus with stylized wings; a male bust with a rooster head whose beak is elongated into an erect penis with scrotum; and a limp phallus and scrotum with "wings" consisting of a phallus shape with rings or rolls of flesh *(right)* and a clenched hand with thumb between the index and middle fingers (*left*—still a common obscene gesture). Blake executed winged penis designs on *FZ* 26 and 42, a bird with phallic neck and scrotum-breast on the former page, and long, phallic bird-necks, though not phallus-beaks, in other works (see chapter 3). Jean H. Hagstrum notes priapean figures in an earlier Neapolitan publication as possible sources for the phalli and serpents ridden by cupids or children in designs like *T* 5, *A* 11, and *FZ* 4, 21, 40, 134 (*William Blake* 89, figure 49A). G. S. Rousseau notes that by the 1820s "Knight's radical anticlericalism, pronounced in the name of a serious primitive phallic religion, had become legendary and notorious" ("Sorrows" 133); it seems likely, then, that Blake would have known of him at least by reputation.

18. For *Vathek*'s reviews, see Lonsdale xix-xxi; see Elfenbein 50–58 for a reading of the Gulchenrouz material. See Rousseau, "Sorrows" 118–31 for *Priapus*'s reception. On *Vathek*'s additional "Episodes," not published in Beckford's lifetime, see Lonsdale xiv, xvi-xvii, xxii, xxxiv; Haggerty 150–51 and nn.

19. Linda Dowling notes that antihomosexuality was part of "a classical republican discourse that . . . exercised a powerful hold over the English cultural imagination for over two hundred years," from the seventeenth to nineteenth centuries (xv); I owe my use of Dowling to a reference by Haggerty, who himself briefly refers to republican antihomosexuality (4, 16).

20. See Gen. 19:1–11 (Sodom) and Judg. 19 (Gibeah). In the latter, the host pleads, "unto this man do not so vile a thing," and at last the traveler offers his concubine, whom the men "abused . . . all the night," leaving her dying (24, 25). Two chapters of *De doctrina Christiana* mention homosexual practices. The first, on "a man's duty toward himself," includes "sodomy" ("Sodomia") among practices "[o]pposed to chastity"; the second, on duties to one's neighbor, includes "homosexuality" ("masculorum concubito," i.e., "lying together of men") among violations of his chastity. Milton's attached biblical references cite Gen. 19:5 and Judg. 19:22 (the incidents of Sodom and Gibeah) in relation to the latter offence but not the first, since these incidents add the sin of violation to that of sodomy (*Prose Works* 6: 726, 756; *Works* 17: 218, 290). In some other citations Milton's translators exaggerate his specific emphasis on homosexuality by using "sodomites" where he pairs the terms "meretrix" and "meretorius" and their derivatives, apparently referring to female and male prostitutes. (See discussion of the Hebrew texts, Boswell 98–99.) Nevertheless, Milton's citation of Paul is unambiguous: "no fornicators, or adulterers, none who are effeminate or homosexual ["necque qui concumbunt cum masculis"—"nor those who lie with males"] . . . will inherit the kingdom of God" (*Prose Works* 6: 727; *Works* 17: 220). See brief discussion in Rumrich 131; for recent debates over Milton's authorship of this work and a defense of the traditional view, see Fallon.

21. See also *Prose Works* 1: 893, 941; 2: 264–65; 3: 342; 7: 296.

22. Milton frequently refers to Salmasius as effeminate, a eunuch, or henpecked, and compares him to Salmacis (the nymph who tried to seduce Hermaphroditus), Elpenor (thrall to Circe), etc.; see *Prose Works* 4: 312, 428, 471, 476, 483, 518 (*Defence*); 4: 556, 579 (*Second Defence*); for similar slurs against More, supposed author of the work he was answering in the *Second Defence*, see 4: 571, 630.

23. My interpretation of the Sodom notes differs from Bredbeck's (225). The notes for tragedies date probably from 1639–42; the prose treatises mentioned above date from 1641–60.

24. For background, see D. Smith xv and passim; Hill 11–16. Nol is Cromwell. In 1669 Samuel Parker had published the antitoleration *A Discourse of Ecclesiastical Politie,* followed by similar works in 1671 and 1672. In 1672, Marvell wrote *The Rehearsal Transpros'd,* defending indulgences for Dissenters; the title was a takeoff on a phrase in a contemporary play, *The Re-*

hearsal. Leigh's work was a reply, and it followed responses by Parker and several others; Marvell, it was generally agreed, finished them all off in *The Rehearsall Transpros'd: The Second Part* (1673). Besides toleration, the polemics concerned Milton's political role and issues of poetics. I am indebted to Joseph Wittreich for bringing the Leigh reference to my attention.

25. See Hughes's note to *PL* 1:501. For the conflicting interpretive traditions concerning the Sodom and Gibeah stories, see Boswell 92–98.

26. Werner's topic is Blake's illustration of this scene (see chapter 4), but here she comments on Milton's own presentation.

27. Bredbeck's is the fullest, most thoroughly contextualized discussion of homoeroticism in the banquet temptation (189–231); he discusses *PL*'s Belial passage briefly as part of this treatment (214–15). I follow Bredbeck's reading of the generic and vernacular associations of Ganymede and Hylas, though not fully accepting his conclusions. Bredbeck's further argument that while common glosses "establish homoeroticism as the other *within* patriarchal meaning, Milton's banquet specifies it as the other to patriarchy" (224–25) should also be noted. Unfortunately, Bredbeck does not fully elaborate this important idea.

28. See G. S. Rousseau, "Introduction to the *Love-Letters* 69–79, for discussion of the possible anti-Walpole purposes of this pamphlet.

29. The lines apparently were popular; they were pirated in the anonymous "Œconomy of Love," 1766 (Norton 117, 272 n. 5).

30. On this genre and the opposition to it see Rosso, "Empire of the Sea."

31. Among Churchill's other works, see *Night* 169–78, attacking catamites who gain advancement through sex (also a concern of Chatterton); *Gotham* 2:378, 435–44, on homosexual influence in the courts of James I and Charles I; and *The Rosciad,* on effeminacy on the stage. See also Rowland's discussions of this poem and *The Times,* and of the anonymous rejoinder to the latter, *The Anti-Times,* which accused Churchill of promoting vice by talking about it. Rowland emphasizes antihomosexual satires' polyvalency, meaning that they stir interest in homosexuality even while denouncing it. He notes Churchill's emphasis on privilege but does not really find it significant.

32. Overall, Chatterton's satire is directed at Bute's supposed liaison with the Princess Dowager (hence the title) and takes aim at a wide variety of figures, including Johnson (for his anti-Wilkes pamphlet "The False Alarm"). For other antihomosexual references in Chatterton, see "Whore" 365–66, "Kew Gardens" 865–66 (a cognate passage), and "The Exhibition" 313–16. A comparable use of the amalgam appears a few years later in *Sodom and Onan,* by William Jackson (1776). Lifting some examples from Churchill, Jackson charges that "G——e the seal majestic hath disgrac'd / . . . / To pardon Sodomites and damn the Nation" (qtd. in Norton 178). The interest here lies in the author's career as a reformer: As founder of *The Morning Post* the same year, he printed the American Declaration of Independence, and in 1794–95 he was arrested and convicted of treason as a spy trying to facilitate the French invasion of England (Norton 174–82).

33. Blake owned Chatterton's "Rowley" poems in a 1778 edition that does not include the poems mentioned here (*BB* 685). "Whore" was first printed in 1803; the others (or their relevant lines) after Blake's lifetime. Blake refers to Chatterton in *IM* and in annotations to Wordsworth, but only on the issue of the authenticity of the Rowley poems (*E*665–66). S. Foster Damon identifies Chatterton speculatively as Bristol (where he was born) in Blake's listing of cathedral cities (*Dictionary* 71–72).

34. For Cowper's early opinions, see, e.g., "On the Trial of Admiral Keppel" and "An Address to the Mob . . ." (1779); "The Modern Patriot," "On the Burning of Lord Mansfield's Library . . . ," "On the Same" (1780), in *Poems* 1: 211–13, 408, 411–12. Cowper refers admiringly to Chatham's opposition to peace with America, *The Task* 2:240–44 (*Poems* 2). In some late works, perhaps influenced by his own recurrent madness, he ingratiatingly praises King George's recovery from that malady; see *Poems* 3: 34–37, 44. On slavery, see "The Negro's Complaint," printed at least ten times between 1789 and 1793; "Sweet Meat Has Sour Sauce: Or, the Slave-Trader in the Dumps"; and "The Morning Dream" (1788–89; *Poems* 3: 13–18, 284n); and see also "Charity" (1782) 131–244 (*Poems* 1: 340–43).

35. For the classic treatment of this political trend, see Robbins.

36. See *The Task* 1:730–38, 4:267–332, 4:676–83, etc.

37. Hayley was Blake's patron and Cowper's biographer, but the remark does not seem insincere. In angrier moments, Blake also privately held Hayley a false friend to Cowper (*E*507).

38. *Poems* 1: 296–316. The poem as a whole warns England of God's vengeance through an extended parallel with ancient Israel (33–271). Cowper's specific targets are praise of arms rather than God; the conquest of India, and resulting moral corruption; corruption in the church; the hypocrisy of fast-days; and sodomy (346–427). He venerates Magna Charta and credits God's grace with saving England from the Armada and James II (596–601; 568–79).

39. Cowper also praised Churchill in measured terms ("Table Talk" 670–89) and later included *The Times* among his greatest poems, "except that the subject is disgusting to the last degree" (qtd. in James Laver, Introduction, C. Churchill 1: xliv). See Elfenbein 63–89 for a discussion of Cowper (centered on *The Task*), which fails to note his antisodomitic passages.

40. For the information on Bentham that follows, see Crompton, *Byron* 2, 19–21, 26–31, 39–53, 252–83. Crompton's appendix, 383–86, describes the mss. Crompton published excerpts from the 1785 ms. in two issues of *Journal of Homosexuality* (1978), under the title "Offences Against One's Self: Paederasty"; redacted excerpts from the 1814–16 mss. were published by C. K. Ogden (1931) as "Offences Against Taste." My quotations are from these sources.

41. Crompton transcribes Bentham's comments on Jesus slightly differently than Ogden (*Byron* 260); see 274–75, 279–80 for Blake's Jesus and Bentham's.

Chapter 2.
Blake and the Poetics of Masculinity

1. See *OED, prolific, prolifical,* and derivatives. While a majority of senses are nongendered or applicable to both sexes, one regular meaning was "[c]ausing abundant production, fertilizing," and, as a verb (*prolificate*), "to render prolific or fruitful; to fertilize"; most instances of this meaning refer to males. Some other exempla, e.g., one involving the suppressive effects of French wines, indicate that male functions are being thought of. Few uses of these words referred specifically to females.

2. See *FZ* 122:27–123:32; Exod. 13:21–22; Ezek. 37:2–12; Isa. 14:29–30. For discussion, see Tannenbaum 196–98. Because Hezekiah first destroyed the Mosaic brazen image of a serpent and then was emblematized as a serpent himself, Tannenbaum views these lines as implying Orc's cyclic degeneration.

3. These differences appear in the five copies viewable (May 2000) at the on-line *William Blake Archive.* Copies D and I (Library of Congress; Fitzwilliam Museum, Cambridge) use color to suggest elongated shapes along the right lover's thigh; in the others (C and F, Morgan Library; H, Fitzwilliam Museum), color suggests indeterminate or moundlike forms. See the detailed description by Erdman and others in "Reading the Illuminations" 164–69. Mitchell refers to the figures both as "androgynous" and as either female or "sexually ambiguous" (*Composite Art* 11n., 10). See also Eaves, Essick, and Viscomi 130–31.

4. See contrasting evaluations by Hagstrum (*Poet and Painter* 94; see also 56, 79 on "The Ecchoing Green") and by Erdman and others ("Reading the Illuminations" 169–71); see also Eaves, Essick, and Viscomi 131–32. Hagstrum sees the upper figure as male.

5. Blake might have known the lines in Dryden's translation: "His snowy neck reclines upon his breast, / Like a fair flower by the keen share oppressed" (9.581–82). But he also knew some Latin, as his later citations of Vergil according to the Latin lineation show (*E*270, 274). "Purpureus" literally means purple; figuratively, it signifies brilliantly colored, beautiful.

6. In stressing the overall male-centeredness of the proverbs, I would not deny their dialogic quality, stressed by Andrew Cooper, Gavin Edwards, Michael F. Holstein, and others. But it is hard to disagree with Bruder that even in the proverbs, dialogue over gender is at best a "dissenting undercurrent" (122).

7. This point omits a discussion of whether other forms of sexuality, and/or less hierarchized sexual relations, are suggested in the implied renewal of "innocence" in several of the *Songs.* I also postpone, for the moment, a discussion of sexual categorization in Blake's later doctrine of "emanations."

8. Treatments of this situation were legion. Ann Radcliffe, Mary Darby Robinson, Mary Wollstonecraft (in *The Wrongs of Woman,* written after *VDA*), and others dealt with it, as did other male writers—see Chatterton's "Maria Friendless Letter" (*Works* 1: 594–97), itself largely plagiarized from Johnson's *Rambler* 170 (*Works* 5: 135–39).

9. Warren Stevenson cites two lyrics from *PS* (pub. 1783), "To Spring" and "How sweet I roam'd," as exemplifying the "androgynous sublime" (18, 23, 24). His arguments are not fully persuasive to me, and in any case, Stevenson does not contend that these poems refer to homoeroticism.

10. See Schuchard, "Blake's 'Mr. Femality.'" Erdman, with the archness of early responses to homosexuality in Blake, says, "I shan't venture a guess" about his identity (*Prophet* 124n).

11. See also Mellor, "Sex, Violence, and Slavery" 266n, citing Jack Goody; Worrall, "*Botanic Garden*" 402–405; *IB* 128, citing Elaine M. Kauvar.

12. Bruder further argues that Oothoon's "virgin fears" (iii:3) are not of her approaching heterosexual initiation but of the hostility her open sexuality may provoke (74); but "virgin" surely suggests the conventional reading.

13. See *FZ* 7b, 91–93, where she is so identified in a revision of *A* 1–2.

14. See also Blackstone 55; Bloom, *Apocalypse* 120; Damon, *Dictionary* 438; Margoliouth 95. Despite its early date (1924) Damon's discussion in *Philosophy* (99–100, 105–108) is the most complex of these.

15. Besides Peterson, Aers, and Mellor, see Anderson and Haigwood for negative assessments; Wilkie 73–84 for a critical but more sympathetic view. See Morris Eaves's rejoinder to Mellor, "On Blakes We Want" 433–35.

16. Bruder here extends an extraordinarily provocative reading of *T,* which contends that male critics have misread Thel's flight back to the vales of Har as a refusal of experience when it is actually a positive protest against patriarchy ("The Sins of the Fathers," revised as chapter 2 of *Daughters*).

17. Brenda S. Webster, for example, uses the offer as evidence that "Blake's ideal female freely provides her husband with other men like Oothoon in *Visions*" ("Blake, Women, and Sexuality" 205; see 212–13 for further discussion of the speech).

18. Linkin argues that perhaps Oothoon means to lie "beside Theotormon 'in lovely copulation' while the pair watch the wanton play of the girls" (190). But this argument seems to proceed from embarrassment. The two lines already quoted (7:25–26) do bear this interpretation, but line 28, "Oothoon shall view his [Theotormon's] dear delight," seems to rule it out and sustain most readers' view that Oothoon refers to voyeurism.

19. See Castle, *Masquerade,* chapters 1–2; *IM* 8, E457 ("they go in Post chaises & Stages to Vauxhall & Ranelagh"); *J* 8:2, discussed in chapter 6 below.

20. To cite one modern example, Christopher Isherwood's *A Single Man* (1964), an early affirmative treatment of male homosexuality, ends with a masturbation scene in which the protagonist achieves orgasm by fantasizing sex between two college boys.

21. Though they are not strictly material to my argument, it is well to have the several distinct versions of Urizen's creation in mind. In chapter 4 [b] of *U,* Los creates time but does not directly cobble together Urizen's body; rather, in the passages I quote below, Urizen's fantasies surge and his "bounded" mind begins to roll, creating "chains of the mind" (10:19, 25). Though possibly Los's rivets, etc., materialize as these chains, the rest of the formation of

Urizen's body in seven "ages" is self-generated. On the other hand, chapter 4 [a], present in six of *U*'s eight known copies, starts with Urizen's "hurtling bones" and states that Los "bound every change [of Urizen] / With rivets of iron & brass" (8:2, 10–11; precedes plate 10 in copies ADG, follows 10 in BEF, and is omitted in CJ). This phrase gives the impression that Los rivets together the parts of Urizen's body as they self-generate in 4 [b]. In the section of *Ah* that I consider below, Urizen's nerves and (apparently) semen have already created "hurtling bones" (4:24) when Los appears and throws nets around the bones (4:29–30), in a process like that in *U* 4 [a]. Finally, in *BL,* not considered further below, Los perceives Urizen's already formed spine, forges the sun, and binds sun to spine, in *nine* ages (5:12–14, 27–30, 41–47).

22. David Simpson has previously noted that this passage refers to masturbation but has discussed only lines 11–14. His point, I take it, is that masturbation encapsulates Urizen's character as writer of his books, since writing, like masturbating, replaces a present partner (audience) by "an absent or at best phantasized public" (16). Simpson further notes the passage's syntactic ambiguity and asserts that Los (mentioned in line 15) may be hiding Urizen, rather than Urizen hiding his fantasies (16). Though barely possible, the resulting gloss, "Los hiding Urizen in dark secresy [and hiding] his [Urizen's or Los's] fantasies in surging sulphureous fluid," is the most contrived of several possibilities.

23. For some treatments of *U*'s structure see Simmons; Ault, "De-Formation"; Mitchell, *Composite Art* chapter 4.

24. For a discussion of Freud's theory of masturbation as applied to Blake, in reference to the *VDA* scene already discussed, see George 135–40.

25. See Dörrbecker 182–84 for an extended discussion of this design. See also *IB* 161–62. Bruder suggests that the image represents the contemporary allegation that Marie Antoinette taught the eight-year-old dauphin to masturbate (*Daughters* 164–65).

26. For the children's roles, see Damon, *Dictionary,* under various names; Ferber, "Finite Revolutions" 223–27; Dörrbecker 277–78. Ferber nicely remarks that the children are "staying out later than they should like any children" (226). These writers do not discuss the implication of autoerotic activity. Damon's symbolic identifications of the children (Sotha is war resulting from sexual frustration, Ethinthus is "the mortal flesh," etc.) are often schematic, and his overall view of the children as representing "the progressive frustration of sex under the domination of the female" (*Dictionary* 130) ignores the sexual rebellions of both Antamon and Oothoon here.

27. Aers criticizes the passages I have quoted as showing a "thoroughly traditional . . . division of sexual roles" ("Sex, Society and Ideology" 36). Though he does not notice their masturbatory implications, he is right about their male-centeredness.

28. S. A. A. D. Tissot's *Onanism or, a Treatise upon the Disorders Produced by Masturbation* (trans. 1761), which likewise focused on the act's purported

physiological sequelae, made similar claims (Porter and Hall 101–102). I quote *Onania* from the sixteenth edition (1737), incorporating the seventh edition of the *Supplement,* originally published separately. Only 68 of the 332 pages of this edition (excluding front matter) are expository text; the rest consist of letters from readers, with commentary, and the constant expansion of this material ensured the work's frequent editions. *Onania* sold well on both sides of the Atlantic; the tenth edition was reprinted in Boston in 1724 (Brit. Lib. Cat.).

29. See *The Chained Boy,* chapter 3.

30. For some other examples, see Edmiston 15, on Sade's belief that the Qur'án tolerates sodomy; Norton 124, for sodomites' "Turkish crimes" in polemical verse. For the medieval Christian view that Islam was lax toward marriage and divorce, see Daniel 158–63; on the same view regarding hetero- and homosexual sodomy and lesbianism, see 164–68, 179–80, 226–27, 351–53. Daniel focuses on the period when medieval Christians first seriously studied Islam, 1100 to 1350; the conceptions then formed apparently changed little in five hundred years. The *Phoenix,* for example, was reflecting a view formed early on that the Qur'án effectually tolerated sodomy because it failed to condemn it severely enough (see Daniel 166, 353). See also Said 62–63.

31. This quick discussion scants the complexity of Blake's presentation, but it has to be said that previous commentaries haven't done much better. For some representative discussions, see Howard, *Infernal Poetics,* chapter 8; Tannenbaum, *Biblical Tradition,* chapter 7; Mee, *Enthusiasm* 129–31. Dörrbecker usefully suggests that the "secluded places" section is "a double-edged critique of the monastic system and of the repression of sexual desire," and wonders if Blake "thought of the Koran as . . . 'loose' in its narrative structure and contents if compared with the Old and New Testament[s]" (349). Mee reads this reference as a negative comment on "the monstrous consequences of repression . . . lust and violence: the 'loose Bible' of Mahomet and Odin's 'Code of War'" (130–31); but he misses the opposition between the two and the sex-positive resonance of Islam and Arab lands in much contemporary usage. See *OED, looseness* 3 and *loose* a./adv. 7: "[f]ree from moral restraint; lax in principle, conduct, or speech; chiefly in narrower sense, unchaste, wanton, dissolute, immoral," with exempla from 1470.

32. Erdman concedes, "[I]f [the women] have a secret child they are not showing it" (*IB* 154); the invisible child and Dörrbecker's belief that the women must be sisters seem to enter the picture only because each makes a lesbian embrace less likely. *BB*'s "a nude woman who is clasping two younger nude women" (98) is not euphemistic, as this commentary sticks to pictographic description and avoids interpretation. Keynes and Wolf believe the women "cower" in the flames (*Census* 41), which is at least possible. Much of the critical discussion has centered on whether the ensemble of illustrations should be read as a sequence rising up the page (possibly with negative implications, since the above-ground figure at top seems to be in a despairing

huddle) or should be taken separately or in another configuration, e.g., with the bottom figures counterposed to those at top. (See Dörrbecker 67–68 for representative quotations.) However important this issue may be for *A*'s political themes, in relation to the portrayal of homosexuality it makes little difference whether the tableau is taken by itself, as showing lesbian awakening in the flames of revolt, or as part of a sequence ending in female isolation and despair.

Chapter 3.
Homosexuality, Resistance, and Apocalypse:
The Four Zoas

1. Blake wrote two texts headed "Night the Seventh," conventionally termed 7a and 7b. Erdman's 1982 and later editions of Blake's works *(E)*, now standard, depart from the practice of earlier editors, including Erdman himself, in arranging these into a hypothetical single text. With several other writers, I regard this emendation as unsatisfactory and continue to refer to 7a and 7b, but the issue does not greatly affect my argument.

2. The shape over Orc's belly is about 2 cm long on its dorsal edge, 2.5 cm on the ventral edge; assuming Orc's 27.6-cm figure (toe to forehead) to be five feet, six inches tall, the "penis" would be about 4.8 inches dorsally and 6 inches ventrally, consistent with penises in other images (see chapter 5). Orc also has sketch marks for an alternative, flexed left leg (Magno and Erdman 69). To the right and above Orc's head are moundlike shapes that may be rocks but that also suggest a third torso or an alternative sketch for Orc's upper body: a large upper chest and shoulders turned slightly toward us and a suggestion of a head turned to the figure's left side. This figure would represent a slightly more conventional posture for a male receiving fellation; the redrawing may also indicate some problems in dealing with perspective. Of the two facsimiles, Bentley's *Vala* shows most details; Magno and Erdman's *The Four Zoas*, shot in infrared to bring up erasures, paradoxically produces a dark blur. The kneeling figure is described by Butlin (1: 285), and, with qualifications, Magno and Erdman (69); neither description notes the two possible penises. Some other commentaries do not note the kneeling figure at all (Bentley, *Vala* 79; Webster, *Psychology* 234). Webster sees the recumbent figure as Urizen and unaccountably states that he has "large genitals" (234).

3. Direct allusion seems unlikely. Blake may well have been acquainted with Churchill's poems, though we do not know this. He did not own the 1803 volume in which some of Chatterton's antihomosexual verses first appeared (chapter 1); moreover, inferences about *FZ*'s composition would probably date the page 78 sketch earlier than 1803 (Essick, "Intention"). But the general situation was a familiar one.

4. I cite Robertson from the first edition, *The History of America;* Bidney quotes the cognate passage from the fifth edition, London, 1788, 2: 389–90 (Bid-

ney 196). Guatimozin is another name for Cuauhtémoc, still the chief resistance hero in Mexican tradition (Cuauhtémoc Cárdenas, leader of the leftist electoral opposition in the 1980s and 1990s, was named for him).

5. Bidney interprets this line as referring to Aztec practices of ritual sacrifice; he does not comment at all on what occurs *between* Guatimozin and the "favourite."

6. The text reads, *"Da cay fasy?"* but is corrected in an erratum and in the second edition (1806). Blake is likely to have known Stedman's written account, certainly after publication, since he owned the published book. His engraving, facing the following page (110), includes only one prisoner, a simplification that may be his or Stedman's (Stedman's watercolors are lost). Blood flows from the hook and drips to the ground in uncolored copies; in a hand-tinted copy at the Huntington Library, the figure is medium dark brown and the blood is crimson.

7. For an extended discussion, see *The Chained Boy,* chapter 4.

8. See *NT* 163 (Night 5, p. 8), which illustrates Young's "Wit, a true Pagan, deifies the Brute." Blake depicts a cowled Wit bowing to a rising snake, ignoring Young's emphasis on how wit dignifies base pleasures, or "Swine-enjoyments," as the next line says. For some treatments of Blake's procedures in illustrating other authors, see Tayler, *Gray,* and Grant, Rose, and Tolley.

9. Blake produced *FZ* on folio-size sheets, working on both sides and including sketches in varying stages of finish. Starting with page 43, he used proof sheets from his earlier engraved illustrations for *NT,* writing his text in the blank rectangles left for the printed text and continuing on the verso sides, where he added further sketches. With a few exceptions the rest of *FZ* conforms to this format; see Magno and Erdman for particulars.

10. In suggesting that Blake's illustrations may ignore narrative context, I do not contravene the general view that they often comment critically or expand on the works he is illustrating; rather, I am suggesting one way that they do this. The main page-by-page commentary on *The Four Zoas* designs, Magno and Erdman's, consistently (and often ingeniously) relates the designs directly to the text narrative. I am suggesting a freer relationship, one in which Blake could give a word or phrase a meaning not present in the narrative at all.

11. The woman has a goofy, delighted expression as she cups the man's testicles with her left hand and manipulates his penis with her right; the drops are not visible to the eye or in Magno and Erdman's photograph, though they are supplied in their accompanying sketch (47).

12. Besides others discussed below, these include the ascending figure on page 139 and a full-page figure on page 76 with indeterminately male-female breasts and partly erased genitals that may be male or male-female.

13. For descriptions, see Magno and Erdman 39; Butlin 1: 278; Grant, "Visions" 153–60 (also summarizing earlier commentaries), which sees the figure embracing the winged penis as female; Hilton, *Imagination* 165; Storch,

Sons 71–73, which sees this whole figure as a female, "menacing and castrating" like others on the page (73).

14. This and some other fragments, bound at the end of the *FZ* manuscript, are described in *E*, Bentley's *Vala*, and Lincoln 293–95. No placement within the main text is indicated; though the fragments contain three short lines ending "&c" (Blake's usual procedure for showing how an addition fit together with existing lines), there are no likely candidates for continuing the lines. Since the fragments are written on a sheet of notepaper, either side could begin the mini-narrative, if indeed the two sides are related. Erdman notes a rejected passage on page 7 referring to "two forms of horror" as part of the birth scene (*E*821; see Lincoln 294–95). Seemingly, Blake tried one version of a hermaphroditic birth in that passage, another in the separate fragments, and abandoned both. Schuchard speculates that page 141 may reflect interest in the hermaphrodism of the Chevalier D'Éon ("Mr. Femality" 64; see chapter 2).

15. The actual rape occurs two pages after Orc's initial temptation. The intervening war song sung by "Elemental Gods" and "demons of the deep"—on one level, those of English naval imperialism—evokes Urizen's power manifested through the ages and also celebrates Vala as a sexually enticing war goddess (91:21–93:20). This narrative order implicitly presents Orc's action as a capitulation to overwhelming tyrannic power and the sexual lures of collaboration, while maintaining the critique of sexual aggression. For the specific revisions of *A*, compare *A* 2:1–2, incorporated as 91:13 and 17 with interlinear and marginal additions (91:10–17). On sexual violence in *A*, see chapter 2.

16. For other views of these designs, see Magno and Erdman 27–28, 74; Butlin 1: 276, 287; Grant, "Visions" 150, 152, 189 (brief references). Magno and Erdman perceive "eyes, nose, and mouth on the head of the penis" in 88 [96] (74); I do not see these in the ms. or in their reproduction. Page 4 includes a lightly sketched extension of the snake into the upper margin, ending with a more literal serpent head. Magno and Erdman try to view both phallic images positively: On 4, the cupid myth's sexual meaning becomes "manifest and therefore innocent and human," while on 88 [96], Jesus' presence in the design for facing page 89 [97] suggests that "the bowing figures [may] be the Three Wise men" (28, 74). But the cupid's fierce brow speaks for itself, and figures bowing to the earth are nearly always negative in Blake—see "A Little Boy Lost"; *NT* 163, mentioned earlier; and "The Overthrow of Apollo and the Pagan Gods" in both sets of illustrations for Milton's "Nativity" ode (Butlin 538.4, 542.4). In addition, the bowing figures are facing away from Jesus' image on 89 [97].

17. See Hagstrum, "Babylon" 109–11 for an early suggestion that Orc and Vala's treatment in Nights 7a and 7b criticizes aggressive heterosexuality.

18. The issues have been extensively debated. The generative statements remain Fox, "Woman as Metaphor"; George, *Blake and Freud;* Mellor, "Blake's Portrayal of Women"; Storch, *Sons;* Webster, "Blake, Women, and Sexuality"

and *Prophetic Psychology,* all cited elsewhere. On female will, see Essick, "Blake's 'Female Will,'" which also ably summarizes the critical literature as of 1991 (615–17, 627 nn. 1, 2, 4). See Freed for a restatement of the case against "female will" (44–59, 69–71, 74, and elsewhere).

19. On the erasure of females in the speech, see Ault, *Narrative Unbound* 421 and 425. For a reading opposed to mine, see Freed 44.

20. For discussion of Vala's role in *J,* see chapter 6; on the destructive daughters of Albion in that work, see Sturrock.

21. The same idea is varied by Luvah and Vala in their own pastoral dream (127:14–16).

22. For these views, see Nicholas Venette, trans. 1707; Thomas Gibson, 1682 (qtd. above); George Arnauld, 1750, all cited in Donoghue 38, 39, 51.

23. My attention was drawn to this statement by Donoghue (44), who quotes it (in slightly different form) from the tenth edition of *Supplement.*

24. Reproduced in Donoghue, frontispiece.

25. Butlin also sees the clitoris in the page 22 [20] figure as a penis, or an arm protruding from the vagina (1: 278). John E. Grant believes that the woman has been "urinating into a large, tilted tapered-neck jug" ("Visions" 150, endorsed by Magno and Erdman 37). I am unable to see the jug either in reproduction or in the original. Magno and Erdman do not note the erect penis on the male figure in 110 [106]. Elsewhere in the poem, possible suggestions of lesbianism have apparently been overlooked simply through a preconception that suggestive poses must be male-female. On page 28, for example, Blake shows a kneeling and a reclining figure, both naked, neither with visible sexual organs. The kneeling figure (at left) is broad-hipped and curls one arm over its head, a pose Blake uses for females on pages 3, 112 [108], and 118. The other figure has curly shoulder-length hair, and, when it reappears on page 31, well-defined breasts. Magno and Erdman denominate the figures on 28 as female and male respectively and the second, as it appears on 31, as "hermaphroditic." Butlin sees just the opposite—a male on the left and a female on the right on 28, and a female on 31. Grant sees the page 31 figure as "an evanescent youth" but does not comment on page 28. Since the identifications are so uncertain, and each of the page 28 figures has been seen as female by some viewers, the possibility that both are female should be considered. This possibility seems simply not to have occurred to Magno and Erdman or Butlin, perhaps because the texts of pages 28 and 31 concern Luvah and Vala. Yet, as we know, Blake's drawings do not necessarily illustrate his texts directly. See Magno and Erdman 40–41; Butlin 1: 278–79; Grant, "Visions" 184.

26. *E* reads "Shadowly" in line 24, evidently a misprint for clearly legible "Shadowy" in the ms.

27. Magno and Erdman instead connect this fecundity to Urizen's creative activity (41–42).

28. See *OED, consummate* (past participle and verb); *consummation.* Senses signifying completion, perfection, or ending are found from 1390 onward, and

the apocalyptic sense of the "consummation of the world, of all things, etc.," from 1541; the sexual sense is found from 1530 onward.

29. The two pages, a recto-verso pair, must have been conceived as a unit; they were added to Night 9 after it was first drafted, as shown by the erased title for the night visible on page 119 under the continuation of the text episode beginning on 117. See *E*783.

Chapter 4:
History, Homosexuality, and Milton's Legacy

1. For general studies of the Blake-Milton relationship, see DiSalvo; Sandler; Wittreich, *Angel.* On Milton's doctrine of election, see Fallon. Blake's view of the matter is probably based on *PL* 3:183–202, which combines a statement of election of those "of peculiar grace" with offered possible salvation for "The rest" (183–85); *De doctrina Chrisiana,* now usually considered as affirming the Arminian tenets of conditional election and unlimited atonement, was unknown until 1823–25. In any case Blake rejects election altogether and seems to associate it with the rise of ruling classes (*M* 25:31–32).

2. On *M*'s dating, see Viscomi, chapter 32 and discussion below, chapter 5.

3. For some versions of this interpretation, see Damon, *Philosophy* 168–76, 407–411 and *Dictionary* 179, 277, 357; Elfenbein 154; Essick and Viscomi 15–17; Fox, *Poetic Form* 32, 57 (as one context among others); Frye, *Symmetry* 325–37; Storch, *Sons* 131–33; Webster, *Psychology* 253–55. Not all include the homosexual element. Frye's later "Notes for a Commentary on *Milton,"* while retaining some biographical reference, reads the Bard's Song mainly in terms of interacting mental or imaginative faculties; there is no reference to homosexuality (103–4, 129–33). Blake does use a version of *M*'s dictum about Satan, "Corporeal Friends are Spiritual Enemies," in reference to Hayley in a letter (*M* 4:26; *E*728). Blake, then, saw a similarity between Hayley and his conception of Satan. But this does not mean Satan is Hayley.

4. For example, Otto writes that Charles I, Cromwell, and James II were all of the Reprobate when challenging authority (Charles when facing execution) but of the Elect when in power (48). These points and the underlying assumption that whoever is outside the power structure of the day is of the Reprobate may be valid, but Otto does not try to show that Blake uses the terms this way.

5. See Erdman, *Prophet* 423–26, 424n, 516. Frye adopts the "twelve-book *Milton"* theory in "Notes" 102–103. Among historical readings of the Bard's Song, G. A. Rosso's in "Newton's Pantocrator and Blake's Recovery of Miltonic Prophecy" has affinities with mine while stressing an element I do not, the consolidation of natural religion and its relation to English imperialism.

6. See Thompson, *Making* 157–71; Hone, *Cause of Truth* 147–219.

7. "States" are Blake's way of distinguishing between persons and the acts they perpetrate; individuals enter into the "state" of Satan, for example, but may escape it. Besides the passage above, see *FZ* 107 [115]:23–51, *E*380–81, *J*

49:65–75. For commentaries, see Damon, *Dictionary* 386–87; Erdman, *Prophet* 401; Paley, *Energy* 155–56, none terribly useful, and Damrosch, *Symbol and Truth* 154, an acute comment. For specific treatments of "states" in *M*, see Otto; Bracher 200–207.

8. For modern accounts, see Jones, *First Whigs* 155; Ogg, *Charles II* 2: 206; Prall 66. The accusation was repeated by the Duke of Monmouth in his futile anti-James rebellion in 1685 (van der Zee 193).

9. See Winston S. Churchill 286–301; Jones, *Revolution of 1688* 231; Ogg, *James II and William III* 216; Prall 229–32. Blake could have known of these episodes from many sources, e.g., Hume 12: 272–74, which describes how James, hearing of Anne's defection, "burst into tears . . . [foreseeing] the total expiration of his royal authority," and quotes him: "God help me, my own children have forsaken me!" (12: 274). Catherine Macaulay Graham tells the story in much the same way, including the same quote (8: 245–48). Churchill, created Earl of Marlborough by William, and Duke in 1702, flirted again with James's cause in the 1690s, and remained closely allied with Anne.

10. See Damon, *Dictionary* 329–30 ("Plow"); for a recent discussion, see Otto 50–54 and references.

11. At the assembly "Two Witnesses," Palamabron and Rintrah, appear; Palamabron appeals for judgment, and "it fell on Rintrah and his rage"; then Rintrah's rage "flam'd high & furious in Satan against Palamabron," Los responds in "wrath" and rearranges the earth's geography (a Blakean sign of "fall"), Satan "Accus'd Palamabron before the Assembly of ingratitude! of malice[,]" then "created Seven deadly Sins," became "Opake against the Divine Vision," to the assembly's "Astonishment," and "sunk down a dreadful Death" in the "Space" already mentioned (9:8, 10, 11, 13, 20, 21, 31, 36, 48, 52). At least two aspects of this tale are ambiguous: whether Rintrah and Palamabron are allies or opponents, and whom the judgment favors. There is a related passage in *FZ* in which Rintrah defends Palamabron and Satan is condemned (107:32–37, *E*381), but it is of little help here, for it becomes clear retrospectively that the judgment "fell" negatively on Rintrah (11:23 states that the "wrath [fell] on Rintrah"), which would mean either that Satan is exonerated or that he and Rintrah are allied and both are condemned. The same later passage refers to Satan's receiving "condemnation" (11:28), but it is not clear if this was the import of the initial judgment or a response to Satan's subsequent fall. My own view is that Rintrah and Palamabron are probably on the same side, as they also are at 8:14–24 and 9:43–45, and as the biblical reference to the Two Witnesses (Rev. 11:3–12) seems to imply (possibly, though, Rintrah changes sides twice); the judgment is against Rintrah, as 11:23 indicates, and so implicitly, but not specifically, vindicates Satan and hangs Palamabron out to dry; and Satan rages against Palamabron to consolidate his position (simultaneously becoming blind to the Divine Vision, losing his place in Eden for one in this world, and establishing this world's moral laws), leaving the assembly

"Astonish[ed]" over the unforeseen result of their judgment. All this corresponds, mutatis mutandi, to the process by which Parliament, with popular support and repudiating the "wrath" of the Commonwealth era, invited Charles II to return following his promises of toleration (in the Declaration of Breda, 1660), only to find him persecuting dissenters, executing Commonwealthmen, and attempting to reconstruct absolutism. The Great Solemn Assembly is still in session on plates 11–13, but the emphasis shifts to Leutha's tale, discussed below. For representative views of the textual intricacies, see Bloom, *Apocalypse* 351–53; Damon, *William Blake* 175 and *Dictionary* 321; Essick and Viscomi 127–28; Fox, *Poetic Form* 45; Frye, *Symmetry* 335; Howard, *Milton* 147; Otto 57. Most but not all these commentators have transferred the *FZ* summary to *M,* but there is no support for this reading and it is inconsistent with some details, as noted above. Damon initially felt that "Satan wins the verdict; announces himself as God; and Puritanism is triumphant" (*William Blake* 175) but later believed Satan was condemned; Otto believes Rintrah opposes Palamabron and is condemned but that the result is "one more victory for Satan" (57). It should be noted that the role of the army (possibly identifiable as Rintrah) was highly ambiguous in this period; it initally tried to defend the Commonwealth, but then General George Monck masterminded Charles's return. If one takes the alternative view from mine, Otto's, and Damon's initial view, and believes that Satan is condemned by the assembly, then the outcome of the episode still represents the founding of the Restoration system, but the assembly itself must be viewed less representationally, as a mythic, ambiguous conclave that purges Eden at the cost of inflicting oppression on earth.

12. Suggested by Rosso, in correspondence, March 1999. Rosso further proposes that Leutha's narrative (plates 11–13) focuses on this aspect of the state-church amalgam.
13. On Oothoon's role here, see chapter 6.
14. After 1705 the duchess lost favor, partly because of Anne's turn to a peace policy; she was dismissed in 1711.
15. See, for example, Storch, *Sons* 137; Webster, *Psychology* 253–55.
16. My main sources for this account are van der Zee 414–27 and passim; Rubini 358–81; for the verse, *POAS* vols. 5–6. The van der Zees' biography takes a cautious view, feeling that "[i]f William's feelings for Portland had homosexual overtones, this was almost certainly not the case with Portland," but that the rumors about Keppel most likely had some basis (421–23). For denials, see Baxter 326–27, 348–52, and Horwitz 203–204; for rebuttal, see Rubini 361–62.
17. See *POAS* 5: 38, 60; 6: 244. The satires abound in references to Bentinck; naturally, given his prominent and controversial role in William's diplomacy, not all refer to his alleged sodomy, but many do. Keppel is mentioned less frequently, but in hostile works he nearly always appears as a catamite. See *POAS* 5: 38, 366n (Keppel), 42, 60, 121–22, 153, 154n, 221, 333, 386 (all Bentinck); 6: 16–17 (Bentinck), 18, 244 (Keppel). The term *bardash,* with

the sense of *catamite*, was already current (see *OED*, with exempla from 1548). The satire last quoted affects a biblical locale, hence the Hebraized name. *POAS* tends to explain away these references: "The persistence with which the satirists accuse William of homosexuality may very well result from xenophobia. When confronted by William's baffling refusal to trust any but a few chosen men with his political or private opinions, and by his statesmanlike care to see that young men of promise were preferred rather than old men rewarded [i.e., in the Keppel-Bentinck quarrel], poets and poetasters joined themselves to the common opinion" (W. J. Cameron, *POAS* 5: 38). On the other hand, maybe they knew something Cameron doesn't.

18. I owe this point to van der Zee 424. Swift annotated both volumes of Burnet (1724, 1734), the second rather lightly. The comment quoted, in vol. 1, thus dates from 1724 or later.

19. William's relations with Parliament are too complex to trace here in detail. Very roughly, he largely tried to rule independently from 1690 to 1693, then made a rapprochement with Whig forces and governed through the Whig "Junto" (Somers, Orford, Wharton, and Montagu, with Shrewsbury as an ally) until about 1697, only to break with the Junto and struggle on and off with shifting parliamentary majorities from about 1698 to his death in 1702. The opposition to William was primarily Whig in the first part of his reign, mainly Tory in the last (these terms were just coming into use, and the party organizations they denote were likewise just evolving). For detailed histories, see Horwitz; Ogg, *James II and William III;* Plumb.

20. Plate 9 specifies that Satan reposes "Dead . . . on his Couch" while his "Spectre" descends into the "Space" (49, 52). On plate 13, the Spectre is on the couch; "he" who calls individual law holy, etc., may be either the Spectre or Satan. However important elsewhere in Blake, the distinction between an entity and its Spectre is minimal here. The couch is situated in Rome, Babylon, and Tyre, while Satan's "Mills" are in a "Space" amid "the Rocks of Albions Temples"—likewise a locale of this world—and Satan himself, not his Spectre, is active there (9:51, 11:6–11). For Canaan's meaning, see Frye, "Notes" 121–22.

21. See Blake's remark to Crabb Robinson that atonement is "a horrible doctrine— If another man pay your debt I do not forgive it" (*BR* 337).

22. See Hagstrum's perceptive comment on "monomaniacal heterosexuality" as a quality of the "Babylonian citizen" ("Babylon" 106).

23. Comprehensive studies of all Blake's Milton series include those by Dunbar (1980), Werner (1986), and J. M. Q. Davies (1993), in my view the most carefully nuanced as well as the most provocative; I draw heavily on Davies below. Wittreich (1975) and Behrendt (1983) have discussed the Milton designs in general with detailed studies of those for *PR* (Wittreich) and *PL* (Behrendt, with briefer comments on *Comus* and *PR*). Important discussions of particular sets or topics include Tayler, "Blake" (on the first *Comus* series) and Hagstrum, "Christ's Body." Dates for the groups I discuss are those proposed by Martin Butlin: 1801 and ca. 1815 for the two *Comus* sets; 1816 or

later for *Il Penseroso;* ca. 1816–20 for *PR* (1: 373, with further particulars in the entries for each set). Davies proposes 1825, when the group was sold, as a possible terminal date for *PR* (*Designs* 153). The sets are reproduced as Butlin 527.1–8 and 528.1–8 *(Comus),* 543.1–12 *(L'Allegro* and *Il Penseroso),* and 544.1–12 *(PR).*

24. See the third and tenth (last) designs, "Two boys wandering in the woods by Eton College" and "Boys playing at top." Irene Tayler believes the group as a whole criticizes Gray's sentimental regret for past innocence; while Gray sees the Eton boys as "little victims" ("Ode" 52), Tayler argues, "to Blake they are little fools, accepting the balm of ignorance" (*Illustrations* 41). Tayler does not deal with possible homoeroticism in the designs. For the series' date, see Butlin 1: 255. On "irregular" sexuality in eighteenth-century English public schools, see G. S. Rousseau, "Pursuit" 138, 143–46, and note Bentham's comments (chapter 1); see G. S. Rousseau, "In the House of Madam Vander Tasse," for a university homosocial club.

25. For a vigorous defense of Milton's presentation of virginity, see Fletcher 209–26. To oversimplify a complex argument, Fletcher's point is twofold: first, virginity is a higher virtue than chastity, since it represents the integrity of the person rather than a socially negotiated behavior; second, as used in Milton's masque, chastity stands for the social virtues of conservation and memory while virginity, precisely because it is impermanent, signifies renewal and transcendence. For the possible influence on *Comus* of the execution for sodomy and rape of the Earl of Castlehaven, related by marriage to the Bridgewater family for whom *Comus* was written, see Breasted. For a possible homosexual attraction in Milton's youth, see Shawcross 33–60, esp. 50–54 on *Comus;* see Rumrich for a distinct view.

26. Dunbar suggests the swords' possible homosexual significance (20); she, Werner, and Davies all note the connection between handing down grapes and sexual initiation (19; 28, 39; *Designs* 37). All cite the second design for "The Ecchoing Green" as an example of this motif; Davies adds the similarly handled linnet's nest in the fifth Gray design (*Designs* 37). Werner suggests that in the early design Comus is focusing on the weapons (28). On the grapes in "The Ecchoing Green," see for example Hagstrum, *Poet and Painter* 59, 76; Keynes, *Songs* 134; Leader 85–86; on the similar design in *MHH* 2, see chapter 2 above. One must be cautious in interpreting details. Comus's gaze, for example, cannot be followed precisely. In the Boston design it is indeed a bit walleyed—his right eye seems to look out in a higher plane than the left. Unless Blake is making an exceptionally witty visual pun, the discrepancy would seem to suggest that he did not lavish much care on such details.

27. There are three major versions, with associated sketches. Butlin 531 (signed and dated 1806) shows a phallic snake slithering voluptuously at the couple's feet; Butlin 529.5 and 536.4 (1807, 1808) both show Satan enfolded by the snake, though with other differences in composition and color.

28. Besides the cleavage, what would be the right (closer) breast shows a well-defined bottom contour, and the left an angled contour in profile: these are

more likely breasts than male chest muscles. The right figure's hair is golden-yellow, a little lighter than the background coloring of gold with gold-orange; the "bun" is not clearly defined by color but may be made out in hazy outline. The left figure has no sexually determinate body contours, but its short hair, also yellow-gold, seems to define it as male. Among interpreters I cite, only Davies calls the bound figures male (*Designs* 141); Dunbar does not guess at their sex (150–51), while Werner sees them as Adam and Eve (160).

29. It is interesting to correlate both Jesus' and the woman's gestures with the seventeenth- and eighteenth-century models for hand gestures Janet Warner reproduces in *Blake and the Language of Art.* Jesus' palms-outward gesture is quite close to the gesture John Bulwer (1644 and later) called "castigo" (censure, reproof, chastisement, correction), while the woman's bears some similarity to "rationes profert" (citing reasons, offering explanations). (Warner 56, 50.) Warner's thesis that these and other traditional models offered "a common language that all men could understand" (4) is overstated, but Warner does establish a rough correspondence between these models and many of Blake's uses of gesture. The woman's gesture, then, should perhaps be read as offering justification or inviting consideration, rather than directly enticing.

30. For the *Il Penseroso* design, see Behrendt 32; Davies, *Designs* 132–35; Dunbar 143–46; Werner 154–56. If one reads this design ironically, as these commentaries tend to, Melancholy emerges as a figure who separates what should come together. Not only does she keep females from males, but her influence keeps the two males separate from each other: the nearer, who might become a guide/lover for his notably vacuous companion, instead gazes up reverently at her figure. Melancholy's hooded form has affinities with the cowled females of *A* 14 and *J* 4. For some commentaries on the latter, see Paley, *Jerusalem* 135; Mitchell, *Composite Art* 206; Hoagwood 73–74, whose interpretation is opposite to mine. Overall, my view of the *Il Penseroso* series is closest to Behrendt's: in the last design, "Milton in Old Age," the poet "[t]ranscending the various physical, intellectual, and imaginative limitations the first eleven designs suggest . . . bursts forth in timeless prophetic *song*" (31).

31. Davies adapts Dunbar's suggestion (183–84) that Jesus in both designs appears within a mandorla (almond-shaped aureole), or vesica piscis, a framing convention in much medieval sacred art.

Chapter 5:
The Cruelties of Moral Law:
Homosexuality and the Revision of Milton

1. For varying dates for the poem's composition and printing, see Viscomi chapter 32 passim; Essick and Viscomi 37–41; *E*806; *BB* 304–309. There is consensus that copies AB were printed first, with most of C printed about

the same time, D some years later, and the additional plates sometime in between. Viscomi offers the fullest hypothetical reconstruction of this sequence, which I follow. He argues that A, B, and the first version of C were
all printed ca. late 1810-early 1811; that A and then B were sold around this
time to Philip Hurd and Thomas Butts; and that all the added plates were
etched later than copies AB and the bulk of C—rather than some having
been etched at the same time, as assumed by *BB* and *E.* Hence, added plates
3–5, 10, and 18 (along with 32, which will not concern me) would all date
from some time subsequent to early 1811. Plate 5, initially added to both C
and D (which Blake probably produced on commission for James Vine in
1818), was later removed from C, which Blake kept in his studio at least
until 1826, when it may have been sold to Thomas Wainewright. (See in
particular Viscomi 320–25, 325–29.) I use *E*'s numbers for the added plates,
designated *a, b, f, c, d,* and *e* in standard bibliographical nomenclature. The
salient differences in artwork, detailed below, involve suggestions of aroused
male genitals in some figures in copy A, a more generalized treatment in B,
and the presence of drapery in C and D. These are most easily explained as
a progressive shift from A to D, known to be the latest copy. Viscomi's general thesis on Blake's production method—that he printed and colored his
works simultaneously, in batches—would mean B and C were originally colored with A, presumably similarly, and later altered. Some details in B and
C could easily be additions; others are less easy to explain in this way. Alternatively, A-C may have been printed together but colored separately. Least
easy to imagine is that these images in A-C were given widely differing treatments in a single printing-coloring session. Below, I assume that these details
as now seen in A-C reflect finishing at different dates.

2. The narrative (excluding the preface) contains 1,733 lines in thirty-five text
plates in copies AB, 1,963 in forty-one text plates in D—13.3 percent more.

3. Louis Crompton, *Byron and Greek Love* 161–71, contains apparently the
first modern account of the Vere-street events. (See my preface.) Though excellent, it has some small-scale errors and does not fully convey the broad-
ness of the repression. Norton also has a discussion (187–98). My account
is based on contemporary newspapers, with supplemental detail from
Crompton and Norton as noted.

4. For the locations of Vere-street and Clare-market, see *A to Z of Regency London,* map 13, Db and Dc (based on *Horwoods Plan of London,* 1813); see
also the 1820 map reproduced in Damon, *Dictionary* plate 6. For streets
mentioned in the press accounts, I retain the contemporary style: "Vere-
street"; for others I use modern style: "Oxford Street." The evidence does not
suggest that the Swan's patrons were an organized "society" *(Times)* but
rather some habitual and some casual patrons, as in any other public house;
yet similar terms were used in several newspapers. The events described
below were reported in at least four London newspapers: the *Times* and
Morning Chronicle, both published Monday through Saturday; *Bell's,* published Sunday; and another, unidentified Sunday paper from which a sheaf

of clippings is reproduced in *Sodomy Trials*. (These occupy thirteen unpaginated leaves and are cited below as *Sodomy Trials*, with date.) Many of the stories crib from one another. For instance, the undercover cops' descriptions "of too gross a nature to meet the public eye" in *Bell's* (and much of the rest of this article) are the same in a *Sodomy Trials* clipping; much but not all of the account is the same in *Morning Chronicle* (July 10, 1810: 3), where the descriptions are "of too horrible a nature" (etc.). The *Morning Chronicle* also reports twenty-three persons taken into custody, but gives only twenty-one names; the same error appears in the two Sunday papers, whereas the *Times* has the right number. Presumably then the two Sunday papers pirated and sometimes rewrote the dailies (usually the *Morning Chronicle* but sometimes the *Times*), but the Sunday accounts may differ from each other as well. According to Norton (apparently relying on *Phoenix*, which, however, does not give a date), the White Swan had been a molly house for less than six months when it was raided (190).

5. One, "as not having appeared so active as the others," received one year without pillorying; the rest two years with pillorying, except for a repeat offender, who received three years (*Sodomy Trials*, Sept. 30, 1810).

6. Crompton says seven papers called for death for attempted sodomy, including the *Morning Chronicle* and *Bell's* (*Byron* 167–68). Neither of these, however, specified what legal changes it favored. The former argued that "the horrible exhibition of yesterday must prove to every considerate spectator the necessity for an immediate alteration in the law," adding the remarks quoted above; *Bell's* paraphrased much of this paragraph, including this sentence, but without the points on the war and manners. These remarks are compatible with favoring imprisonment without pillorying, or something similar—a position held by a few contemporaries, as noted below. Crompton further mistakes the *Chronicle's* boast that "illustrious persons" have adopted its views on cultural decline as a claim of support for the death penalty.

7. Sources are as already mentioned, supplemented by Norton 129–31, 196. Of the forty-eight defendants, three were sentenced to death, all mentioned below (Cole, whose execution itself I have not found reported, and Hepburn and White). One received a five-year sentence and thirteen got between one and three years, seven of these with pillorying (six were Vere-street defendants). One received pillorying and prison, the length of sentence not reported; five were sentenced to the pillory without prison, two were given six months, and another was sentenced to three without pillorying. Five (including two Vere-street prisoners) were committed for trial with no outcome reported, and two acquitted, of whom one was held to bail "for a distinct offence of a like nature" (*Sodomy Trials*, July 29, 1810). Two were charged but never prosecuted. Twelve Vere-street prisoners, as noted earlier, were discharged for lack of evidence. One person was convicted of extortion for threatening to prosecute a wealthy merchant on "a charge of an abominable nature," and sentenced to seven years' transportation (*Sodomy Trials*, Nov. 4,

1810). In addition, one person never arrested committed suicide after being hounded by a mob; Richard Barnes's pillorying was reported in *Bell's*, Jan. 20, 1811: 24, but I have not found an earlier report of his arrest or trial.

8. *Sodomy Trials*, Oct. 14, 1810, gives additional details: Carter accosted the young man, Purdy, on a park bench, followed him and tried again, and was arrested with the aid of a passerby.

9. Accounts in *Bell's* and the *Sodomy Trials* clippings (both Dec. 9) are nearly identical. For earlier phases of this prosecution, see *Sodomy Trials*, July 29, 1810; *Bell's*, Sept. 23, 1810: 303. Crompton, Harvey, and Norton all assume or state that Hepburn and White were among those charged in the July 8 raid (169; 943; 194); other accounts have repeated the error. The descriptions of White occur in a letter to Byron from Charles Skinner Matthews, who visited White and Hepburn in prison (qtd. in Crompton, *Byron* 169) and in *Phoenix* 14.

10. The *Times* account was reprinted with minor editing by *Bell's* (Mar. 10, 1811: 80). Crompton gives a slightly different transcription (*Byron* 171). The *Morning Chronicle* carried a briefer and, as Crompton notes, more "stereotyped" account (Mar. 8, 1811: 3; *Byron* 171).

11. Cambridge is not named but is identifiable from details in the story.

12. See also *Times*, Mar. 14, 1811: 3 (death sentence of Cox, also known as Jacob Fisher, at the Oxford Assizes); *Bell's*, Jan. 20, 1811: 24 (pillory), Mar. 3, 1811: 72 (pillory), Mar. 17, 1811: 85 (death sentence of Cox). No details are given about Cox's case. None of these cases is reported in the *Morning Chronicle*, the third paper I have read for this period. See also *Bell's*, Sept. 13, 1811: 295, for a later case (execution of Thomas James, convicted at the Stafford Assizes). I have not read the *Times* or *Morning Chronicle* for July-Dec. 1811.

13. For trends over time, see Harvey 939–40, 947–48. Harvey's data differ in detail from mine, perhaps because of different definitions and coverage. For instance, where I have found three executions (and a death sentence) in 1811, Harvey's sources show two but perhaps count Hepburn and White in 1810. Harvey's figure of twenty-nine convictions in all of England and Wales in 1810 for "assault with intent to commit sodomy, and other unnatural Misdemeanours" (939) is not inconsistent with my tabulation of twenty noncapital convictions for July-Dec. 1810, mainly in London—though perhaps too low. Harvey's sources, parliamentary reports commissioned in 1818 and later, may themselves have missed some older cases. But the overall trends seem clear. For yet another compilation, differing slightly from Harvey's, see Norton 132.

14. Viscomi's argument that C and not D (as assumed by most earlier writers) represents Blake's final editorial intentions is obviously relevant here. Viscomi, joined by Robert N. Essick, argues on chronologic rather than thematic grounds: C stayed in Blake's possession after D was sold, and Blake rearranged plates (and dropped plate 5) during this period, perhaps for nonthematic reasons (to avoid having to renumber plates). While the reader

should consult Essick and Viscomi's arguments, their evidence suggests as easily that C became a kind of "working" copy (containing, for example, doubled plate numbers) and was finally sold "as is," whereas D was finished with great splendor and numbered consecutively throughout. (D was probably produced on commission and sold ca. 1818. C may have been finally sold in 1826.) At any rate, it is not clear that plate 5 was dropped for thematic reasons, though perhaps Blake was again juggling the relative weight to be given Moral Law among other concerns. See Viscomi chapter 32 passim and Essick and Viscomi 37–38.

15. If following the designs, the reader should examine *IB* plates 2, 6–10, and 12–16 (numbered continuously as 3–13 in AB), and then the full sequence 2–16.

16. As noted later, the syntax of this passage is ambiguous.

17. Bloom also views "Naked Beauty!" as true art opposed to Lockean perception and Hayley's supposed formalism (*Apocalypse* 345). Essick and Viscomi view the cherubim as figures of restraint (119), as does Bloom (*E*911), who, however, also sees them as Erdman's soldiers as noted above. Blake, however, refers to cherubim in both positive and negative contexts (see Damon, *Dictionary* 80.) Webster also associates the mocking of mathematical proportion with the triumph of Blake's art, and, more fancifully, the animals with animal illustrations Blake made for Hayley (*Psychology* 253).

18. Damon notes that their wings elsewhere become the female labia (*Dictionary* 80; e.g., *J* 44/30:35). Though there is no reference to wings here, this hint of androgyny would fit the interpretation I place on this passage.

19. For a possible reference to art methods, see *Laocoön:* "Art can never exist without Naked Beauty displayed" (*E*275). The echo in *J,* however, "Art & Science cannot exist but by Naked Beauty displayed" (32/36:49), broadens the statement by adding a second intellectual context; evidently Blake is thinking of overall culture, not simply of art practices. Among other uses of animals for impulse and desire, see *FZ* Night 5, 61:24–26, referring to Orc. Arrows can also represent female protectiveness, as the "arrows of Elynittria," *M* 5:43 and 11:38, as well as other qualities.

20. See tabulation above, pp. 116, 214–15n7.

21. *Bell's* reform sympathies can be gauged from its sympathetic attention to reform parliamentary candidates like Richard Brinsley Sheridan and Sir Francis Burdett, the space given to items by or about Burdett and William Cobbett, etc. I am indebted to Keri Davies for the suggestion of *Bell's* as a source for Blake, which has been fruitful indeed. Davies also notes that a daily paper, at 6–1/2 pence in 1810–11, or 3s. 3d. a week, would have been expensive for Blake, and suggests reading in a public house as an alternative. The same consideration would make a weekly paper attractive—*Bell's* cost 8d.

22. For Blake's residence with Basire, see *BB* 556. For Vere-street and Great Queen Street, see *A to Z of Georgian London,* maps 3Bc and 11Ba; on the map reproduced in *BB,* plate 59, Vere-street may be seen at the right edge,

about 1-1/4 inches (by the route indicated) from 31 Great Queen Street (on this map 1 inch = about 250 yards). This area has been much rebuilt; Kingsway cuts across where Vere-street was, at about the intersection of Kemble and Wild streets.

23. For the Tyburn's location, see Lysons' *The Environs of London*, vol. 3 (1795): "This brook or bourn runs on the south side of Hampstead, and passes near Bellsize to Barrowhill-farm; thence through Marybone-park to Marybone-lane; it crosses Oxford-road near Stratford-place, and Piccadilly under a bridge near Hay-hill . . . [then] passing through the park near Buckingham-house, and through Tothill-fields, falls into the Thames" (242n). Besant, *London North of the Thames* (1911), gives the most complete account of its course, in separate references; see 135, 163, 170, 176, 177, 227, 276, 354. A branch seems to have emptied into the Thames a little north, at present Downing Street. Lysons and Besant both mention the Westbourne, but not the tributary Tyburn Brook. Nevertheless, Blake's references seem to bespeak a local tradition locating the brook there, where it is placed by a modern source, Weinreb and Hibbert (898, 941). Bebbington says the River Tyburn crossed Oxford Street at Vere Street (331), but other sources mention Stratford Place, just west of this, where I place it. Bebbington's end-map 7 traces the river's course. The Tyburn could not in any case follow the course Damon indicates, from Hyde Park south to St. James's Park and then north in a hairpin turn to South Molton Street–Stratford Place; nor, apparently, did it sink below ground there. For other Tyburn references, see *FZ* 25:7–8; *M* 6:9–11, 11:4–5, 13:35 ("the fatal Brook of Albions River"), 39:36–39; *J* 12:26–28, 27 "The fields" 33–34, 34/38:55–59, 37/41:7–8, 43/29:2–3, 62:34, 63:33, 90:47–48. *J* 34/38:55–35/39:3 mention the gate Satan's watch-fiends cannot find (in this context the Blakes' home) bending across Oxford Street as a refuge from "Tyburns deathful shades"; 74:75 mentions South Molton Street–Stratford Place as the place of a "wound," amid references to "Moral Virtue" (74:35).

24. In copy C, without plate 5, Satan's temporary defeat does not occur—nor does this plate's discussion of Moral Law.

25. The twelve daughters are not named in *M* and do not appear before *J* except in a lined-in addition to *FZ* (25:29–30).

26. In discussing these plates, I use the numbering in *IB*, corresponding to copy D. The reader can infer the relative positions of text and visual plates by referring to the second, bracketed number in *E* citations. (See preface.) As full-page visuals, these plates are not numbered in *E* but follow 29 [31] (at the end of Book 1), 33 [36], 39 [44], and 40 [46]. They are 29, 33, 41, and 43 in Essick and Viscomi's facsimile of C. The first three are in the same positions with respect to the basic text order in all copies; the differences in plate numbers result from interpolation of new plates (in C, transposition of one pair of plates). The last, however, moves in CD from its earlier position as 21 in AB (following AB 20, or 22 [24] in *E*'s numbering).

27. The penis in "Robert" is quite visible in A, and rather large for Blake—.95 cm along its dorsal edge, in scale about 6.5 inches. That in "William" is smaller, about .5 cm along the dorsal edge.

28. For Blake's comments on what he felt as Robert's spiritual guidance, see his letter to Hayley, May 6, 1800 (*E*705). A possible further context for these images lies in Schuchard's argument that English Swedenborgian and occultist circles, with which Blake had some connection in the 1780s and perhaps later, practiced "techniques of Yogic-Cabalism that could produce a prolonged erection and state of orgasmic trance. . . . [T]his visionary sexual technique was crucial to the achievement of 'spiritual influx'" ("Secret Masonic History" 45; see also idem, "Blake's Healing Trio" 27). Schuchard has suggested the relevance of this discipline to the images in *M* (personal communication, April 1998). If she is right about the practices she describes, they do more or less fit the depictions in "William" and "Robert." However, the Los-Blake plate reverses what I take to be the techniques' focus on "influx" through genital arousal; here, the "influx" is experienced by the passive, nonaroused partner. In any case this plate's suggestion of a homoerotic posture is too direct to deny, whether or not the techniques mentioned are an influence on "William" and "Robert."

29. For other comments, see Ackroyd 313; Behrendt 25; Kaplan 168–69, discussed below; Mitchell, "Style" 66–68; Storch, *Sons* 146–51 and "Fiend" 133–34; Webster, *Psychology* 261. Storch states flatly that plate 47 depicts "fellatio" (*Sons* 148), as does Kaplan about both scenes (165, 168–69); others are more cautious. Elfenbein, curiously, does not deal with these images, or with "Robert," though he briefly mentions "William" (162).

30. The text in question (on plate 39 [44]) immediately precedes the image (on 45). The fainting figure has been seen both as Urizen and as Ololon and therefore as referring to different texts on the pages before and after the illustration—"Urizen faints" in the former case, "Before Ololon Milton stood" in the latter (40 [46]:1). For commentaries, see, e.g., Behrendt 25; Damon, *Philosophy* 432; Essick and Viscomi 32–33; *IB* 261; Mitchell, "Style" 56. The iconographic details supporting identification as Ololon (see Wittreich, *Angel* 270) are offset by the absence of a textual suggestion that Ololon swoons.

31. In A, Los's penis is about .5 cm long, colored pink-gray. There is darker rounded pink-gray shading at its top, possibly an extension of it, with a darker mark where the opening of the urethra would be.

32. For commentary, see Essick and Viscomi 33–34; *IB* 263–64; Kaplan 169; Mitchell, "Style" 67; Webster, *Psychology* 261–62. For the precursor verses on which the *Milton* incident is based, included in Blake's letter to Thomas Butts, Nov. 22, 1802, see *E*720–22.

33. In "William," there is gray and pink-gray wash over the end of the "penis" shape, and black shadow from the line of the figure's left thigh rises irregularly to merge with the inked shape, obscuring its contour. "Robert" allows a clear view of Blake's procedure. The lines along the two sides of the

pelvis appear on close visual inspection to be parts of the original printed impression. They are continued by counterpart lines above the waist, bending in toward the sternum. The original impression, then, apparently contained an outline of the basic pelvic and rib bone structure—a lozenge shape somewhat like a tennis racket frame. Coloring and shading are used *both* to emphasize the erection-like form along the figure's right thigh while covering the similar form on its left, in A, and, in B, along with ink lines, to achieve the opposite effect. Blake's techniques include using pink-gray wash in patterns that do *not* outline the shape and using pen lines that extend the shape up to the waistband so that it appears as part of the shorts' folds.

34. In C, for example, above Blake's cheekbone, where a fairly defined penis and possible scrotum appear in A, Los's pelvis is colored in with dark gray-pink and lighter pink under a fold-line in the transparent shorts. On Blake's figure, the darkish gray-green of the shorts on his thighs, and possibly line repainting, have provided the line of his right thigh and the shape of his pubic area basically as they would appear under shorts.

35. See further discussion in chapter 6.

36. Elfenbein's discussion of *M* is, in part, a response to Kaplan's. Elfenbein's main focus is on *M*'s treatment of gender hierarchy. He argues that the female Ololon, a collective and, in his view, gender-fluid entity that plays a crucial role in the poem's second book, contributes independently to the prophetic-apocalyptic ending, and hence that Kaplan and other feminist interpreters have been too quick to charge *M* with subordinating women. Elfenbein also criticizes Kaplan and others for implying that "gay sex is really about misogyny," a view he calls "seriously inadequate as a reading of Blake because it ignores his strenuous criticism of conventional male roles" (162). But Elfenbein's discussion of male homosexuality in *M* has its own weaknesses. He limits himself to a discussion of what he considers the "overblown homoeroticism" (169) in the scenes of Milton entering Blake's foot (the "William" plate) and Milton wrestling with Urizen (plate 15 [A-C]/18 [D]); he does not discuss the images of "Robert," Milton and the fainting Urizen, or Blake and Los (162–65). He overlooks the "Calvarys foot" scene and, surprisingly, the textual implications of homosexuality in the Bard's Song. Finally, he misunderstands Blake's references to hermaphrodism, which either ignore or invert the term's ordinary gender sense (161–62; see chapter 6 below).

Chapter 6.
Blake's Synthesis: *Jerusalem*

1. Castle comments that the *Remarks* "is as much a piece of antihomosexual writing as it is a critique of masquerades" (*Masquerade* 47). On homosexuality and the masquerade, see *Masquerade* 45–50; on Ranelagh, *Masquerade* 2, 4, 12, 14, 21, 98; Castle, "Culture" 159–60, 166, 172; G. S. Rousseau,

"Pursuit" 155. For other literary references, see Castle, "Culture" 160–61 and nn, 166–67, 170–71 and nn.

2. The gardens have also been seen as "symptomatic of Albion's social diseases" (Paley, *Jerusalem* 141–42). But doing so requires reading Hand's self-righteousness as Blake's.

3. The place the watch fiends cannot find has several meanings in *M* and *J*: sexual fulfillment, as here (*M* 23:38–40, 29:47–53); any moment used with industry (*M* 35:42–45); and endurance in the face of injustice (*J* 34/38:54–35/39:3).

4. The passage is cognate with *FZ* 119:32–36.

5. "Unnatural consanguinities" undoubtedly refers to incest. In *J*'s finished state (1820), the phrase may allude to English condemnation of Byron, driven into exile for this transgression in 1819. Blake's sympathy for Byron's victimization is evident in his later treatment of him as a prophetic though mistaken voice "in the Wilderness" in *The Ghost of Abel* (*E*270; 1822).

6. Hagstrum, "Babylon" 109 n. 20; Mitchell, *Composite Art* 206–207; and Stevenson 39, 40 all assume the lesbian content of the scene; Doskow 59 leaves its sexual nature unclear; Grant, "Two Flowers" 355, sees the text scene as lesbian but argues at length that plate 28 depicts Albion and Jerusalem (354–62). Webster, *Psychology,* on the other hand, does not mention the scene (in a book on Blake's view of women). For summaries of views of the plate 28 design, see Mitchell, *Composite Art* 206–207; Paley, *City* 169–70 and *Jerusalem* 173–74.

7. For a joint biography, see Mavor; for the newspaper incident, see Mavor 73–77, Donoghue 107 and 129, and Trumbach, "Sapphists" 133; see also Donoghue 149–50, 222; Faderman, *Surpassing* 120–25. Wordsworth's "To the Lady E. B. and the Hon. Miss P." (1824) emphasizes rural withdrawal and idealized friendship. I am indebted to Stuart Curran for calling Seward's poem to my attention.

8. See Witke 46–47 for a view of the veil as wholly negative.

9. Alternatively, one may take the "covering" as a recuperative response to Eden's loss, for which Vala, as nature, is primarily responsible. The "covering" would then be an ambiguous phenomenon, as would Vala's role in "produc[ing] the bodies." But this view implies that Vala's role is fully negative in Eden but more mixed in Generation (the world of experience, production, commerce, and reproduction). The poem's general tenor is just the reverse.

10. "Then" may refer only to the time of Vala and Jerusalem's love; more likely, it includes the seizure, which the rest of this passage rationalizes.

11. Note that this form of the veil appears *before* Jerusalem's account of the veil of "pity & love," a retrospective view.

12. Lines 14–15 repeat Enion's at the start of *FZ* (4:26–27), turning Tharmas's adultery with Jerusalem into Vala and Jerusalem's homosexual union. Casting Vala in Enion's role confirms Vala's relative innocence at the outset. However, while Enion meant she had found sinful intent in Tharmas, Vala

means she has seen her own sin reflected or repeated in Albion. Jerusalem, speaking to Albion, gets some of Tharmas's lines (22:20–24; *FZ* 4:29–33).

13. Webster apparently feels that the speech voices Blake's responses to homosexuality (*Psychology* 278). She is aware that the disgust is Albion's, but here and elsewhere she identifies Albion's condemnations of women and homosexuality as Blake's (275–81).

14. See chapter 2, and discussion in *The Chained Boy,* chapter 4.

15. Tannenbaum (203–204, 326 nn. 6–7) and McGann (*Social Values* 152–72) argue, with differing emphases, that Blake knew of contemporary biblical interpretations stressing the presence of distinct ur-texts in Genesis. Blake could have learned, for example, of J. G. Eichhorn's view of Gen. 1–2:3 and 2:4–25 as distinct threads from a reference in Alexander Geddes's 1792 bible translation (McGann, *Social Values* 168; Geddes xix-xx). Neither Tannenbaum nor McGann discusses the alternative accounts of women's creation. Blake could also have been aware of Milton's distinct emphases in *PL* 7:505–34 and 8:460–77.

16. For Shiloh as peace, and a précis of his appearances, see Damon, *Dictionary* 371–72; for Shiloh as France's emanation, see Erdman, *Prophet* 309, 313, and *IB* 342, which explains his masculinity as "protocol" (France was traditionally female, so her emanation had to be masculine). Paley (*City* 181) sees Shiloh as the "masculine soul" in Vala and Jerusalem's collaboration to produce bodies and souls (18:7, discussed earlier, and illustration). Paley also mentions Shiloh as the promised messiah in the prophecies of Joanna Southcott, parodied in separate material in *J* that does not refer to Shiloh the emanation (*City* 133, 272; "Prince" 285–92). The references in *FZ* come in the "messengers of Beulah" section of Night 1, a late addition; thus Shiloh, like the whole theoretical apparatus I consider here, belongs to Blake's late work.

17. *M* 37:11; *J* 38/43:65, 47:5–8. See Damon, *Dictionary* 447.

18. The terms are used four times in *FZ*, all in Night 8, among its late sections; three times in *M*, twelve in *J*, and once each in the explanatory verses to *For the Sexes* (ca. 1820–25) and the annotations to Thornton (1827).

19. I am indebted to G. A. Rosso for this point.

20. Blake's uses of these terms are not necessarily all consistent. Elsewhere in *J*, he recounts what seems to be a scene of sexual division for the purpose of war and oppression: "The Daughters of Albion. divide & unite in jealousy & cruelty / The Inhabitants of Albion . . . / . . . / And while the Sons of Albion by severe War & Judgment, bonify / The Hermaphroditic Condensations are divided by the Knife / The obdurate Forms are cut asunder by Jealousy & Pity." Subsequently Los, "To Create a World of Generation from the World of Death: / Divid[es] the Masculine & Feminine: for the comingling / Of Albions & Luvahs Spectres was Hermaphroditic"; we are told, finally, that the zoas create the world of generation "out of / The Hermaphroditic Satanic World of rocky destiny" (58:5–12, 18–20, 50–51). Here hermaphrodism seems to be a state of social and sexual amalgamation subsequently "divided" by the daughters, with the divided forms then fixed

in separate sexes by Los. Yet the "Hermaphroditic Satanic World" should be the world of war and oppression created by the daughters, i.e., a sexually riven world, and perhaps "divide" does not signify splitting an original hermaphroditic form, but dividing *out* from a social whole *as* "Hermaphroditic Condensations," in the senses indicated earlier; see a use of "divided" apparently in this sense at 74:36. This meaning would match the idea that "the comingling / Of Albions & Luvahs Spectres was Hermaphroditic," for this commingling, in *J*, would signify the European war (compare 60:1–3). For other uses in *J*, with varying nuances, see 13:8, 64:18–31, 88:58–89:4, and below.

21. Schematically, Blake's familiar conception is fourfold, involving the states of Eden, Beulah, Generation, and Ulro, but these further divisions need not concern us here.

22. Warren Stevenson apparently views this passage as implying androgyny in "Eden" by contrast (45). But, as noted above, the presence of male and female "emanations" indicates that the "human" state in "Eden" does not involve erasure of physical sexual difference.

23. Tayler already noted that emanations are both male and female in this passage, but without exploring the implications concerning homosexuality ("Woman Scaly" 552).

Conclusion

1. For the symbolism of Moses, Og, Anak, Sihon, Joshua, and Caleb, used to convey some of these ideas, see the appropriate entries in Damon, *Dictionary*.

2. For discussion of these points, see *The Chained Boy*, chapter 6.

3. In the morning paper one might read of a "young woman of interesting appearance," charged at law "with being pregnant of a bastard child, which [parish officers] were apprehensive would become a burthen on their parish." The mother was forced to name the father, a Northamptonshire clergyman, and the magistrate ordered the parish exempted from the infant's upkeep, but no other action was taken (*Morning Chronicle*, July 9, 1810: 3).

4. Blake's treatment of the guardian principle, more complex than I can discuss here, is embodied in a reference to the "Seven Eyes of God" (and a latent eighth), elected here for such a guardianship (55:31–33) as in several similar passages in other works. It is not clear, however, that the eyes are activated; the electors, who "were about to make a Separation" (line 30)—apparently, to abandon the mortal realm to the eyes' guardianship—reconsider and, in the speech quoted here, resolve to remain part of our lives and struggles.

5. For an extended presentation, see Lerner.

6. Available as a chapbook, "The Genitals Are Beauty," from House of William Blake, 17 South Molton Street, London W1Y 1DE.

Works Cited

The A to Z of Georgian London. Notes by Ralph Hyde. Lympne Castle, Kent: Harry Margary; London: Guildhall Library, 1981. Map adapted from John Roche's *Plan of the Cities of London and Westminster and the Borough of Southwark.* London, 1747.

The A to Z of Regency London. Introduction by Paul Laxton. N.p. [London]: London Topographical Society, 1985. Map reproduced from [Richard] *Horwoods Plan of London.* 3rd ed. London, 1813.

Ackroyd, Peter. *Blake.* London: Sinclair-Stevenson; New York: Knopf, 1995.

Aers, David. "Blake: Sex, Society and Ideology." *Romanticism and Ideology: Studies in English Writing 1765–1830.* By David Aers, Jonathan Cook, and David Punter. London: Routledge and Kegan Paul, 1981. 27–43.

———. "Representations of Revolution: From *The French Revolution* to *The Four Zoas.*" Miller, Bracher, and Ault 244–70. Citations are to this ed. Rpt. (abridged), *William Blake.* New Casebooks series. Ed. David Punter. New York: St. Martin's, 1996. 165–77.

Alberts, Robert C. *Benjamin West: A Biography.* Boston: Houghton Mifflin, 1978.

[Allen, Rev. John, M.D.] *The Destruction of Sodom improved; as a Warning to Great-Britain. A Sermon Preached on the Fast-Day, Friday, February 6, 1756, at Hanover-Street, Long-Acre. By the Rev. Dr. Allen*[,] *Morning Preacher there.* London: printed for A. Millar and J. and S. Johnson, 1756. [Microfilm: Eighteenth Century, Reel 3645.28. Woodbridge, CT: Research Publications, 1989.]

Anderson, Mark. "Oothoon: Failed Prophet." *Romanticism Past and Present* 8 (1984): 1–21.

The Annual Register, or a View of the History, Politics, and Literature, For the Year 1806. London: printed for W. Otridge [et al.], 1808.

Ault, Donald. "Blake's De-Formation of Neo-Aristotelianism." Miller, Bracher, and Ault 111–38.

———. *Narrative Unbound: Re-Visioning William Blake's* The Four Zoas. Barry-town, NY: Station Hill, 1987.

Baxter, Stephen B. *William III.* London: Longman's, 1966.

Bebbington, Gillian. *London Street Names.* London: B. T. Batsford, 1972.

[Beckford, William.] *An Arabian Tale, from an Unpublished Manuscript: with Notes Critical and Explanatory. The History of the Caliph Vathek*[,] *with Notes.* London: J. Johnson, 1786. Facsimile ed., William Beckford, *Vathek: an Arabian Tale.* Menston: Scolar P, 1971.

Behrendt, Stephen C. *The Moment of Explosion: Blake and the Illustration of Milton.* Lincoln and London: U of Nebraska P, 1983.

Bell's Weekly Messenger. London. July-Dec. 1806, July-Dec. 1810, Jan.-June 1811.

Bentham, Jeremy. "Offences Against One's Self: Paederasty." Introduction by Louis Crompton. Part 1, *Journal of Homosexuality* 3.4 (Summer 1978): 383–405. Part 2, "Jeremy Bentham's Essay on 'Paederasty,' Part 2." *Journal of Homosexuality* 4.1 (Fall 1978): 91–107.

———. "Offences Against Taste." *The Theory of Legislation.* Ed. C. K. Ogden. New York: Harcourt, Brace; London: Kegan Paul, Trench Trubner, 1931. 476–97. [Redacted excerpts from mss. of 1814–16.]

Bentley, G. E., Jr. *Blake Books: Annotated Catalogues of William Blake's Writings[etc.].* Oxford: Clarendon, 1977.

———. "Blake and Cromek: The Wheat and the Tares." *Modern Philology* 71.4 (May 1977): 366–79.

———. *Blake Records.* Oxford: Clarendon, 1969.

———. *Blake Records Supplement: Being New Material Relating to the Life of William Blake Discovered since the Publication of* Blake Records *(1969).* Oxford: Clarendon, 1988.

———. *William Blake, Vala or The Four Zoas: A Facsimile of the Manuscript[,] a Transcript of the Poem[,] and a Study of Its Growth and Significance.* Oxford: Clarendon, 1963.

Besant, Sir Walter. *London North of the Thames.* London: Adam and Charles Black, 1911.

Bidney, Martin. "Urizen and Orc, Cortés and Guatimozin: Mexican History and *The Four Zoas* VII." *Blake: An Illustrated Quarterly* 23.4 (Spring 1990): 195–98.

Blackstone, Bernard. *English Blake.* Cambridge: Cambridge UP, 1949. Rpt., with new foreword, Hamden, CT: Archon, 1966.

Blake, William. *The Complete Poetry and Prose of William Blake.* Ed. David V. Erdman, commentary by Harold Bloom. Rev. ed. New York: Anchor-Doubleday, 1988.

Bloom, Harold. *Blake's Apocalypse: A Study in Poetic Argument.* 1963. Garden City: Anchor, 1965.

Boswell, John. *Christianity, Social Tolerance, and Homosexuality: Gay People in Western Europe from the Beginning of the Christian Era to the Fourteenth Century.* Chicago: U of Chicago P, 1980; Phoenix ed., 1981.

Bracher, Mark. *Being Form'd: Thinking Through Blake's* Milton. Barrytown, NY: Station Hill, 1985.

Bray, Alan. *Homosexuality in Renaissance England.* 2nd ed. London: Gay Men's P, 1988.

Breasted, Barbara. "*Comus* and the Castlehaven Scandal." *Milton Studies* 3 (1971): 201–24.

Bredbeck, Gregory W. *Sodomy and Interpretation: Marlowe to Milton.* Ithaca and London: Cornell UP, 1991.

Bronowski, J. *William Blake and the Age of Revolution.* Orig. pub. as *William Blake 1757–1827: A Man Without a Mask.* London: Secker and Warburg, 1943. Rev.

ed., New York: Harper and Row, 1965; London: Routledge and Kegan Paul, 1972.

Bruder, Helen P. "The Sins of the Fathers: Patriarchal Criticism and *The Book of Thel.*" *Historicizing Blake*. Ed. Steve Clark and David Worrall. London: Macmillan; New York: St. Martin's, 1994. 147–58.

———. *William Blake and the Daughters of Albion*. Houndmills, Basingstoke: Macmillan; New York: St. Martin's, 1997.

Burg, B. R. "Ho Hum, Another Work of the Devil: Buggery and Sodomy in Early Stuart England." *Journal of Homosexuality* 6.1–2 (Fall-Winter 1980–81): 69–78.

[Burnet, Gilbert.] *Bishop* Burnet's *History of His Own Time*. 2 vols. London: vol. 1, Thomas Ward, 1724; vol. 2, Joseph Downing, Henry Woodfall, 1734.

———. *Bishop Burnet's History of His Own Time*. [With notes by Dartmouth, Swift, and others.] Vol. 3. Oxford: Clarendon, 1823.

Butlin, Martin. *The Paintings and Drawings of William Blake*. 2 vols. New Haven: Yale UP, 1981.

Cady, Joseph. " 'Masculine Love,' Renaissance Writing, and the 'New Invention' of Homosexuality." Summers 9–40.

Castle, Terry. "The Culture of Travesty: Sexuality and Masquerade in Eighteenth-Century England." Rousseau and Porter 156–80.

———. *Masquerade and Civilization: The Carnivalesque in Eighteenth-Century English Culture and Fiction*. Stanford: Stanford UP, 1986.

Chatterton, Thomas. *The Complete Works of Thomas Chatterton: A Bicentenary Edition*. Ed. Donald S. Taylor in association with Benjamin B. Hoover. 2 vols. Oxford: Clarendon, 1971.

Chaucer, Geoffrey. *The Canterbury Tales*. *The Riverside Chaucer*. 3rd ed. Gen. ed. Larry D. Benson. Boston: Houghton Mifflin, 1987. 23–328.

Churchill, Charles. *Poems of Charles Churchill*. Ed. James Laver. 2 vols. London: Eyre and Spottiswoode, 1933.

Churchill, Winston S. *Marlborough: His Life and Times*. 2 vols. London: Harrap, 1933.

Cleland, John. *Memoirs of a Woman of Pleasure*. Ed. Peter Sabor. Oxford and New York: World's Classics–Oxford UP, 1985.

Cooper, Andrew. "Irony as Self-Concealment in *The Marriage of Heaven and Hell.*" *Auto/Biography Studies* 2.4 (Winter 1986–87): 34–44.

Cowper, William. *The Poems of William Cowper*. Ed. John D. Baird, Charles Ryskamp. 3 vols. Vol. 1, Oxford: Clarendon, 1980. Vols. 2–3, Oxford: Clarendon, 1995.

Crompton, Louis. *Byron and Greek Love: Homophobia in Nineteenth-Century England*. Berkeley and Los Angeles: U of California P, 1985.

Curran, Stuart and Joseph Anthony Wittreich, eds. *Blake's Sublime Allegory: Essays on The Four Zoas, Milton, Jerusalem*. Madison: U of Wisconsin P, 1973.

Damon, S. Foster. *A Blake Dictionary: The Ideas and Symbols of William Blake*. Providence: Brown UP, 1965. Rev. ed., Hanover and London: UP of New England, 1988.

————. *William Blake: His Philosophy and Symbols.* Boston: Houghton Mifflin; London: Constable, 1924. Rpt., London: Dawsons, 1969.

Damrosch, Leopold, Jr. *Symbol and Truth in Blake's Myth.* Princeton: Princeton UP, 1980.

Daniel, Norman. *Islam and the West: The Making of an Image.* Rev. ed. Oxford: Oneworld, 1993.

Davies, J. M. Q. *Blake's Milton Designs: The Dynamics of Meaning.* West Cornwall, CT: Locust Hill, 1993.

Davies, Keri. "Mrs Bliss: A Blake Collector of 1794." *Blake in the Nineties.* Ed. Steve Clark, David Worrall. Houndmills and London: Macmillan; New York: St. Martin's, 1999. 212–30.

Dinshaw, Carolyn. *Chaucer's Sexual Poetics.* Madison: U of Wisconsin P, 1989.

DiSalvo, Jackie. *War of Titans. Blake's Critique of Milton and the Politics of Religion.* Pittsburgh: U of Pittsburgh P, 1983.

DiSalvo, Jackie, Christopher Z. Hobson, and G. A. Rosso, eds. *Blake, Politics, and History.* New York: Garland, 1998.

Donoghue, Emma. *Passions Between Women: British Lesbian Culture, 1668–1801.* London: Scarlet, 1993; New York: HarperCollins, 1995.

Dörrbecker, D. W., ed. *The Continental Prophecies*[:] *America: a Prophecy*[,] *Europe: a Prophecy*[,] *The Song of Los.* By William Blake. Princeton: William Blake Trust and Princeton UP, 1995. Vol. 4 of *Blake's Illuminated Works.* David Bindman, Gen. Ed. [Facsimiles of *America* copy H, *Europe* copy B, *The Song of Los* copy A.]

Doskow, Minna. *William Blake's* Jerusalem: *Structure and Meaning in Poetry and Picture.* Rutherford: Fairleigh Dickinson UP; London and Toronto: Associated U Presses, 1982.

Dowling, Linda. *Hellenism and Homosexuality in Victorian Oxford.* Ithaca and London: Cornell UP, 1994.

Dunbar, Pamela. *William Blake's Illustrations to the Poetry of Milton.* Oxford: Clarendon, 1980.

Dryden, John, trans. *The Aeneid of Virgil.* Ed. Robert Fitzgerald. New York: Macmillan; London: Collier-Macmillan, 1965.

Eaves, Morris. "On Blakes We Want and Blakes We Don't." *Huntington Library Quarterly* 58:3, 4 (1997): 413–39.

Eaves, Morris, Robert N. Essick, and Joseph Viscomi, eds. *The Early Illuminated Books.* By William Blake. Princeton: William Blake Trust and Princeton UP, 1993, rpt. 1998. Vol. 3 of *Blake's Illuminated Works.* David Bindman, Gen. Ed. [Facsimiles of *Marriage* copy F and other works.]

Edmiston, William F. "Shifting Ground: Sade, Same-Sex Desire, and the One-, Two-, and Three-Sex Models." *Illicit Sex: Identity Politics in Early Modern Culture.* Ed. Thomas DiPiero, Pat Gill. Athens and London: U of Georgia P, 1997. 143–60.

Edwards, Gavin. "Repeating the Same Dull Round." *Unnam'd Forms: Blake and Textuality.* Ed. Nelson Hilton, Thomas A. Vogler. Berkeley and Los Angeles: U of California P, 1986. 26–48.

Elfenbein, Andrew. *Romantic Genius: The Prehistory of a Homosexual Role.* New York: Columbia UP, 1999.

Erdman, David V. *Blake, Prophet Against Empire: A Poet's Interpretation of the History of His Own Times.* 1954. 3rd ed., Princeton: Princeton UP, 1977.

———. *The Illuminated Blake.* Garden City: Anchor-Doubleday, 1974. Rpt. with corrections, New York: Dover, 1992.

Erdman, David V., with Tom Dargan and Marlene Deverell-Van Meter. "Reading the Illuminations of Blake's *Marriage of Heaven and Hell.*" Paley and Phillips 162–207.

Essick, Robert N. "*The Four Zoas:* Intention and Production." *Blake: An Illustrated Quarterly* 18.2 (Spring 1985): 216–20.

———. "William Blake's 'Female Will' and Its Biographical Context." *SEL* 31.3 (Autumn 1991): 615–30.

Essick, Robert N., and Joseph Viscomi, eds. *Milton a Poem and the Final Illuminated Works: The Ghost of Abel[,] On Homers Poetry [and] On Virgil[,] Laocoön.* By William Blake. Princeton: William Blake Trust and Princeton UP, 1993. Vol. 5 of *Blake's Illuminated Works.* David Bindman, Gen. Ed. [Facsimile of *Milton* copy C, with other works as listed, introduction, and commentaries.]

Faderman, Lillian. *Scotch Verdict: Miss Pirie and Miss Woods v. Dame Cumming Gordon.* 1983. New York: Columbia UP-Morningside, 1993.

———. *Surpassing the Love of Men: Romantic Friendship and Love Between Women from the Renaissance to the Present.* New York: Morrow, 1981.

Fallon, Stephen M. "Milton's Arminianism and the Authorship of *De doctrina Christiana.*" *Texas Studies in Literature and Language* 41.2 (Summer 1999): 103–27.

Ferber, Michael. "The Finite Revolutions of *Europe.*" DiSalvo, Hobson, and Rosso 212–34.

Fletcher, Angus. *The Transcendental Masque: An Essay on Milton's* Comus. Ithaca: Cornell UP, 1971.

Forster, E. M. *Maurice.* With "Terminal Note" (1960) by Forster. New York: Norton, 1971.

Foucault, Michel. *The History of Sexuality. Vol. 1: An Introduction.* Trans. Robert Hurley. New York: Pantheon, 1978; rpt. New York: Vintage, 1990.

Fox, Susan. "The Female as Metaphor in William Blake's Poetry." *Critical Inquiry* 3.3 (Spring 1977): 507–19. Rpt. in *Essential Articles for the Study of William Blake, 1970–84.* Ed. Nelson Hilton. Hamden, CT: Archon, 1986. 75–90. Citations are to this edition.

———. *Poetic Form in Blake's* Milton. Princeton: Princeton UP, 1976.

Freed, Eugenie R. *"A Portion of His Life": William Blake's Miltonic Vision of Women.* Lewisburg: Bucknell UP; London and Toronto: Associated U Presses, 1994.

Frye, Northrop. *Fearful Symmetry: A Study of William Blake.* Princeton: Princeton UP, 1947. Rpt., with new preface, Princeton: Princeton UP, 1969; rpt., 1974.

———. "Notes for a Commentary on *Milton.*" *The Divine Vision: Studies in the Poetry and Art of William Blake.* Ed. Vivian de Sola Pinto. 1957. Rpt., New York: Haskell House, 1968. 99–137.

Geddes, Alexander, trans. *The Holy Bible, or the Books Accounted Sacred by Jews and Christians; Otherwise Called the Books of the Old and New Covenants* [etc.]. 2 vols. London: J. Davis, 1792, 1797.

"The Genitals Are Beauty." Graphic arts chapbook. London: House of William Blake, 1995.

George, Diana Hume. *Blake and Freud*. Ithaca and London: Cornell UP, 1980.

Gerard, Kent, and Gert Hekma, eds. *The Pursuit of Sodomy: Male Homosexuality in Renaissance and Enlightenment Europe*. New York and London: Harrington Park, 1989.

Gilbert, Arthur N. "Conceptions of Homosexuality and Sodomy in Western History." *Journal of Homosexuality* 6.1–2 (Fall-Winter 1980–81): 57–68.

Gleckner, Robert F. *Gray Agonistes: Thomas Gray and Masculine Friendship*. Baltimore and London: Johns Hopkins UP, 1997.

[Goldsmith, Oliver.] *The History of England, From the Earliest Times to the Death of George II*. By Dr. Goldsmith. 4 vols. London: printed for T. Davies, Becket and De Hondt, and T. Cadell, 1771.

Goldsmith, Steven. *Unbuilding Jerusalem: Apocalypse and Romantic Representation*. Ithaca and London: Cornell UP, 1993.

Graham, Catherine Macaulay. *The History of England from the Accession of James I. to the Revolution*. 8 vols. [Title varies; that of vol. 1, . . . *from the Accession of James I to that of the Brunswick Line,* reflects the intention to carry the story through to 1714, abandoned after vol. 5.] London: various printers, 1763–83.

Grant, John E. "Two Flowers in the Garden of Experience." *William Blake: Essays for S. Foster Damon*. Ed. Alvin H. Rosenfeld. Providence: Brown UP, 1969. 333–67.

———. "Visions in *Vala*: A Consideration of Some Pictures in the Manuscript." Curran and Wittreich 141–202.

Grant, John E., Edward J. Rose, and Michael J. Tolley, coordinating ed. David V. Erdman. *William Blake's Designs for Edward Young's Night Thoughts: A Complete Edition*. 2 vols. Oxford: Clarendon, 1980.

Haggerty, George E. *Men in Love: Masculinity and Sexuality in the Eighteenth Century*. New York: Columbia UP, 1999.

Hagstrum, Jean H. "Babylon Revisited, or the Story of Luvah and Vala." Curran and Wittreich 101–18.

———. "Christ's Body." Paley and Phillips 129–56.

———. "Gray's Sensibility." *Fearful Joy: Papers from the Thomas Gray Bicentenary Conference at Carleton University*. Ed. James Downey, Ben Jones. Montreal and London: McGill-Queen's UP, 1974. 6–19.

———. "William Blake: 'Arrows of Desire' and 'Chariots of Fire.'" *The Romantic Body: Love and Sexuality in Keats, Wordsworth, and Blake*. Knoxville: U of Tennessee P, 1985. 109–45.

———. *William Blake: Poet and Painter. An Introduction to the Illuminated Verse*. Chicago: U of Chicago P, 1964.

Haigwood, Laura Ellen. "Blake's *Visions of the Daughters of Albion:* Revising an Interpretive Tradition." *San Jose Studies* 11 (1985): 77–94. Rpt. *William Blake*. New Casebooks series. Ed. David Punter. New York: St. Martin's, 1996. 94–107.

Halperin, David M. *"One Hundred Years of Homosexuality" and Other Essays on Greek Love*. New York and London: Routledge, 1990.

Harris, Walter. *The History of the Life and Reign of William-Henry, Prince of Nassau and Orange, Stadtholder of the United Provinces, King of England, Scotland, France and Ireland, &c.* Dublin: Edward Bate, 1749.

Harvey, A. D. "Prosecutions for Sodomy in England at the Beginning of the Nineteenth Century." *Historical Journal* 21.4 (1978): 939–48.

Hell upon Earth: or the Town in an Uproar. Occasion'd by The late horrible Scenes of Forgery, Perjury, Street-Robbery, Murder, Sodomy, and other shocking Impieties. London: printed for J. Roberts and A. Dodd, 1729. [Microfilm: The Eighteenth Century, Reel 2522.12. Woodbridge, CT: Research Publications, 1987.]

Hill, Christopher. "Milton and Marvell." *Approaches to Marvell: The York Tercentenary Lectures.* Ed. C. A. Patrides. London: Routledge and Kegan Paul, 1978. 1–30.

Hilton, Nelson. *Literal Imagination: Blake's Vision of Words.* Berkeley and Los Angeles: U of California P, 1983.

Hoagwood, Terence Allan. *Prophecy and the Philosophy of Mind: Traditions of Blake and Shelley.* Tuscaloosa: U of Alabama P, 1985.

Hobson, Christopher Z. *The Chained Boy: Orc and Blake's Idea of Revolution.* Lewisburg: Bucknell UP-Associated U Presses, 1999.

———. "The Myth of Blake's 'Orc Cycle.'" DiSalvo, Hobson, and Rosso 5–36.

Holstein, Michael F. "Crooked Paths Without Improvement: Blake's Proverbs of Hell." *Genre* 8 (1975): 26–41.

Hone, J. Ann. *For the Cause of Truth: Radicalism in London 1796–1821.* Oxford: Clarendon, 1982.

Horwitz, Henry. *Parliament, Policy and Politics in the Reign of William III.* Manchester: Manchester UP, 1977; Newark: U of Delaware P, n.d. [1977].

Howard, John. *Blake's* Milton: *A Study in the Selfhood.* Rutherford, NJ: Fairleigh Dickinson UP; London and Toronto: Associated U Presses, 1976.

———. *Infernal Poetics: Poetic Structures in Blake's Lambeth Prophecies.* Rutherford: Fairleigh Dickinson UP; London and Toronto: Associated U Presses, 1984.

Hume, David, [Tobias] Smollett, T. A. Lloyd. *The History of England, from the Invasion of Julius Cæsar to the Abdication of James the Second, by David Hume, Esq. With the Author's last Corrections and Improvements. To which are added A Continuation, from the Abdication to the Death of George II. By Dr. Smollett; And a farther Continuation, From George II to the Present Time, by T. A. Lloyd, Esq.* Cooke's Edition. 24 vols. London: C. Cooke, 1794.

Huussen, Arend H. Jr. "Sodomy in the Dutch Republic During the Eighteenth Century." Maccubbin 169–78.

Isherwood, Christopher. *A Single Man.* New York: Simon and Schuster, 1964.

Johnson, Samuel. *The Yale Edition of the Works of Samuel Johnson.* Vol. 5. *The Rambler,* vol. 3. Ed. W. J. Bate, Albrecht B. Strauss. New Haven and London: Yale UP, 1969.

Jones, J. R. *The First Whigs: The Politics of the Exclusion Crisis, 1678–1683.* London: Oxford UP, 1961.

———. *The Revolution of 1688 in England.* London: Weidenfeld and Nicolson, 1972.

Juvenal. *The Sixteen Satires.* Trans. Peter Green. London: Penguin, 1974.

Kaplan, Marc. "Blake's *Milton:* The Metaphysics of Gender." *Nineteenth-Century Contexts* 19 (1995): 151–78.

Keynes, Geoffrey. Introduction and commentary. *Songs of Innocence and of Experience.* By William Blake. [Rpt. of Trianon Press facsimile, 1967.] Oxford and New York: Oxford UP; Paris: Trianon, 1970. Rpt., 1988. 7–15, 131–55.

Keynes, Geoffrey, and Edwin Wolf 2nd. *William Blake's Illuminated Books: A Census.* New York: Grolier Club, 1953.

Kimmel, Michael S. "'Greedy Kisses' and 'Melting Extasy': Notes on the Homosexual World and Early 18th Century England as Found in *Love Letters Between a certain late Nobleman and the famous Mr. Wilson.*" Kimmel, *Love Letters* 1–9.

———, ed. *Love Letters Between a Certain Late Nobleman and the Famous Mr. Wilson.* [1723 pamphlet with commentary.] New York and London: Harrington Park: 1990.

Knight, R[ichard] P[ayne]. *An Account of the Remains of the Worship of Priapus, lately Existing at Isernia, in the Kingdom of Naples: in Two Letters . . . to which is Added, A Discourse on the Worship of Priapus, and Its Connexion with the Mystic Theology of the Ancients.* London: T. Spilsbury, 1786. [Microfilm: The Eighteenth Century, Reel 986.10. Woodbridge, CT: Research Publications, 1985.]

Kopelson, Kevin. "Seeing Sodomy: *Fanny Hill's* Blinding Vision." Summers 173–83.

Lanser, Susan S. "Sapphic Subjects and Enlightenment Politics." Paper presented at American Society for Eighteenth-Century Studies, April 2000.

Leader, Zachary. *Reading Blake's* Songs. Boston, London, and Henley: Routledge and Kegan Paul, 1981.

[Leigh, Richard.] *The Transproser Rehears'd: Or the Fifth Act of Mr. Bayes's Play Being a Postscript to the Adimadversions on the Preface to Bishop Bramhall's Vindication, &c. Shewing What Grounds there are of Fears and Jealousies of Popery.* Oxford, 1673.

Lerner, Gerda. *The Creation of Patriarchy.* New York: Oxford UP, 1986.

Levinson, Marjorie. *Wordsworth's Great Period Poems: Four Essays.* Cambridge: Cambridge UP, 1986.

Lincoln, Andrew. *Spiritual History: A Reading of William Blake's* Vala *or* The Four Zoas. Oxford: Clarendon, 1995.

Linkin, Harriet Kramer. "Revisioning Blake's Oothoon." *Blake: An Illustrated Quarterly* 23.4 (Spring 1990): 184–94.

Lonsdale, Roger. Introduction. William Beckford, *Vathek.* Oxford and New York: Oxford UP–World's Classics, 1983. vii–xxxi.

Lysons, Rev. Daniel. *The Environs of London: Being an Historical Account of the Towns, Villages, and Hamlets, Within Twelve Miles of that Capital: Interspersed with Biographical Anecdotes.* 3 vols. London, 1792–95. Vol. 3: *County of Middlesex.* London: printed for T. Cadell, Jr., and W. Davies, 1795.

Maccubbin, Robert P., ed. *'Tis Nature's Fault: Unauthorized Sexuality during the Enlightenment.* Cambridge: Cambridge UP, 1987.

Magno, Cettina Tramontano, and David V. Erdman. The Four Zoas *by William Blake: A Photographic Facsimile of the Manuscript with Commentary on the Illustrations.* Lewisburg: Bucknell UP; London: Associated U Presses, 1987.

Margoliouth, H. M. *William Blake.* Oxford: Oxford UP, 1961. Rpt., n.p. [Hamden, CT]: Archon, 1967.

Mavor, Elizabeth. *The Ladies of Llangollen: A Study in Romantic Friendship.* London: Michael Joseph, 1971; Harmondsworth: Penguin, 1973, rpt. 1976.

McGann, Jerome J. *The Romantic Ideology. A Critical Investigation.* Chicago and London: U of Chicago P, 1983.

———. *Social Values and Poetic Acts: The Historical Judgment of Literary Work.* Cambridge and London: Harvard UP, 1988.

Mee, Jon. *Dangerous Enthusiasm: William Blake and the Culture of Radicalism in the 1790s.* Oxford: Clarendon, 1992.

Mellor, Anne K. "Blake's Portrayal of Women." *Blake: An Illustrated Quarterly* 16.3 (Winter 1982–83): 148–55.

———. *Romanticism and Gender.* New York and London: Routledge, 1993.

———. "Sex, Violence, and Slavery: Blake and Wollstonecraft." *Huntington Library Quarterly* 58.3, 4 (1997): 345–70.

Mellor, Anne K., and Richard E. Matlak, eds. *British Literature 1780–1830.* Fort Worth: Harcourt Brace College Publishers, 1996.

Mengay, Donald H. "The Sodomitical Muse: *Fanny Hill* and the Rhetoric of Cross-dressing." Summers 185–98.

Miller, Dan, Mark Bracher, and Donald Ault, eds. *Critical Paths: Blake and the Argument of Method.* Durham and London: Duke UP, 1987.

Milton, John. *Complete Prose Works of John Milton.* Various eds. 8 vols. New Haven and London: Yale UP, 1953–82.

———. *Paradise Lost.* Ed. Merritt Y. Hughes. New York: Odyssey, 1935.

———. *Paradise Regained, The Minor Poems, and Samson Agonistes.* Ed. Merritt Y. Hughes. New York: Odyssey, 1937.

———. *The Works of John Milton.* Vol. 17. *De Doctrina Christiana,* vol. 2. Ed. James Holly Hanford, Waldo Hilary Dunn, with the translation of Charles R. Sumner (1825). New York: Columbia UP, 1934.

Miss Marianne Woods and Miss Jane Pirie Against Dame Helen Cumming Gordon. [Facsimiles of court proceedings, 1811–20.] New York: Arno, 1975.

Mitchell, W. J. T. *Blake's Composite Art: A Study of the Illuminated Poetry.* Princeton: Princeton UP, 1978.

———. "Dangerous Blake." Symposium, "Inside the Blake Industry: Past, Present, and Future." Ed. Morris Eaves. *Studies in Romanticism* 21.3 (Fall 1982). 410–16.

———. "Style and Iconography in the Illustrations of Blake's *Milton.*" *Blake Studies* 6.1 (Fall 1973): 47–71.

The Morning Chronicle. London. July 1810-June 1811.

Murray, Stephen O. "Homosexual Acts and Selves in Early Modern Europe." Gerard and Hekma 457–77.

Norton, Rictor. *Mother Clap's Molly House: The Gay Subculture in England 1700–1830.* London: GMP, 1992.

Ogg, David. *England in the Reign of Charles II.* 2 vols. Oxford: Clarendon, 1934.

———. *England in the Reigns of James II and William III.* Oxford: Clarendon, 1955.

Onania: or, the Heinous Sin of Self-Pollution, and All its Frightful Consequences, in Both Sexes consider'd, &c. With Spiritual and Physical Advice to those who have already injur'd themselves by this abominable Practice. The Sixteenth Edition, as also the Seventh Edition of the Supplement [etc.]. London: Printed for the Author, 1737. [Microfilm: Eighteenth Century, Reel 4409.20. Woodbridge, CT: Research Publications, 1990.]

Otto, Peter. *Constructive Vision and Visionary Deconstruction: Los, Eternity, and the Productions of Time in the Later Poetry of William Blake.* Oxford: Clarendon, 1991.

Paley, Morton D. *The Continuing City: William Blake's Jerusalem.* Oxford: Clarendon, 1983.

————. *Energy and the Imagination: A Study of the Development of Blake's Thought.* Oxford: Clarendon, 1970.

————, ed. *Jerusalem*[:] *The Emanation of the Giant Albion.* By William Blake. Princeton: William Blake Trust and Princeton UP, 1991. Vol. 1 of *Blake's Illuminated Works.* David Bindman, Gen. Ed. [Facsimile of Copy E.]

————. "William Blake, The Prince of the Hebrews, and The Woman Clothed with the Sun." Paley and Phillips 260–93.

Paley, Morton D. and Michael Phillips. *William Blake: Essays in Honour of Sir Geoffrey Keynes.* Oxford: Clarendon, 1973.

Patterson, Craig. "The Rage of Caliban: Eighteenth-Century Molly Houses and the Twentieth-Century Search for Sexual Identity." *Illicit Sex: Identity Politics in Early Modern Culture.* Ed. Thomas DiPiero, Pat Gill. Athens and London: U of Georgia P, 1997. 256–69.

Peterson, Jane E. "The *Visions of the Daughters of Albion:* A Problem in Perception." *Philological Quarterly* 52.2 (April 1973): 252–64.

The Phoenix of Sodom, or the Vere Street Coterie. Being an Exhibition of the Gambols Practised by the Ancient Lechers of Sodom and Gomorrah, embellished and improved with the Modern Refinements in Sodomitical Practices, by the members of the Vere Street Coterie, of detestable memory. [By Robert Holloway.] London, 1813. *Sodomy Trials,* n.p.

Plumb, J. H. *The Growth of Political Stability in England, 1675–1725.* London: Macmillan, 1967.

Poems on Affairs of State: Augustan Satirical Verse, 1660–1714. [POAS] 7 vols. *Volume 5: 1688–1697.* Ed. William J. Cameron. New Haven and London: Yale UP, 1971. *Volume 6: 1697–1704.* Ed. Frank H. Ellis. New Haven and London: Yale UP, 1970.

Pope, Alexander. "Epistle to Dr. Arbuthnot." *Poetical Works.* Ed. Herbert Davis. Oxford and New York: Oxford UP, 1978, rpt. 1985. 327–40.

Porter, Roy, and Lesley Hall. *The Facts of Life: The Creation of Sexual Knowledge in Britain, 1650–1950.* New Haven and London: Yale UP, 1995.

Prall, Stuart E. *The Bloodless Revolution: England, 1688.* Madison: U of Wisconsin P, 1985.

Pressly, Nancy L. *Revealed Religion: Benjamin West's Commissions for Windsor Castle and Fonthill Abbey.* San Antonio: San Antonio Museum Association, San Antonio Museum of Art, 1983.

Rey, Michel. "Parisian Homosexuals Create a Lifestyle, 1700–1750: The Police Archives." Trans. Robert A. Day and Robert Welch. Maccubbin 179–91.

Robbins, Caroline. *The Eighteenth-Century Commonwealthman: Studies in the Transmission, Development, and Circumstance of English Liberal Thought from the Restoration of Charles II until the War with the Thirteen Colonies.* Cambridge: Harvard UP, 1961.

Robertson, William. *The History of America.* 2 vols. London: W. Strahan, T. Cadell, J. Balfour, 1777.

Rose, Edward. "Blake's Human Insect: Symbol, Theory, and Design." *Texas Studies in Literature and Language* 10.2 (Summer 1968): 215–32.

Rosso, G. A. "Empire of the Sea: Blake's 'King Edward the Third' and English Imperial Poetry." DiSalvo, Hobson, and Rosso 251–72.

———. "Newton's Pantocrator and Blake's Recovery of Miltonic Prophecy." *Milton, the Metaphysicals, and Romanticism.* Ed. Lisa Low, Anthony John Harding. Cambridge: Cambridge UP, 1994. 47–64.

Rousseau, G. S. " 'In the House of Madam Vander Tasse, on the Long Bridge': A Homosocial University Club in Early Modern Europe." Gerard and Hekma 311–47.

———. "An Introduction to the *Love-Letters:* Circumstances of Publication, Context, and Cultural Commentary." Kimmel, *Love Letters* 47–90.

———. "The Pursuit of Homosexuality in the Eighteenth Century: 'Utterly Confused Category' and/or Rich Repository?" Maccubbin 132–168.

———. "The Sorrows of Priapus: Anticlericalism, Homosocial Desire, and Richard Payne Knight." Rousseau and Porter 101–53.

Rousseau, G. S., and Roy Porter, eds. *Sexual Underworlds of the Enlightenment.* Chapel Hill: U of North Carolina P., 1988.

Rousseau, Jean-Jacques. *The Confessions of Jean-Jacques Rousseau.* 1781. Trans. J. M. Cohen. Harmondsworth: Penguin, 1953.

Rowland, Jon Thomas. *"Swords in Myrtle Dress'd": Toward a Rhetoric of Sodom: Gay Readings of Homosexual Politics and Poetics in the Eighteenth Century.* Madison, NJ: Fairleigh Dickinson UP; London: Associated U Presses, 1998.

Rubini, Dennis. "Sexuality and Augustan England: Sodomy, Politics, Elite Circles and Society." Gerard and Hekma 349–81.

Rumrich, John R. "The Erotic Milton." *Texas Studies in Literature and Language* 41.2 (Summer 1999): 128–41.

Sabor, Peter. Introduction and notes. *Memoirs of a Woman of Pleasure.* By John Cleland. vii–xxxii, 189–204.

Said, Edward W. *Orientalism.* New York: Vintage-Random House, 1979.

Sandler, Florence. "The Iconoclastic Enterprise: Blake's Critique of 'Milton's Religion.'" *Blake Studies* 5 (Fall 1972): 13–57. Rpt., with revisions, in *Essential Articles for the Study of William Blake, 1970–84.* Ed. Nelson Hilton. Hamden, CT: Archon, 1986. 33–55. Citations are to this edition.

A Satyr upon King William; Being the Secret History of His Life and Reign. Written by a Gentleman that was near his Person for many Years. 2nd. ed. London: n.p., 1703.

Sayre, Robert, and Michael Löwy. "Figures of Romantic Anticapitalism." With response by Michael Ferber and "The Fire Is Still Burning: An Answer to Michael

Ferber." *Spirits of Fire: English Romantic Writers and Contemporary Historical Methods.* Ed. G. A. Rosso, Daniel P. Watkins. Rutherford: Fairleigh Dickinson UP; London and Toronto: Associated U Presses, 1990. 23–68, 85–91.

Schuchard, Marsha Keith. "Blake's Healing Trio: Magnetism, Medicine, and Mania." *Blake: An Illustrated Quarterly* 23:1 (Summer 1989): 20–32.

————. "Blake's 'Mr. Femality': Freemasonry, Espionage, and the Double-Sexed." *Studies in Eighteenth-Century Culture* 22 (1992): 51–71.

————. "The Secret Masonic History of Blake's Swedenborg Society." *Blake: An Illustrated Quarterly* 26:2 (Fall 1992): 40–51.

Seward, Anna. "Llangollen Vale." *Llangollen Vale, With Other Poems.* London: G. Sael, 1796. 1–11.

Shakespeare, William. *Macbeth.* Ed. Kenneth Muir. Arden edition. London and New York: Methuen, 1951; revised ed., 1984, rpt. 1986.

Shawcross, John. *John Milton: The Self and the World.* Lexington: UP of Kentucky, 1993.

Shelley, Percy Bysshe. *The Complete Works of Percy Bysshe Shelley.* Ed. Roger Ingpen and Walter E. Peck. Vol. 7. London: Ernest Benn; New York: Scribner, 1930.

————. "A Discourse on the Manners of the Antient Greeks Relative to the Subject of Love." 1818. *The Platonism of Shelley.* Ed. James A. Notopoulos. Durham: Duke UP, 1949. 404–413.

Simmons, Robert E. "*Urizen:* The Symmetry of Fear." *Blake's Visionary Forms Dramatic.* Ed. David V. Erdman and John E. Grant. Princeton: Princeton UP, 1970. 146–73.

Simpson, David. "Reading Blake and Derrida—Our Caesars Neither Praised nor Buried." *Unnam'd Forms: Blake and Textuality.* Ed. Nelson Hilton, Thomas A. Vogler. Berkeley and Los Angeles: U of California P, 1986. 11–25.

Smith, Bruce R. "Premodern Sexualities." *PMLA* 115.3 (May 2000): 318–29.

Smith, D. I. B. Introduction. *The Rehearsal Transpros'd and The Rehearsal Transpros'd: The Second Part.* By Andrew Marvell, ed. D. I. B. Smith. Oxford: Clarendon, 1971.

Smollett, T[obias]. *The History of England; from Revolution in 1688 to the Death of George II. Designed as a Continuation of Hume.* 5 vols. London: J. F. Dove, 1822.

Sodomy Trials: Seven Documents. [Ed. Randolph Trumbach.] New York and London: Garland, 1986.

Stedman, John Gabriel. *Narrative, of a five years' expedition, against the Revolted Negroes of Surinam, in Guiana, on the Wild Coast of South America; from the year 1772, to 1777* [etc.]. 2 vols. London: printed for J. Johnson and J. Edwards, 1796.

Stevenson, Warren. *Romanticism and the Androgynous Sublime.* Madison and Teaneck, NJ: Fairleigh Dickinson UP; London: Associated U Presses, 1996.

Storch, Margaret. *Sons and Adversaries: Women in William Blake and D. H. Lawrence.* Knoxville: U of Tennessee P, 1990.

————. "The 'Spectrous Fiend' Cast Out: Blake's Crisis at Felpham." *Modern Language Quarterly* 44 (1983): 115–35.

Sturrock, June. "Maenads, Young Ladies, and the Lovely Daughters of Albion." DiSalvo, Hobson, and Rosso 339–49.

Summers, Claude J., ed. *Homosexuality in Renaissance and Enlightenment England: Literary Representations in Historical Context*. New York: Haworth, 1992.

Swift, Jonathan. *Miscellaneous and Autobiographical Pieces, Fragments, and Marginalia*. Ed. Herbert Davis. Oxford: Basil Blackwell, 1969.

Tannenbaum, Leslie. *Biblical Tradition in Blake's Early Prophecies: The Great Code of Art*. Princeton: Princeton UP, 1982.

Tayler, Irene. *Blake's Illustrations to the Poems of Gray*. Princeton: Princeton UP, 1971.

———. "Say First! What Mov'd Blake? Blake's *Comus* Designs and *Milton*." Curran and Wittreich 233–58.

———. "The Woman Scaly." *Bulletin of the Midwest Modern Language Association* 6.1 (Spring 1973): 74–87. Rpt. in *Blake's Poetry and Designs*. Ed. Mary Lynn Johnson and John E. Grant. New York: Norton, 1979. 539–53. Citations are to this edition.

Thompson, E. P. *The Making of the English Working Class*. New York: Pantheon, 1963. Rpt., New York: Random House, Vintage, 1966.

The Times. London. Jan.-Dec. 1798, July 1810-June 1811, other selected issues.

The Trial of Richard Branson, for An Attempt to commit Sodomy, On the Body of James Fassett, One of the Scholars belonging to God's-Gift-College, in Dulwich. London: H. Serjeant, T. Drake, 1760. *Sodomy Trials*, n.p.

Trumbach, Randolph. "The Birth of the Queen: Sodomy and the Emergence of Gender Equality in Modern Culture, 1660–1750." *Hidden From History: Reclaiming the Gay and Lesbian Past*. Ed. Martin Bauml Duberman, Martha Vicinus, George Chauncey, Jr. New York: Penguin-New American Library, 1989. 129–40.

———. "London's Sapphists: From Three Sexes to Four Genders in the Making of Modern Culture." *Body Guards: The Cultural Politics of Gender Ambiguity*. Ed. Julia Epstein, Kristina Straub. New York and London: Routledge, 1991. 112–41.

———. "London's Sodomites: Homosexual Behavior and Western Culture in the Eighteenth Century." *Journal of Social History* 11.1 (Fall 1977): 1–33.

———. *Sex and the Gender Revolution*. Vol. 1. *Heterosexuality and the Third Gender in Enlightenment London*. Chicago and London: U of Chicago P, 1998.

———. "Sodomitical Assaults, Gender Role, and Sexual Development in Eighteenth-Century London." Gerard and Hekma 407–29.

———. "Sodomy Transformed: Aristocratic Libertinage, Public Reputation and the Gender Revolution of the 18th Century." Kimmel, *Love Letters* 105–24.

Van der Zee, Henri and Barbara. *William and Mary*. London: Macmillan, 1973.

Vergil. *The Aeneid*. Loeb Classical Library. Latin with Engl. trans. by H. Rushton Fairclough. 2 vols. London: Heinemann; New York: Putnam, 1927, 1930.

Viscomi, Joseph. *Blake and the Idea of the Book*. Princeton: Princeton UP, 1993.

Warner, Janet. *Blake and the Language of Art*. Kingston and Montreal: McGill-Queen's UP; Gloucester: Alan Sutton, 1984.

Webster, Brenda S. "Blake, Women, and Sexuality." Miller, Bracher, and Ault, 204–24.

———. *Blake's Prophetic Psychology*. Athens, GA: U of Georgia P, 1983.

Weinreb, Ben, and Christopher Hibbert. *The London Encyclopædia*. Bethesda, MD: Adler and Adler, 1986.

Werner, Bette Charlene. *Blake's Vision of the Poetry of Milton: Illustrations to Six Poems*. Lewisburg, PA: Bucknell UP; London and Toronto: Associated U Presses, 1986.

Wilkie, Brian. *Blake's* Thel *and* Oothoon. Victoria: English Literary Studies, U of Victoria, 1990.

The William Blake Archive. Online. Ed. Morris Eaves, Robert N. Essick, and Joseph Viscomi. <http: www.iath.virginia.edu/blake/>

Witke, Joanne. *William Blake's Epic: Imagination Unbound*. New York: St. Martin's, 1986.

Wittreich, Joseph. *Angel of Apocalypse: Blake's Idea of Milton*. Madison: U of Wisconsin P, 1975.

The Women-Hater's Lamentation: A New Copy of Verses on the Fatal End of Mr. Grant, a Woollen-Draper, and two others that Cut their Throats, or Hang'd themselves in the Counter . . . To the Tune of, Ye pretty Sailors all. London: J. Robinson, 1707. *Sodomy Trials*, n.p.

Wordsworth, William. "To the Lady E.B. and the Hon. Miss P." *Poems, Volume 2*. Ed. John O. Hayden. London: Penguin Classics, 1989. 602.

———. *The Prelude* (1805–1806). *The Prelude: A Parallel Text*. Ed. J. C. Maxwell. New Haven and London: Yale UP, 1981.

Worrall, David. *Radical Culture: Discourse, Resistance and Surveillance, 1790–1820*. Detroit: Wayne State UP, 1992.

———. "William Blake and Erasmus Darwin's *Botanic Garden*." *Bulletin of the New York Public Library* 78.4 (Summer 1975): 397–417.

Index

*Blake works in the list of abbreviations are indexed separately; other Blake works are listed under Blake. Characters and concepts in Blake (e.g., Albion, emanation) are indexed separately. Visual designs are indicated by plate/page number in **boldface**. Notes are indexed selectively.*

Ackroyd, Peter, 191 n. 4
Aers, David, 26, 32, 201 n. 27
Ahania, 40, 42–44, 54, 163; as
  Urizen's "parted soul" (*Ah*), 163
Ahania, The Book of, 37, 38, 39–40,
  41, 42–44, 45, 163, 188, 201 n.
  21
Akenside, Mark, 11
Albion, 54, 66, 124, 146, 149, 150,
  162, 163, 164–65, 168, 169, 172,
  177, 178, 179–80, 181; death
  couch, etc., mentioned in Bard's
  Song, 83, 87, 92, 94; fall, 151,
  155, 158; recognition of
  brotherhood (*J* 96), 150; rejection
  of mutuality (*J* 4), 146, 148–49,
  151, 173, 186, 188; river of, as
  Thames, 162; in riverbank scene
  (*J*) and its aftermath, 150–52,
  153, 154, 155, 156, 157–58,
  159–62; "terrible surfaces" of,
  164, 177, 181; seizure of Vala,
  153, 155–57, 158

—, daughters of: as British women in
  general, 128, 149, 186; as
  characters, 146, 157, 206 n. 20,
  217 n. 25, 221–22 n. 20; as
  "emanations" of his sons, 163;
  Gwendolen, Cambel, 169
—, "Friends of," 149
—, sons, children, or Spectre Sons of,
  79, 149, 150, 151, 163, 164–65,
  186, 221 n. 20; Hand, 146–47,
  148, 149, 151, 160, 161, 169,
  172, 176, 220 n. 2; Hyle, 169
All Religions are One, 25
America, 25–26, 29, 46, 52, 62;
  Preludium, 25–26, 31–32, 59,
  60–61, 176; visual designs: **1**, 51;
  6, 45–46; **8**, 46; **10**, 26, 46; **14**,
  212 n. 30; **15**, 47, 107, 202–203
  n. 32
American Revolution, 178
Anne, Princess (1688) and Queen
  (1702–13), 15, 84, 85, 87, 89,
  94, 208 n. 9, 209 n. 14
Antamon, 31, 42, 46, 87, 201 n. 26
Antichrist, 78, 79, 168, 169, 170–71.
  See also Covering Cherub
apocalypse (Last Judgment) and the
  apocalyptic, 23, 26, 50, 64,
  72–73, 74–75, 81, 150, 169, 176,
  177, 178, 181, 219 n. 36
atonement, 85, 92, 119, 126, 127,
  150, 207 n. 1; Blake's view of,

—, England, eighteenth–early nineteenth centuries (general), xviii-xxi, 4–10

—, lesbian, eighteenth–early nineteenth centuries: 7–9, 10, 148; conceptions of, 9, 63, 67, 167, 193–94 n. 10; female cohabitation and, 8–9, 152–53; literary treatments, 9, 30–31, 152 (*see also* Cleland, John, and other authors); "romantic friendship" and, 8–9; "sapphic," "sapphist," and other terms for, 8, 152, 156; self-conceptions, 8. *See also* Woods-Pirie v. Gordon

—, male (sodomy), eighteenth–early nineteenth centuries: clandestine culture (London and elsewhere), 4–5, 192–93 nn. 3, 5; defenses of, infrequency in general culture, 9–10, 194–95 n. 13 (*see also* Bentham, Shelley); in military forces, 4, 6, 7, 114, 116–17, 122, 125; molly houses, etc., 4–5 (*see also* White Swan); penalties, prosecution, etc., 5–7, 115–16, 118, 193 n. 6, 214–15 nn. 7, 13; pillory, opposition to, 117–18, 188; and republican tradition, *see* republican tradition; seen as foreign, "Italian," etc., 7, 9, 13, 16, 90; as target of satire, sermons, etc., 7, 9, 142, 193 n. 9, 194 n. 13, 197 n. 31 (*see also* specific authors and titles); toleration of, in Bentham's writings, 19–20; —, in France, 164; —, in Islam (attributed), 46, 202 nn. 30, 31

—, male (sodomy), eighteenth–early nineteenth century, trials and other repression: Branson, Richard, 5, 193 n. 6; Cambridge, Richard, 116, 117; Carter (first name unknown), 116, 215 n. 8;

Cole, John Carey (death sentence), 116, 142; Cox, Thomas (or Jason Fisher; death sentence), 117; Dawson, Edward, and John Hall, 6; Hepburn, John N., and Thomas White, trial and execution, 116–17, 122–23, 124, 125–26, 142 (Hepburn), 166 (White), 172, 215 n. 9; Hitchin, Isaac, and others, Warrington (death sentences and reprieves), 7, 123, 193 n. 8; Norton, John, 5. *See also* Vere-street persecutions

—, theories of (current), xv-xxi

House of William Blake, The, 189

Hume, David, *History of England,* 90, 208 n. 9; qtd., 84

Isherwood, Christopher, *A Single Man,* 200 n. 20

"An Island in the Moon," 35, 147, 198 n. 33, 200 n. 19; Mr. Femality, 29, 200 n. 10

Jackson, William, *Sodom and Onan* (1776), 197 n. 32

Jacob, Giles, *A Treatise of Hermaphrodites* (1718), 67

James (*M* 5), 82, 84–85, 95

James I, 82, 197 n. 31

James II, 84–85, 95, 198 n. 38, 207 n. 4, 208 nn. 8, 9

Jerusalem, xi, xii, xv, 3, 35, 49, 56, 65, 66, 78–79, 93, 106, 112, 142, 145–73, 176, 177–82, 184, 186, 187, 188; cited, 122; prefaces, 179–81

—, central sexual, moral, social, and religious themes: assessed, 145–46; mutuality and communal values, 146, 148–49, 160, 172–73; reconsideration of gender, 162–73, 182–87, 189–90 (*see also* emanations, hermaphrodism, Shiloh); sexual